MAGIC AND RELIGION

MAGIC AND RELIGION

BY

ANDREW LANG

AUTHOR OF

MYTH, RITUAL, AND RELIGION' 'CUSTOM AND MYTH' ETC.

GREENWOOD PRESS, PUBLISHERS
NEW YORK

Originally published in 1901
by Longman's, Green and Co.

First Greenwood Reprinting, 1969

Library of Congress Catalogue Card Number 69-13964

PREFACE

RECENT years have brought rich additions to the materials
for the study of early religion, ritual, magic, and myth.
In proportion to the abundance of information has been
the growth of theory and hypothesis. The first essay in
this collection, ' Science and Superstition,' points out the
danger of allowing too ingenious and imaginative hypotheses to lead captive our science.

As, like others, I have not long since advanced a
provisional theory of my own, the second and third essays
are designed to strengthen my position. The theory is
that perhaps the earliest traceable form of religion was
relatively high, and that it was inevitably lowered in tone
during the process of social evolution. Obviously this
opinion may be attacked from two sides. It may be said
that the loftier religious ideas of the lowest savages are
borrowed from Christianity or Islam. This I understand
to be the theory of Mr. E. B. Tylor. It is with much
diffidence that I venture, at present, to disagree with so
eminent and sagacious an authority, while awaiting the
publication of Mr. Tylor's Aberdeen Gifford Lectures.
My reply to his hypothesis, so far as it has been published
by him, will be found in the second essay, ' The Theory
of Loan-Gods.' Secondly, my position may be attacked
by disabling the evidence for the existence of the higher
elements in the religion of low savages. Mr. Frazer,

in the second edition of his 'Golden Bough,' has advanced an hypothesis of the origin of religion, wherein the evidence for the higher factors is not taken into account. Probably he may consider the subject in a later work, to which he alludes in his Preface. 'Should I live to complete the works for which I have collected and am collecting materials, I dare to think that they will clear me of any suspicion of treating the early history of religion from a single narrow point of view.'[1]

Meanwhile, however, Mr. Frazer has advanced a theory of the origin of religion wherein evidence which I think deserving of attention receives no recognition. I hope, therefore, that it is not premature to state the evidence, or some of it, which I do in the third essay, 'Magic and Religion.'

Fourth comes a long criticism of Mr. Frazer's many hypotheses, which are combined into his theory of the origin, or partial origin, of the belief in the divine character of Christ. This argument demands very minute, and, I fear, tedious examination. I fear still more that my labour has not, after all, been sufficiently minute and accurate. It seems to be almost impossible to understand clearly and represent fairly ideas with which one does not agree. If I have failed in these respects it is unconsciously, and I shall gratefully accept criticism enabling me to recognise and correct errors.

Fifthly, I examine, in 'The Ghastly Priest,' Mr. Frazer's theory of the Golden Bough of Virgil as connected with the fugitive slave who was 'King of the Wood' near Aricia. I offer a conjecture as to the origin of his curious position, which seems to me simpler, and not less probable, than Mr. Frazer's hypothesis that this outcast 'lived and died as an incarnation of the supreme

[1] *Golden Bough*, i. xvii, 1900.

Aryan god, whose life was in the mistletoe or golden bough.' But my conjecture is only a guess at a problem which, I think, we have not the means of solving.

There follow an essay, ' South African Religion,' and another on the old puzzle of the ' Cup and Ring ' marks on rocks and cists and other objects all over the world.

Next I consider the subject of ' Taboos,' with especial reference to the theory of Mr. F. B. Jevons. An essay follows on the singular rite of the Fire Walk, with the alleged immunity of the performers. This curious topic I have treated before, but now add fresh evidence.

Of these essays the second, in part, appeared in the ' Nineteenth Century,' and most of ' The Ghastly Priest ' was published in ' The Fortnightly Review,' while ' Cup and Ring ' first saw the light in ' The Contemporary Review.' My thanks are due to the Editors of those periodicals for permission to republish. The essay on the ' Fire Walk ' was in the ' Proceedings of the Society for Psychical Research,' though the topic does not appear to be ' psychical.' All the other papers are new, and three Appendices on points of detail are added.

The design on the cover is drawn by Mr. Donnelly, the discoverer of the Dunbuie and Dumbuck sites and relics, from an Australian design, in Messrs. Spencer and Gillen's ' Native Tribes of Central Australia.'

For permission to reproduce this drawing I have to thank the kindness of Messrs. Macmillan & Co. The designs of feet, on the back of the volume (a subject found in Australia), and the ' jew's harp ' ornament (common to Scotland and Hindostan), are also by Mr. Donnelly, from Scottish rock carvings.

Corrigenda and Addenda

Page 4, lines 24, 25, *for* story *read* storey, *for* stories *read* storeys.

Page 13, line 7, compare p. 297, the second paragraph, as to Motagon and Bishop Salvado.

Page 17, line 24, *for* 1871 *read* 1873.

Page 44. To the names of writers who support the idea of an Australian religion should be added that of Dr. John Mathew, in *Eaglehawk and Crow*, p. 147 (1899), ' I was once of opinion that notions about a divinity had been derived from the whites and transmitted among the blacks hither and thither, but I am now convinced that this idea was here before European occupation.' But (pp. 130, 131) Dr. Mathew gives his reasons for thinking importation from Indian mythology possible. But as they rest on his decipherment of certain marks, which may be meant for characters, in Sir George Grey's copy of an Australian wall-painting, the evidence is weak. (Grey, *North-west and Western Australia*, i. 201 *et seq.*). Supposing the characters to be Sumatran, it would be necessary to show that the people of Sumatra do represent their otiose deity as in the painting copied by Grey.

Page 58, line 6, *for* rights *read* rites.

Page 75, note 1, *for* Primitive Culture, i. 379, 1871, *read* Primitive Culture, i. 419, 1873.

Page 112, note 1. ' But so there were in 1000 A.D.' I have been informed that there was no special fear of the end of the world in 1000 A.D. M. Cumont gives good reasons for holding that the martyrdom of St. Dasius in 303 was on record between 362 and 411 (*Man*, May 1901, No. 53).

Page 120. ' Ctesias flourished rather earlier than Berosus, who is about 200 B.C. ; ' *for* 200 *read* 260. Ctesias was a contemporary of Herodotus.

CONTENTS

APPENDICES

MAGIC AND RELIGION

I

SCIENCE AND SUPERSTITION

WE all know what we mean by science; science is 'organised common sense.' Her aim is the acquisition of reasoned and orderly knowledge. Presented with a collection of verified facts, it is the part of science to reduce them to order, and to account for their existence in accordance with her recognised theory of things. If the facts cannot be fitted into the theory, it must be expanded or altered; for we must admit that, if the facts are verified, there is need for change and expansion in the theory. The 'colligation' of facts demands hypotheses, and these may not, at the moment of their construction, be verifiable. The deflections of a planet from its apparently normal course may be accounted for by the hypothesis of the attraction of another heavenly body not yet discovered. The hypothesis is legitimate, for such bodies are known to exist, and to produce such effects. When the body is discovered, the hypothesis becomes a certainty. On the other hand, the hypothesis that some capricious and conscious agency pushed the planet into deflections would be illegitimate, for the existence of such a freakish agency is not demonstrated. Our hypotheses then must be consistent with our actual knowledge of nature and of human nature, and our conjectured causes must be adequate to the production of the effects. Thus, science gradually acquires and organises new regions of knowledge.

Superstition is a word of much less definite meaning. When we call a man 'superstitious,' we usually mean that evidence which satisfies him does not satisfy us. We see examples daily of the dependence of belief on bias. One man believes a story about cruelties committed by our adversaries; another, disbelieving the tale, credits a narrative about the misconduct of our own party. Probably the evidence in neither case would satisfy the historian, or be accepted by a jury. A man in a tavern tells another how the Boers, retreating from a position, buried their own wounded. 'I don't believe that,' says the other. 'Then you are a pro-Boer.'

The sceptic reasoned from his general knowledge of human nature. The believer reasoned from his own prejudiced and mythopœic conception of people whom he disliked. If the question had been one of religion the believer might be called superstitious; the sceptic might be called scientific, if he was ready to yield his doubts to the evidence of capable observers of the alleged fact.

Superstition, like science, has her hypotheses, and, like science, she reasons from experience. But her experience is usually fantastic, unreal, or if real capable of explanation by causes other than those alleged by superstition. A man comes in at night, and says he has seen a ghost in white. That is merely his hypothesis; the existence of ghosts in white is not demonstrated. You accompany him to the scene of the experience, and prove to him that he has seen a post, not a ghost. His experience was real, but was misinterpreted by dint of an hypothesis resting on no demonstrated fact of knowledge.

The hypotheses of superstition are familiar. Thus, an event has happened : say you have lost your button-hook. You presently hear of a death in your family. Ever afterwards you go anxiously about when you have lost a button-hook. You are confusing a casual sequence of facts with a causal connection of facts. Sequence in time is mistaken for sequence of what we commonly style cause and effect. In the same way, superstition cherishes the hypothesis that like affects like. Thus, the sun is round, and a ball of clay is round. Therefore, if an Australian native wishes to delay the course of the round sun in the heavens, he fixes a round ball of clay on the bough of a tree ; or so books on anthropology tell us. Acting on the hypothesis that like affects like, a man makes a clay or waxen image of an enemy, and sticks it full of pins or thorns. He expects his enemy to suffer agony in consequence, and so powerful is 'suggestion' that, if the enemy knows about the image, he sometimes falls ill and dies. This experience corroborates the super-stitious hypothesis, and so the experiment with the image is of world-wide diffusion. Everything is done, or at-tempted, on these lines by superstition. Men imitate the killing of foes or game, and expect, as a result, to kill them in war or in the chase. They mimic the gathering of clouds and the fall of rain, and expect rain to fall in consequence. They imitate the evolution of an edible grub from the larva, and expect grubs to multiply ; and so on.

All this is quite rational, if you grant the hypotheses of superstition. Her practices are magic. We are later to discuss a theory that men had magic before they had religion, and only invented gods because they found that magic did not work. Still later they invented science, which is only magic with a legitimate hypothesis, using

real, not fanciful, experience. In the long run magic and
religion are to die out, perhaps, and science is to have the
whole field to herself.

This may be a glorious though a remote prospect. But
surely it is above all things needful that our science should
be scientific. She must not blink facts, merely because
they do not fit into her scheme or hypothesis of the
nature of things, or of religion. She really must give as
much prominence to the evidence which contradicts as to
that which supports her theory in each instance. Not
only must she not shut her eyes to this evidence, but she
must diligently search for it, must seek for what Bacon
calls *instantiæ contradictoriæ*, since, if these exist, the
theory which ignores them is useless. If she advances an
hypothesis, it must not be contradictory of the whole
mass of human experience. If science finds that her
hypothesis contradicts experience, she must seek for an
hypothesis which is in accordance with experience, and,
if that cannot be found, she must wait till it is found.
Again, science must not pile one unverified hypothesis
upon another unverified hypothesis till her edifice rivals
the Tower of Babel. She must not make a conjecture on
p. 35, and on p. 210 treat the conjecture as a fact.
Because, if one story in the card-castle is destroyed by
being proved impossible, all the other stories will ' come
tumbling after.' It seems hardly necessary, but it is not
superfluous, to add that, in her castle of hypotheses, one
must not contradict, and therefore destroy, another. We
must not be asked to believe that an event occurred at
one date, and also that it occurred at another ; or that an
institution was both borrowed by a people at one period,
and was also possessed, unborrowed, by the same people, at
an earlier period. We cannot permit science to assure us
that a certain fact was well known, and that the knowledge

produced important consequences ; while we are no less solemnly told that the fact was wholly unknown, whence it would seem that the results alleged to spring from the knowledge could not be produced.

This kind of reasoning, with its inferring of inferences from other inferences, themselves inferred from conjectures as to the existence of facts of which no proof is adduced, must be called superstitious rather than scientific. The results may be interesting, but they are the reverse of science.

It is perhaps chiefly in the nascent science of the anthropological study of institutions, and above all of religion, that this kind of reasoning prevails. The topic attracts ingenious and curious minds. System after system has been constructed, unstinted in material, elegant in aspect, has been launched, and has been wrecked, or been drifted by the careless winds to the forlorn shore where Bryant's ark, with all its crew, divine or human, lies in decay. No mortal student believes in the arkite system of Bryant, though his ark, on the match-boxes of Messrs. Bryant and May, perhaps denotes loyalty to the ancestral idea.

The world of modern readers has watched sun myths, and dawn myths, and storm myths, and wind myths come in and go out : *autant en emporte le vent.* Totems and taboos succeeded, and we are bewildered by the contending theories of the origins of taboos and totems. Deities of vegetation now are all in all, and may it be far from us to say that any one from Ouranos to Pan, from the Persian King to the horses of Virbius, is not a spirit of vegetable life. Yet perhaps the deity has higher aspects and nobler functions than the pursuit of his ' vapid vegetable loves ; ' and these deserve occasional attention.

The result, however, of scurrying hypotheses and hasty generalisations is that the nascent science of religious origins is received with distrust. We may review the brief history of the modern science.

Some twenty years ago, when the ' Principles of Sociology,' by Mr. Herbert Spencer, was first published, the book was reviewed, in ' Mind,' by the author of ' Primitive Culture.' That work, again, was published in 1871. In 1890 appeared the ' Golden Bough,' by Mr. J. G. Frazer, and the second edition of the book, with changes and much new matter, was given to the world in 1900.

Here, then, we have a whole generation, a space of thirty years, during which English philosophers or scholars have been studying the science of the Origins of Religion. In the latest edition of the ' Golden Bough,' Mr. Frazer has even penetrated into the remote region where man neither had, nor wanted, any religion at all. We naturally ask ourselves to what point we have arrived after the labours of a generation. Twenty years ago, when reviewing Mr. Spencer, Mr. Tylor said that a time of great public excitement as to these topics was at hand. The clamour and contest aroused by Mr. Darwin's theory of the Origin of Species and the Descent of Man would be outdone by the coming war over the question of the Evolution of Religion. But there has been no general excitement ; there has been little display of public interest in these questions. They have been left to ' the curious ' and ' the learned,' classes not absolutely identical. Mr. Frazer, indeed, assures us that the comparative study of human beliefs and institutions is ' fitted to be much more than a means of satisfying an enlightened curiosity, and of furnishing materials for the researches of the learned.' [1]

---

[1] *Golden Bough*, i. xxi., 1900.

But enlightened curiosity seems to be easily satisfied, and only very few of the learned concern themselves with these researches, which Mr. Tylor expected to be so generally exciting.

A member of the University of Oxford informed me that the study of beliefs, and of anthropology in general, is almost entirely neglected by the undergraduates, and when I asked him 'Why?' he replied 'There is no money in it.' Another said that anthropology 'had no evidence.' In the language of the economists there is no supply provided at Oxford because there is no demand. Classics, philology, history, physical science, and even literature, are studied, because 'there is money in them,' not much money indeed, but a competence, if the student is successful. For the study of the evolution of beliefs there is no demand, or very little. Yet, says Mr. Frazer, 'well handled, it may become a powerful instrument to expedite progress, if it lays bare certain weak spots in the foundations on which modern society is built.' We all desire progress (in the right direction), we all pine to lay bare weak spots, and yet we do not seem to be concerned about the services which might be done for progress by the study of the evolution of religion. 'It is indeed a melancholy and, in some respects, thankless task,' says Mr. Frazer, 'to strike at the foundations of beliefs in which, as in a strong tower, the hopes and aspirations of humanity through long ages have sought a refuge from the storm and stress of life.' 'Thankless,' indeed, these operations are. 'Yet sooner or later,' Mr. Frazer adds, 'it is inevitable that the battery of the comparative method should breach these venerable walls, mantled over with the ivy and mosses and wild flowers of a thousand tender and sacred associations. At present we are only dragging the guns into position; they have hardly yet begun to speak.'

Mr. Frazer is too modest: he has dragged into position a work of immense learning and eloquent style in three siege guns, we may say, three volumes of the largest calibre, and they have spoken about 500,000 words. No man, to continue the metaphor, is better supplied than he with the ammunition of learning, with the knowledge of facts of every kind. Yet the venerable walls, with their pleasing growth of ivy, mosses, wild flowers, and other mural vegetation, do not, to myself, seem in the least degree impaired by the artillery, and I try to show cause for my opinion.

Why is this, and why is the portion of the public which lives within or without the venerable walls mainly indifferent?

Several sufficient reasons might be given. In the first place many people have, or think they have, so many other grounds for disbelief, that additional grounds, provided by the comparative method, are regarded rather as a luxury than as supplying a felt want. Again, but very few persons have leisure, or inclination, or power of mind enough to follow an elaborate argument through fifteen hundred pages, not to speak of other works on the same theme. Once more, only a minute minority are capable of testing and weighing the evidence, and criticising the tangled hypotheses on which the argument rests, or in which it is involved.

But there is another and perhaps a sounder argument for indifference. The learned are aware that the evidence for all these speculations is not of the nature to which they are accustomed, either in historical or scientific studies. More and more the age insists on strictness in appreciating evidence, and on economy in conjecture. But the study of the evolution of myth and belief has always been, and still is, marked by an extraordinary use, or abuse, of conjecture. The 'perhapses,' the 'we may supposes,' the 'we must infers' are countless.

As in too much of the so-called 'Higher Criticism' hypothesis is piled, by many anthropologists, upon hypothesis, guess upon guess, while, if only one guess is wrong, the main argument falls to pieces. Moreover, it is the easiest thing, in certain cases, to explain the alleged facts by a counter hypothesis, not a complex hypothesis, but at least as plausible as the many combined conjectures of the castle architects, though perhaps as far from the truth, and as incapable of verification. Of these statements examples shall be given in the course of this book.

We are all, we who work at these topics, engaged in science, the science of man, or rather we are painfully labouring to lay the foundations of that science. We are all trying 'to expedite progress.' But our science cannot expedite progress if our science is not scientific. We must, therefore, however pedantic our process may seem, keep insisting on the rejection of all evidence which is not valid, on the sparing use of conjecture, and on the futility of piling up hypothesis upon unproved hypothesis. To me it seems, as I have already said, that a legitimate hypothesis must 'colligate the facts,' that it must do so more successfully than any counter hypothesis, and that it must, for every link in its chain, have evidence which will stand the tests of criticism.

But the chief cause of indifference is the character of our evidence. We can find anything we want to find people say—not only 'the man in the street' but the learned say—among reports of the doings of savage and barbarous races. We find what we want, and to what we do not want we are often blind. For example, nothing in savage religion is better vouched for than the belief in a being whom narrators of every sort call 'a Creator who holds all in his power.' I take the first instance of this kind that comes to hand in opening Mr. Tylor's 'Primitive Culture.' The being is he whom the natives of Canada 'call " Andouagni," without, however, having any form or method of prayer to him.' The date of this evidence is 1558. It is obvious that Andouagni (to take one case out of a multitude) was not invented in the despair of magic. Mysticism has been called the despair of philosophy, and Mr. Frazer, as we shall see, regards religion as the despair of magic. By his theory man, originally without religion, and trusting in magic, found by experience that magic could not really control the weather and the food supply. Man therefore dreamed that 'there were other beings, like himself, but far stronger,' who, unseen, controlled what his magic could not control. ' To these mighty beings . . . . man now addressed himself . . . . beseeching them of their mercy to furnish him with all good things . . . .'[1]

But nobody beseeched Andouagni to do anything. The Canadians had ' no method or form of prayer to him.'[2] Therefore Andouagni was not invented because magic failed, and therefore this great power was dreamed of, and his mercy was beseeched with prayers for good things. That was not the process by which Andouagni was evolved, because nobody prayed to him in 1558, nor have we reason to believe that any one ever did.

From every part of the globe, but chiefly from among very low savage and barbaric races, the existence of beings powerful as Andouagni, but, like him, not addressed in prayer, or but seldom so addressed, is reported by

[1] *G. B.* i. 77.

[2] Tylor, *Prim. Cult.* ii. 309, citing Thevet, *Singularitez de la France Antarctique*, Paris, 1558, ch. 77.

travellers of many ages, races, creeds, and professions. The existence of the belief in such beings, often not approached by prayer or sacrifice, is fatal to several modern theories of the origin and evolution of religion. But these facts, resting on the best evidence which anthropology can offer, and corroborated by the undesigned coincidence of testimony from every quarter, are not what most students in this science want to find. Therefore these facts have been ignored or hastily slurred over, or the beliefs are ascribed to European or Islamite influence. Yet, first, Christians or Islamites, with the god they introduced would introduce prayer to him, and prayer, in many cases, there is none. Next, in the case of Andouagni, what missionary influence could exist in Canada before 1558? Thirdly, if missionaries, amateur or professional, there were in Canada before 1558 they would be Catholics, and would introduce, not a Creator never addressed in prayer, but crosses, beads, the Madonna, the Saints, and such Catholic rites as would leave material traces.

In spite of all these obvious considerations, I am unacquainted with any book on this phase of savage religion, and scarcely know any book, except Mr. Tylor's 'Primitive Culture,' in which the facts are prominently stated.

The evidence for the facts, let me repeat, is of the best character that anthropology can supply, for it rests on testimony undesignedly coincident, given from most parts of the world by men of every kind of education, creed, and bias. Contradictory evidence, the denial of the existence of the beliefs, is also abundant: to such eternal contradictions of testimony anthropology must make up her mind. We can only test and examine, in each instance, the bias of the witness, if he has a bias, and his opportunities of acquiring knowledge. If the belief does exist, it can seldom attest itself, or never, by material objects, such as idols, altars, sacrifices, and the sound of prayers, for a being like Andouagni is not prayed to or propitiated : one proof that he is not of Christian introduction. We have thus little but the reports of Europeans intimately acquainted with the peoples, savage or barbaric, and, if possible, with their language, to serve as a proof of the existence of the savage belief in a supreme being, a maker or creator of things.

This fact warns us to be cautious, but occasionally we have such evidence as is supplied by Europeans initiated into the mysteries of savage religion. Our best proof, however, of the existence of this exalted, usually neglected belief, is the coincidence of testimony, from that of the companions of Columbus, and the earliest traders visiting America, to that of Mr. A. W. Howitt, a *mystes* of the Australian Eleusinia, or of the latest travellers among the Fangs, the remote Masai, and other scarcely ' contaminated ' races.[1]

If we can raise, at least, a case for consideration in favour of this non-utilitarian belief in a deity not approached with prayer or sacrifice, we also raise a presumption against the theory that gods were invented, in the despair of magic, as powers out of whom something useful could be got : powers with good things in their gift, things which men were ceasing to believe that they could obtain by their own magical machinery. The strong primal gods, unvexed by prayer, were not invented as recipients of prayer.

To ignore this chapter of early religion, to dismiss it as a tissue of borrowed ideas—though its existence is attested by the first Europeans on the spot, and its originality is vouched for by the very absence of prayer,

---

[1] *Journal of Anthropological Institute*, Oct.–Dec. 1900 and N.S. II., Nos. 1, 2, p. 85.

and by observers like Mr. A. W. Howitt, Miss Kingsley, and Sir A. B. Ellis, who proposed, but withdrew, a theory of 'loan-gods'—is not scientific.

My own early readings in early religion did not bring me acquainted with this chapter in the book of beliefs. When I first noticed an example of it, in the reports of the Benedictine Mission at Nursia, in Australia, I conceived, that some mistake had been made in 1845, by the missionary who sent in the report.[1] But later, when I began to notice the coincidence of testimony from many quarters, in many ages, then I could not conceal from myself that this chapter must be read. It is in conflict with our prevalent theories of the development of gods out of worshipped ancestral spirits : for the maker of things, not approached in prayer as a rule, is said to exist where ancestral spirits are not reported to be worshipped. But science (in other fields) specially studies exceptional cases, and contradictory instances, and all that seems out of accord with her theory. In this case science has glanced at what goes contrary to her theory, and has explained it by bias in the reporters, by error in the reporters, and by the theory of borrowing. But such coincidence in misreporting is a dangerous thing for anthropology to admit, as it damages her evidence in general. Again, the theory of borrowing seems to be contradicted by the early dates of many reports, made prior to the arrival of missionaries, and by the secrecy in which the beliefs are often veiled by the savages; as also by the absence of prayer to the most potent being.

We are all naturally apt to insist on and be prepossessed in favour of an idea which has come to ourselves unexpectedly, and has appeared to be corroborated by wider research, and, perhaps, above all, which runs

[1] Max Müller, *Hibbert Lectures*, p. 16.

contrary to the current of scientific opinion. We make a
pet of the relatively new idea; let it be the origin of
mythology in ' a disease of language; ' or the vast religious
importance of totems; or our theory of the origin of
totemism; or the tremendous part played in religion by
gods of plants. We insist on the idea too exclusively;
we find it where it is not—in fact, we are very human,
very unscientific, very apt to become one-idea'd. It is
even more natural that we should be regarded in this
light by our brethren (*est-il embêtant avec son Etre
Suprême !*), whose own systems will be imperilled if our
favourite idea can be established.

I risk this interpretation when I keep maintaining—
what ?—that the chapter of otiose or unworshipped
superior beings in the ' Early History of Religion '
deserves perusal. Not to cut its pages, to go on making
systems as if it did not exist, is, I venture to think, less
than scientific, and borders on the superstitious. For to
build and defend a theory, without looking closely to
whatever may imperil it, is precisely the fault of the
superstitious Khond, who used to manure his field with a
thumb, or a collop from the flank of a human victim, and
did not try sowing a field without a collop of man's flesh,
to see what the comparative crops would be. Or science
of this kind is like Don Quixote, who, having cleft his
helmet with one experimental sword-stroke, repaired it,
but did not test it again.

Like other martyrs of science, I must expect to be
thought importunate, tedious, a fellow of one idea, and
that idea wrong. To resent this would show great want
of humour, and a plentiful lack of knowledge of human
nature. Meanwhile, I am about to permit myself to
criticise some recent hypotheses in the field of religious
origins, in the interests of anthropology, not of orthodoxy.

II

THE THEORY OF LOAN-GODS; OR BORROWED RELIGION

THE study of the origins of religion is impeded by the impossibility of obtaining historical evidence on the subject. If we examine the religious beliefs of extant races, the lowest in material culture, the best representatives of palæolithic man, we are still a long way from the beginnings of human speculation and belief. Man must have begun to speculate about the origins of things as soon as he was a reasoning animal. If we look at the isolated and backward tribe of Central Australia, the Arunta, we have the advantage of perhaps the best and most thoroughly scientific study ever made of such a race, the book by Messrs. Spencer and Gillen.[1]

Here we watch a people so 'primitive' that they are said to be utterly ignorant of the natural results, in the way of progeny, of the union of the sexes. Yet, on the same authority, this tribe has evolved an elaborate, and, granting the premises, a scientific and adequate theory of the evolution of our species, and the nature of life. An original stock of spirits is constantly reincarnated; spiritual pedigrees are preserved by records in the shape of oval decorated stones, and it seems that a man or woman of to-day may be identified as an incarnation of a soul, whose adventures, in earlier incarnations, can be traced back to the Alcheringa, or mythical heroic age of

[1] *Natives of Central Australia*, London, 1899.

the people. Their marriage laws are already in advance
of those of their neighbours, the Urabunna, and their
only magistracy, of a limited and constitutional kind,
descends in the male line.

Thus the Arunta are socially in advance of the Pictish
royal family in Scotland, whose crown descended in the
female line, no king being succeeded by his son. Manifestly
the religious or non-religious ideas of such a people, un-
clothed, houseless, ignorant of metals and of agriculture, and
without domesticated animals though they are, must be
ideas with a long history behind them. The Arunta philosophy is a peculiar philosophy, worked out by thoughtful
men, and elaborated so artfully that there seems neither
room for a god, nor for the idea of a future life, except the
life of successive reincarnations. It is therefore impossible
for us to argue that mankind in general began its speculative career with the singular and apparently godless
philosophy of the Arunta. Their working science is
sympathetic magic ; to the Great Spirit, with a trace of
belief in whom they are credited, they are not said to
pray ; and he seems to be either an invention of the
seniors, for the purpose of keeping the juniors and women
in order, or a being originally of higher character,
belief in whom has died out among the adults. To him
we return in another essay.

As historical information about the early or late evolution of the idea of a superior (not to say supreme) being
is thus unattainable, thinkers both ancient and modern
have derived the idea of God from that of ghost. The
conception of a powerful spirit of a dead father,
worshipped by his children, is supposed to have been
gradually raised to the power of a god. Against this
theory I have elsewhere urged that superior beings are
found among races who do not worship ancestral spirits ;

and again that these superior beings are not envisaged as spirits, but rather as supernormal magnified men, of unbounded power (an idea often contradicted in savage as in Greek mythology) and of limitless duration.

The reply to me takes the form of ignoring, or disabling the evidence, or of asserting that these superior beings are 'loan-gods,' borrowed by savages from Europeans or Islamites. It is to the second theory, that these savage superior beings are disguised borrowings from missionaries, explorers, traders, or squatters, that I now address myself.[1] These beings certainly cause difficulties to the philosophy which derives gods, in the last resort, from ghosts.

It is probable that these difficulties have for some time been present to the mind of Mr. E. B. Tylor (one may drop academic titles in speaking of so celebrated a scholar). When Mr. Tylor publishes the Gifford Lectures which he delivered some years ago at Aberdeen, we shall know his mature mind about this problem. Meanwhile he has shown that the difficulty, the god where no god should be, is haunting his reflections. For example, his latest edition of his 'Primitive Culture' (1891) contains, as we shall show, interesting modifications of what he wrote in the second edition (1871).

There are three ways in which friends of the current theory that gods are grown-up ghosts may attempt to escape from their quandary. (1) The low races with the high gods are *degenerate*, and their deity is a survival from a loftier stage of lost culture. Mr. Tylor, however, of course, knows too much to regard the Australians, in the stone age, as degenerate. (2) The evidence is bad or (Fr. Müller) is that of prejudiced missionaries. But Mr. Tylor

---

[1] With a case of ignoring the evidence I deal in the following essay, *Magic and Religion*.

knows that some of the evidence is excellent, and, at its best, does not repose on missionary testimony.   (3) The high gods of the low races are borrowed from missionary teaching.   This is the line adopted by Mr. Tylor.

I recently pointed out, in 'The Making of Religion' (1898), the many difficulties which beset the current theory. I was therefore alarmed on finding that Mr. Tylor had mined the soil under my own hypothesis.   His theory of borrowing (which would blow mine sky-high if it exploded) is expounded by Mr. Tylor in an essay, 'The Limits of Savage Religion,' published in the 'Journal of the Anthropological Institute' (vol. xxi., 1892).   I propose to examine Mr. Tylor's work, and to show that his own witnesses demonstrate the unborrowed and original character of the gods in question.

Mr. Tylor first opposes the loose popular notion that all over North America the Indians believed in a being named *Kitchi Manitou,* or 'Great Spirit,' a notion which I do not defend.   He says : 'The historical evidence is that the Great Spirit belongs, not to the untutored, but to the tutored mind of the savage, and is preserved for us in the records of the tutors themselves, the Jesuit missionaries of Canada.' [1]   Now as to the *word* 'Manitou,' spirit, Mr. Tylor quotes Le Jeune (1633) : ' By this word "Manitou," I think they understand what we call an angel, or some powerful being.' [2]   Again : 'The Montagnets give the name " Manitou " to everything, whether good or bad, superior to man.   Therefore, when we speak of God, they sometimes call Him "The Good Manitou," while when we speak of the Devil, they call him "The Bad Manitou."' [3]   When then, ninety years later, in 1724, Père Lafitau dilates on 'The Great Spirit,' 'The

[1] *Op. cit.* p. 284.   [2] Le Jeune, *Relations,* 1633, p. 17.
[3] *Ibid.,* 1637, p. 49.

Great Manitou,' we are to see that in ninety years the
term which the Indians used for *our* God—their translation of *le bon dieu*—has taken root, become acclimatised,
and flourished. Lafitau, according to Mr. Tylor, has also
raised the Huron word for spirit, *oki*, to Okki, with a
capital O, which he calls *Le Grand Esprit.* The eleva-
tion is solely due to Lafitau and other Christian teachers.
If all this were granted, all this is far indeed from proving
that the idea of a beneficent Creator was borrowed by
the Indians from the Jesuits between 1633 and 1724.
Mr. Tylor's own book, 'Primitive Culture,' enables us to
correct that opinion. Here he quotes Captain Smith, from
an edition of the 'History of Virginia' of 1632. Smith
began to colonise Virginia in 1607. He says (edition
of 1632) : 'Their chief god they worship is the Devil.
Him they call Okee (Okki), and serve him more of fear
than love.' Mr. Tylor cites this as a statement by 'a
half-educated and whole-prejudiced European' about
'savage deities, which, from his point of view, seem of a
wholly diabolic nature.' 'The word oki,' Mr. Tylor goes
on, 'apparently means "that which is above," and was,
in fact, a general name for spirit or deity.' [1]

The chief deity of the Virginians then (in 1607, before
missionaries came), with his temples and images, was a
being whose name apparently meant 'that which is above.'
Moreover, Father Brébeuf (1636) describes an oki in the
heavens who rules the seasons, is dreaded, and sanctions
treaties.

Consequently Lafitau did not, in 1724, first make oki,
a spirit, into Okki, a god. That had been done in Virginia
before any missionaries arrived, by the natives themselves,
long before 1607. For this we have, and Mr. Tylor has
cited, the evidence of Smith, before Jesuits arrived. What

---

[1] *Prim. Cult.* ii. 310.

is yet more to the purpose, William Strachey, a successor
of Smith, writing in 1611–12, tells us that Okeus (as he
spells the word) was only a magisterial deputy of 'the
great God (the priests tell them) who governs all the
world, and makes the sun to shine, creatyng the sun and
moone his companions, . . . [him] they call Ahone.   The
good and peaceable God requires no such duties [as are
paid to Okeus], nor needs to be sacrificed to, for he
intendeth all good unto them.'   He has no image.[1]
Strachey remarks that the native priests vigorously
resisted Christianity.   They certainly borrowed neither
Okeus nor Ahone, the beneficent Creator who is without
sacrifice, from Jesuits who had not yet arrived.

Do we need more evidence ?   If so, here it is.
Speaking of New England in 1622, Winslow writes about
the god Kiehtan as a being of ancient credit among the
natives.   He 'made all the other gods; he dwells far
westerly above the heavens, whither all good men go when
they die.'   Thus Mr. Tylor himself (*loc. cit.*) summarises
Winslow, and quotes : ' They never saw Kiehtan, *but they
hold it a great charge and dutie that one age teach another.*
And to him they make feasts, and cry and sing for plentie,
and victorie, or anything that is good.'

Thus Kiehtan, in 1622, was not only a relatively supreme
god, but also a god of ancient standing.   Borrowing from
missionaries was therefore impossible.

Mr. Tylor then added, in 1871 : ' Brinton's etymology
is plausible, that this Kiehtan is simply the Great Spirit
(Kittanitowit, Great Living Spirit, an Algonquin word
compounded of Kitta = great, manitou = spirit, termination,
wit, indicating life).'

---

[1] *Historie of Travaile into Virginia.*   By William Strachey, Gent. (a
companion of Captain Smith).   Hakluyt Society.   Date *circ.* 1612–1616.
See *Myth, Ritual, and Religion*, i. xx–xxxix, 1899.

But all this etymology Mr. Tylor omitted in his edition of 1891, probably no longer thinking it plausible.

He did, however, say in 1891 (ii. 342) : 'Another famous native American name for the Supreme Deity is Oki.'

Not content with Okeus, capital O and all, before the arrival of missionaries ; not content with Kiehtan, whose etymology (in 1871) 'apparently' means 'Great Spirit,' before the arrival of Jesuits in New England, Mr. Tylor, in ' Primitive Culture,' adds to these deities ' the Greenlanders' Torngarsuk, or Great Spirit (his name is an augmentative of " torngak," " spirit " [in 1891 " demon "]),' before the arrival of missionaries !   For, says Mr. Tylor, ' he seems no figure derived from the religion of Scandinavian colonists, ancient or modern. . . . He so clearly held his place as supreme deity in the native mind that, as Cranz the missionary alleges, many Greenlanders, hearing of God and His Almighty power, were apt to fall on the idea that it was their Torngarsuk who was meant.' [1]

Now, in 1891, Mr. Tylor dropped out ' he seems no figure derived from the religion of Scandinavian colonists, ancient or modern ; ' and he added that Torngarsuk was later identified, not with our God, but with our Devil : a foible characteristic, I may say—as Mr. Tylor said concerning Captain Smith and Oki—of ' a half-educated and whole-prejudiced European.' For the Algonquin Indians Mr. Tylor cited Father Le Jeune (1633) : 'When the missionary talked to them of an almighty creator of heaven and earth, they began to say to one another Atahocan, Atahocan.' But his name had fallen into contempt and a verb, *Nitatahocan*, meant ' I tell an old fanciful story.' In 1558 Thevet credits the Canadian Indians with belief in ' a creator ' Andouagni, not

---

[1] *Prim. Cult.* ii. p. 308.

approached with prayers. None of these beings can have been borrowed from Europeans. It will presently be seen that between 1871 and 1892 Mr. Tylor became sceptical as to the records of a Great Spirit in America. But he retained Oki in the sense of Supreme Deity.

Here, then, from Virginia to Greenland, Mr. Tylor presented in 1871 evidence for a being of supreme power, called by names which, perhaps, mean ' Great Spirit.' In his essay of 1892 he does not refer to his earlier work and his evidence there for a Great Spirit, nor tell us why he has changed his mind. He now attributes the Great Spirit to missionary influence. We naturally ask in what respect he has found the early evidence on which he previously relied lacking in value. Mr. Tylor, in ' Primitive Culture,' [1] gives a yet earlier reference than the others for a Virginian Creator. He cites Heriot (an author of 1586). Again : ' They believe in one who made all things, but pay him no honour,' writes Père L'Allemant in 1626, in a region where ' il n'y ait point eu de religieux.'

In 1871 Mr. Tylor said : ' It has even been thought that the whole doctrine of the Great Spirit was borrowed by the savages from missionaries and colonists. But this view will not bear examination. After due allowance made for mis-rendering of savage answers and importation of white men's thoughts, it can hardly be judged that a divine being, whose characteristics are so unlike what European intercourse would have suggested, and who is heard of by such early explorers among such distant tribes, could be a deity of foreign origin.' [2] In 1891 ' this view will not bear examination ' is deleted—why?—and the deity, we are told, ' could *hardly* be altogether of

---

[1] *Prim. Cult.* ii. pp. 309, 310 (1873 and 1891).
[2] *Prim. Cult.* ii. p. 308.

foreign origin.' He could not be, when found by the first European discoverers, and, had the creed been borrowed, prayer to the being would have been borrowed with it.

Now, in his essay of 1892, Mr. Tylor never, I think, alludes to his own evidence of 1873, or even of 1891, in favour of a Red Indian creator, evidence earlier than the Jesuits (1558, 1586, 1612–16, 1622, and of Le Jeune, 1633). In the essay of 1892 that authentic evidence 'of such early explorers among such distant tribes' to a savage conception of the Creator is not cited. The coincidence of testimony is the strongest possible evidence to the nature and unborrowed character of the being. Such coincidence is, in fact, Mr. Tylor's own touchstone of trustworthy testimony. Yet in 1892 the Jesuits receive the whole credit of introducing the idea. It would be interesting to know why the early evidence has suddenly become untrustworthy. The essay of 1892 ought, of course, to be regarded as only a sketch. Yet we are anxious to learn the reasons which made Mr. Tylor leave his evidence out of sight, though republished by him only the year before he put forth his tractate in favour of borrowing from Jesuits. I turn to another point on which I cannot accept Mr. Tylor's arguments.

In his essay of 1892 Mr. Tylor dates the Mandan Deluge legend as not before 1700. Why? Because Catlin (in 1830–1840) found iron instruments used ritually in the native Mystery Play of the Flood. They were supposed to represent the tools employed in making the vessel wherein 'the only man' escaped drowning. But the Mandans did not get iron tools before 1700. The Indians, however, we reply, had canoes before they had iron tools, and, in modern times, might naturally employ iron instead of flint instruments (discarded) in the Mystery Play. They might do this, in spite of the marked preference for stone tools in ritual. Perhaps they had none. It must here be observed that Catlin does not use the word ' ark ' (as Mr. Tylor does) for the vessel of ' the only man.' Catlin always says ' the big canoe.' Even if we admit (which we do not) that the Mandans necessarily borrowed their Deluge legend from whites, it does not follow, as Mr. Tylor argues, that because the ' Great Spirit ' appears in the Deluge legend, he ' cannot claim greater antiquity ' than 1700. In the first place, as, in Mr. Tylor's earlier statement, Canadians, Algonquins, Virginians, Massachusetts, and Greenlanders had a Great Spirit before Christian influences began, the Mandans may have been equally fortunate. Nor does it seem safe to argue, like Mr. Tylor, that if the Great Spirit figures in a (hypothetically) borrowed myth, therefore the conception of a Great Spirit was necessarily borrowed at the same time. That more recent myths are constantly being attached to a pre-existing god or hero is a recognised fact in mythology. Nor can mythologists argue (1) that Biblical myth is a modified survival of savage myth, and (2) that such natural and obvious savage myths as the kneading of man out of clay, the origin of death (' the Fall '), and the tradition of the Deluge are necessarily borrowed by savages from the Bible. This is, indeed, to argue in a vicious circle. Again, was the Australian and American myth of a race of wise birds, earlier than man, borrowed from the famous chorus in the ' Birds ' of Aristophanes ? Is the Arunta theory of evolution borrowed from Darwin, or their theory of re-incarnation from Buddhism ? Borrowing of ideas seems only to be in favour when savage ideas resemble more or less those of Christianity.

Mr. Tylor remarks that Prince Maximilian, who knew Mandanese better than Catlin, found among them no

'Great Manitou'—so called. But he did find a Creator
whose name means 'Lord of Earth.' Was He borrowed
from the whites? Finally, on this point, would savages
who remained so utterly un-Christian as the Mandans,
adopt from missionaries just one myth—the Deluge—and
make that the central feature in their national ritual?
Indeed this seems very improbable conduct! Nothing is
more conservative than ritual : that is notorious.

We do not follow Mr. Tylor into South America. If
our case is proved, by his own not repudiated authorities,
for North America, that suffices us. We turn to
Australia.

Let us first take the typical Australian case of Baiame,
Pei-a-mei, or Baiamai, at present alleged by Mr. Howitt
and others to be the moral creative being of many tribes,[1]
and served, without sacrifice, in their mysteries. Mr.
Tylor first finds him mentioned as a creator by Mr. Horace
Hale, whose book is of 1840.[2] Next, in 1850, Baiame
was spoken of by a native to some German Moravian
missionaries as a being who, according to their ' sorcerers
or doctors,' made all things, but was easy to anger, and
was to be appeased by dances. Thus he was accepted by
the most notoriously conservative class, the class most
jealous of missionary influence, the sorcerers. Omitting
for the moment a later description of Baiame as seen by
a black devotee in a vision, we turn to Mr. Tylor's theory
of the origin of this god. Mr. Ridley (who began his
missionary career in Victoria in 1854) gives a pleasing
account of Baiame as a creator, with a paradise for the
good. According to Mr. Ridley, ' Baiame ' is discovered
by Mr. Greenway to be derived from *baia*, ' to make,' and

---

[1] Howitt, *Journal of Anthropological Institute*, 1884, 1885.
[2] *United States Exploring Expedition. Ethnology and Philology*
p. 110.

he concludes that 'for ages unknown' the blacks have
called God 'the Maker.'[1]

Mr. Tylor now asks, 'Was Baiame,' who is, he
avers, 'near 1840 so prominent a divine figure among
the Australians, known to them at all a few years
earlier?' He decides that before 1840 Baiame was
'unknown to well-informed (white) observers.' This,
of course, would not prove that Baiame was unknown
to the blacks. As for the observers, who are three
in number, one, Buckley the convict, in spite of his
thirty-two years with the blacks, is of no real value. We
cannot trust a man who lied so freely as to say that in
Australia he 'speared salmon'! and often saw the fabled
monster, the Bunyip.[2] Buckley could not read, and his
book was made up by a Mr. Morgan out of 'rough notes
and memoranda . . . and by conversation.' If, then, as
Buckley says, 'they have no notion of a Supreme Being'
(p. 57), we may discount that; Buckley's idea of such a
being was probably too elevated. Moreover he never
mentions the confessedly ancient native mysteries, in one
of which among certain tribes the being is revealed.[3]
Mr. Tylor's next well-informed observer before 1840,
Mr. Backhouse, a Quaker, takes his facts straight from
the third witness, Mr. Threlkeld; he admits it for some
of them, and it is true, in this matter, of all of them.[4]
Buckley being out of court, and Backhouse being a mere
copy of Mr. Threlkeld, what has Mr. Threlkeld to say?
What follows is curious. Mr. Threlkeld (1834–1857) does

[1] Ridley, *Kamilaroi Vocabularies*, p. 17 (1875). Also in an earlier
Grammar, 1866.

[2] *The Life and Adventures of William Buckley*, 1852, pp. 40–48.

[3] Howitt, *J. A. I.*, 1885. The Kurnai tribe.

[4] Backhouse, *Narrative of a Visit to the Australian Colonies*, 1843,
p. 555. Compare Threlkeld, *An Australian Language*, 1892, p. 47. This
is a reprint of Mr. Threlkeld's early works of 1831–1857.

not name Baiame, but speaks of a big supernatural black man, called Koin, who carries wizards up to the sky, inspires sorcerers, walks about with a fire-stick, and so on.[1] To honour him boys' front teeth are knocked out in the initiatory stages.

As soon as I read this passage I perceived that Mr. Threlkeld was amalgamating such a goblin as the Kurnai call ' Brewin ' with the high God of the Mysteries. In 1881, when Mr. Howitt, with Mr. Fison, wrote ' Kamilaroi and Kurnai,' he knew no higher being among that tribe than the goblin Brewin. But, being initiated later, Mr. Howitt discovered that the God of the Mysteries is Mungan-ngaur = ' Our Father ' (this shows the slight value of negative evidence). Women know about Brewin, the goblin master of sorcerers, but the knowledge of Mungan-ngaur is hidden from them under awful penalties.[2] Not only I, but Mr. Horace Hale (1840), came to this opinion : that Koin is a goblin, Baiame a god, as we shall see. In the same way, where Baiame is supreme, Dara-mulun is sometimes a goblin or fiend.

Mr. Threlkeld very properly did not use the name of the fiend Koin as equivalent to ' God ' in his translation of the Gospel of St. Luke into the native tongue (1831–1834). He there used for God Eloi, and no doubt did the same in his teaching ; he also tried the word *Jehovaka-birvη*. Neither word has taken with the blacks ; neither word occurs in their traditions. The word, though forced on them, has not been accepted by them. That looks ill for the theory of borrowing.

Here, then, of Mr. Tylor's three negative witnesses, who, before 1840, knew not Baiame, Mr. Threlkeld alone is of value. As Mr. Hale says, Mr. Threlkeld was (1826–1857) the first worker at the dialects of those Baiame-

[1] *Op. cit.* p. 47.   [2] *Journal Anthrop. Inst.*, 1885.

worshipping tribes, the Kamilaroi of the Wellington
Valley, in Victoria. But whence did Mr. Hale get
what Mr. Tylor cites, his knowledge in 1840 of Baiame?
He, an American *savant* on an exploring expedition,
could not well find out esoteric native secrets. I
shall prove that Mr. Hale got his knowledge of Baiame
from Mr. Tylor's own negative witness, Mr. Threlkeld.
Mr. Hale says that 'when the missionaries first came to
Wellington,' Baiame was worshipped with songs. 'There
was a native famous for the composition of these songs
or hymns, which, according to Mr. Threlkeld, were passed
on,' &c. Mr. Hale thus declares (Mr. Tylor probably
overlooked the remark) that when the missionaries first
came to Wellington (where Baiame is the Creator) they
found Baiame there before them ![1] Then, why did Mr.
Threlkeld not name Baiame? I think because Mr. Hale
says that Baiame's name and sacred dance were brought
in by natives from a distance, and (when he is writing)
had fallen into disuse.[2] Had, then, a missionary before
1840 evolved Baiame from Kamilaroi *baia*, 'to make '
(for that is Mr. Tylor's theory of the origin of the word
'Baiame '), and taught the name to distant natives as a
word for his own God; and had these proselytising
distant dancing natives brought Baiame's name and dance
to Wellington? Are missionaries dancing masters?
They would teach prayer and kneeling, or give rosaries;
dances are no part of our religion. To demonstrate
missionary influence here we must find a missionary, not
Mr. Threlkeld, who was studying and working on the
Kamilaroi tongue before 1840. There was no such
missionary. Finally, Mr. Hale runs counter to Mr. Tylor's

---

[1] He was supposed to live on an island, on fish which came at his call,
probably a childlike answer to a tedious questioner.

[2] *Exploring Expedition of U. S.*, 1846, p. 110.

theory of borrowing from whites, though Mr. Tylor does not quote his remark. The ideas of Baiame may 'possibly' be derived from Europeans, 'though,' says Mr. Hale, 'the great unwillingness which the natives always evince to adopt any custom or opinion from them militates against such a supposition.' So strong is this reluctance to borrow ideas from the whites, that the blacks of the centre have not even borrowed the idea that children are a result of the intercourse of the sexes! Here, then, in part of the district studied by Mr. Threlkeld in 1826–1857, an American *savant* (who certainly received the facts from Mr. Threlkeld) testifies to Baiame as recently brought from a distance by natives, but as prior to the arrival of missionaries, and most unlikely to have been borrowed.

Whence, then, came Baiame? Mr. Tylor thinks the evidence 'points rather to Baiame being the missionary translation of the word "creator," used in missionary lesson books for God.' But by 1840, when Baiame is confessedly 'so prominent a divine figure,' Mr. Threlkeld's were the only translations and grammatical tracts in the Kamilaroi tongue. Now Mr. Threlkeld did not translate 'creator' (or anything else) by 'Baiame;' he used 'Eloi' and 'Jehova-ka,' and the natives would have neither of these words. Where is Mr. Tylor's reason, then, for holding that before 1840 (for it must be prior to that date if it is going to help his argument) any missionary ever rendered creator by 'Baiame'? He has just argued that no 'observer' then knew the name Baiame, so no observer could have introduced a name Baiame which he did not know; yet there was the name; Mr. Hale found it there. Mr. Tylor's argument seems to be that Mr. Ridley in 1866, and again in 1877, printed extracts, in which occurs Baiame = God, from the 'Missionary Primers prepared for the Kamilaroi.' We might have expected Mr. Tylor at least to give the dates of the ' Missionary Primers ' that, *ex hypothesi*, introduced Baiame before 1840. He gives no dates, and the primers are of 1856 and are written by Mr. Ridley, who cites them.[1] Thus they must be posterior to the Baiame of 1840, and Baiame was prior to missionaries at Wellington, at the time when Mr. Tylor first notes his appearance. Thus, by Mr. Tylor's own evidence, Baiame is not shown to be a missionary importation ; the reverse.

As to Australia, it is not denied by Mr. Tylor that practically all over the continent the blacks possess religious mysteries of confessed antiquity. It is not denied that the institution of these mysteries is now, in many cases, attributed by the blacks to a moral creative being, whose home is in or above the heavens. It is not denied that his name now usually means, in different dialects, Maker (Baiame), Master (Biamban), and Father (Papang, and many other words). It is not denied that the doctrine of this being is *now* concealed from children and women, and revealed to lads at the *Bora*, or initiatory mystery.[2] But, on the other hand (as I understand Mr. Tylor), while initiatory rites are old (they certainly existed when Dampier touched at the Australian coast in 1688–1689), the names of their institutor (Father, Maker), his moral excellencies (?), and his creative attributes, are all due to missionary influence. The original founder of the Bora, in pre-missionary days, would only be a dead ' head-man ' or leader, now religiously regarded.

To this we first demur. It is not shown—it is denied by Waitz, and it is not even alleged by Mr. Herbert Spencer—that the Australians ' steadily propitiate ' or sacrifice at all to any ghosts of dead men. How can they ?

---

[1] *Gurre Kamilaroi, or Kamilaroi Sayings.* Sydney, 1856. It is a scarce little book, with illustrations and Bible stories.

[2] Howitt, *Journal Anthrop. Institute, ut supra.*

The name of the dead is tabooed, and even where there is in one instance an eponymous human patronymic of a tribe, that patronymic alters in every generation. Now, among such a ghost-worshipping people as the Zulus, the most recently dead father gets most worship. In Australia, where even the recent ghosts are unadored, is it likely that some remote ghost is remembered as founder of the ancient mysteries ? This is beyond our belief, though the opinion is, or at least was, that of Mr. Howitt. The mere institution of female kin among some of these tribes (though paternity is recognised) makes against an ancient worship of a male ancestor where even now ancestors are unworshipped.

As to the aspect of this god, Baiame, Mr. Tylor presently cites a story told to Mr. Howitt by a native, of how with his father he once penetrated in the spirit to Baiame's home, and found him to be ' a very great old man with a long beard,' and with crystal pillars growing out of his shoulders which support a supernal sky. His ' people,' birds and beasts, were around him. Mr. Tylor says : ' These details are, it will have been noticed, in some respects of very native character, while in others recalling conventional Christian ideas of the Almighty.'

The ' Christian ' idea is, naturally, that of the old man of Blake and Michael Angelo—Hartley Coleridge's ' old man with the beard.' Is it likely that the savages had seen any such representations ? Again, is the idea of Baiame as an old man not natural to a race where respect of age is regularly inculcated in the mysteries and prevails in practice ? ' Among the Kamilaroi about Bundurra, Turramulan [another name for this or a lower god] is represented [at the mysteries] by an old man learned in all the laws.' [1] . . .

[1] Greenway, *J. A. I.* vii. p. 243.

As early as 1798 Collins found that the native word
for ' father ' in New South Wales was applied by the
blacks as a title of reverence to the Governor of the nascent
colony.[1] It is used now in many native tribes as the name
of their Supreme Being, and Mr. Tylor thinks it of missionary origin. Manifestly, this idea of age and paternity
in a worshipped being is congenial to the natives, is illustrated in their laws and customs, need not be borrowed,
and is rather inevitable. The vision of Baiame, we may
add, was narrated to Mr. Howitt by a native fellow-initiate.
To lie, in such cases, is ' an unheard-of thing,' says Mr.
Howitt. The vision was a result of the world-wide
practice of crystal gazing. The seer's father handed
to him a crystal. ' When I looked at it,' says the
narrator, all manner of visions appeared, including that
of Baiame.[2]

It is manifest, we think, that when the natives attach
the attributes of fatherhood and antiquity to Baiame, they
need not be borrowing from Christian art notions so
natural, nay, so inevitable, in their own stage of society.
Though in many cases reckoning kinship through women,
they quite undeniably recognise paternity in fact. Thus
the paternal title had no need to be borrowed as a word of
reverence. It was so used before missionaries came.

Mr. Howitt, who is deeply initiated, writes : ' Beyond
the vaulted sky lies the mysterious home of that great
and powerful being who is Bunjil, Baiame, or Taramulan
in different tribal languages, but who in all is known by a
name the equivalent of the only one used by the Kurnai,
which is Mangun-ngaur, Our Father.'[3]

Now, not to multiply evidence which is provided by

[1] Collins, *Account of the Colony of New South Wales*, 1798, vol. ii.
p. 544.
[2] *J. A. I.* xvi. pp. 49, 50.   [3] *Op. cit.*, 1885, p. 54.

other observers as to Central Australia (not so central
as the Arunta country) and the North, Mr. Tylor is
confronted with this problem : Have all the tribes who
regard a powerful being, Baiame or another, as founder of
their ancient mysteries, borrowed his name and attributes,
since 1840 or so, from whites with whom they were
constantly in hostile relations ? Is it probable that,
having hypothetically picked up from Christians the
notion of a moral Father in heaven, their ' priests ' and
initiators instantly disseminated that idea over most of
the continent, and introduced it into their most secret
and most conservative ceremonies ? Would they be likely
to restrict so novel a piece of European information to the
men ? Mr. Dawson, in his ' Aborigines of Australia ' (p. 51),
writes : ' The recent custom of providing food for it (a
corpse) is derided by intelligent old aborigines as " white
fellows' gammon " ! ' Thus do they estimate novelties !
Yet in Mr. Tylor's theory it is the most conservative
class of all, the medicine-men and learned elders—everywhere rivals and opponents of Christian doctrine—who
pick up the European idea of a good, powerful father or
master, borrow a missionary name for him (we have
shown that the name, Baiame, is not of missionary origin),
and introduce him in precisely the secret heart of the
mysteries. This knowledge is hidden, under terrible
penalties, from women and children : to what purpose ?
Do missionaries teach only the old rams of the flock, and
neglect the ewes and lambs ? Obviously the women and
children must know any secret of divine names and
attributes imparted by missionaries. Again, it is not
probable that having recently borrowed a new idea from
the whites the blacks would elaborately hide it from its
authors, the Europeans. So well is it hidden that, till he

was formally initiated, Mr. Howitt had no suspicion of its existence.[1]

Mr. Tylor may rest in his hypothesis of borrowing, but for the reasons assigned we think it impossible in our, and his, selected North American cases, and inconceivable as an explanation of the Australian phenomena.

Finally, Mr. Tylor candidly adduces a case in which Mr. Dawson, taking great and acknowledged trouble to collect evidence, learned from the blacks that they had believed in a benevolent being, Pirnmeheal, 'whose voice is the thunder,' 'before they knew of the existence of Europeans,' who 'have given them a dread of Pirnmeheal.'[2] We add Mr. Howitt's testimony to a supreme being ruling 'from Omeo to Shoalhaven River, from the coast to Yass Gundagai,' concerning whom ' old men strenuously maintained that it was so before the white men came,' they themselves, now aged, having only learned the secret when they were initiated 'and made men' at about the age of fourteen.[3] In the same essay of 1885 [4] Mr. Howitt tells of a native whose grandfather initiated him as to an all-seeing personality, Bunjil, 'up there,' who would mark his conduct. ' This was said before the white men came to Melbourne' (1835). Bunjil, said William Beiruk, a black, was called ' our father' ' before white men came to Melbourne.'

I might give other evidence in favour of the unborrowed character of Australian belief in some such being as Baiame. Thus Mrs. Langloh Parker, the careful collector of ' Australian Legendary Tales,'[5] was herself interested in the question. She approached the

---

[1] For concealment from women and children, see Howitt, *J. A. I.* xiii. p. 192.

[2] Dawson, *Aborigines of Australia*, p. 49.

[3] *J. A. I.* xiii. 1885, p. 142.

[4] *Op. cit.* p. 194.   [5] Two volumes. Nutt.

subject as a disciple of Mr. Herbert Spencer, who allows hardly a germ of religion to the Australians.   On hearing what she did hear, as to Baiame, from the tribesmen, she asked one of them whether the idea was not borrowed from Europeans.   The old warrior answered that if it were so the young men would know most about Baiame. But they know nothing, apparently because the old rites of initiation have fallen into disuse.   Nor are they much more familiar with Christian doctrine.   This black man had logic in him.   Mrs. Langloh Parker came, contrary to her prepossessions, to the same opinion as our best authority, Mr. Howitt, that the Australian belief is unborrowed.

This lady, who has taken very great pains in criticising and collecting her evidence, kindly sent me an essay of Mr. Manning's from 'The Journal of the Royal Society of New South Wales,' vol. xvi. p. 159, 1883.   Mr. Manning was an early settler in the north border of the southern colony.   About 1832 he was in Europe, and met Goethe, whose undiminished curiosity, he being then about eighty-five, induced him to bid Mr. Manning examine Australian beliefs.   He did, but lost his notes, made in 1845–1848.   In these notes, which he later recovered, Mr. Manning used Christian terminology, instead of making a verbatim report.   Struck by the certainly singular savage idea of a son (begotten in some cases, in others a kind of 'emanation') of the superior being, he employed theological phrases.   The son, in his story, sprang from a liquid like blood, which Boyma (Baiame) placed in a vessel within a crystal oven.   The myth of such a birth, as Mr. Hartland remarks, is familiar to Zulus and Red Indians.[1]   It is therefore not likely to be of European origin.   But Mr. Manning's evidence,

[1] *Legend of Perseus*, i. 97.

despite its terminology, so far agrees with Mrs. Langloh
Parker's account of the extant Baiame belief as to 'make
a case for further inquiry;' so Mr. Hartland concedes.
I ask for no more.[1] Thus Mr. Manning has Ballima,
Mrs. Langloh Parker has Bullimah, for a kind of floral
paradise of souls, very beautifully described in the lady's
'More Australian Legendary Tales.'

Both authorities mention prayers for the dead; Mrs.
Langloh Parker quotes what Mr. Hartland calls 'very interesting funeral rites and prayers for the dead.' He adds:
'We want to be assured whether these are usual, by means
of an accurate description of the customary ceremonies, and
that she does not give us.' I shall make inquiry; but what
does it matter whether the rites, in the overthrow of native
manners, are now usual or not? Baiame is unknown to
the new generation, as we have seen. Prayers to him,
then, cannot be usual. The point is that Mr. Manning
in 1845, and Mrs. Langloh Parker in 1898, both mention
the prayers for the dead, certainly not borrowed from
Protestants. There is a similar account, only that of an
unnamed runaway convict who lived with the black
fellows in North-Western Australia.[2] By a mythical
contradiction, the soul of the hero Eerin, prayed for in
Mrs. Langloh Parker's tale, now inhabits a little bird.

Another curious point needs to be considered by the
advocates of the theory of borrowing. Mr. Hartland
offers some deserved censures on Mr. Manning's terminology in his report of Australian religion (1845–1848).
Mr. Manning says: 'They believe in the existence of a
Son of God, equal with him in omniscience, and but
slightly inferior to his Father in any attribute. Him
they call "Grogoragally." His divine office is to watch over
all the actions of mankind, and to bring to life the dead

---

[1] *Folk Lore*, March 1899, p. 55.   [2] Ridley, *J. A. I.*, 1872, p. 282.

to appear before the judgment seat of his Father, who alone pronounces the awful judgment of eternal happiness in heaven (Ballima) or eternal misery in "Oorooma" (hell), which is the place of everlasting fire (gumby). The Son . . . acts as mediator for their souls to the great God, to whom the good and bad actions of all are known.' As Mr. Hartland truly says, 'this is not an accurate scientific account.' Even Mr. Manning's ' capital letters ' are censured.

Probably the native theologian really said something like this : 'Boyma' (Baiame) big man; very budgery man. Him sit on big glass stone. Him son Grogoragally can see everything and go everywhere. See budgery man, like him ; see bad man, plenty too much devil devil. Likes budgery man ; no likes bad man : he growl too much. Budgery man die, Grogoragally tell Boyma ; Boyma say, 'Take him Ballima way, plenty budgery place.' Bad man 'die ; Boyma say, 'Take him Oorooma way, plenty too hot, him growl there.' Grogoragally plenty strong, him not so strong as Boyma.

This, or something like this, would be the actual statement of the dusky theologian. It is easily rendered into Mr. Manning's terminology ; but at the same time the native, in his rude *lingua franca*, or pidgin English, could hardly do justice to his creed. It *was* his creed ; Mr. Hartland himself recognises the original character of the native version of the Supernatural Birth.[1]

Here are certainly ' Biblical analogies,' as Mr. Tylor recognises, but they are as certainly unborrowed.

Now let us fancy that a traveller, not a Greek scholar, is storm-driven to a hitherto unknown island. He finds a race of heathen white men. He describes their religion. ' Despite their polytheism, they have certainly been

[1] *Folk Lore*, March 1899, pp. 52, 53.

visited by Christian missionaries, or are descended from a Christian colony. They believe in a supreme being whom they call Zeus. He has a son named Apollon or Phœbus Apollon, who is all-knowing and all-seeing. He acts as a kind of mediator between Zeus and men, to whom, as one of the native hymns says, he "delivers the counsels of the Father, and his unerring will." This Apollo is consulted through an hysterical woman, who lives in a cave. After being convulsed, like other savage mediums, she speaks in a kind of verse. Her advice is often obscure and ambiguous, but generally of a moral tendency.

' This son of Zeus is believed to be the only god who really knows the future and the will of his father. There is another son, Hermes, one of whose duties is to conduct the souls of the dead into the presence of their judge, who is not Zeus, but another god.

' There is also a son of Apollo, whom I take to be only a kind of double of that god; he sometimes appears to his worshippers as a serpent: his name is Asclepius.

' This reminds us of what Winslow writes about the Red Indians of New England. They have a supreme being, Kiehtan, whose son, Hobamok, appears in their assemblies as a serpent. Ridley has the same story about the blacks of Australia. I infer, then, that the natives of this island have inherited or been taught some elements of Christianity, as in the case of Apollo, the mediator between Zeus and men; and Hermes, the Guide of Souls as they call him, *psychopompos* in their language. But they have mixed up all this with degrading superstitions.'

Of course our traveller has arrived among Greeks, and quotes the Homeric hymn to Apollo. But the Greeks, being prior to Christianity, did not borrow from it, as our traveller supposes. On the other hand, the Greek beliefs which he describes resemble Australian and American beliefs more closely than Australian and American beliefs resemble the creed taught by missionaries. Yet neither Mr. Tylor nor any other friend of the borrowing theory asserts that the Australians or Americans borrowed their tenets from Greece.

The truth seems to be that where a supreme being is regarded as too remote and impassive, he is naturally supplied with a deputy. Ahone has Oki, Kiehtan has Hobamok, Boyma has Grogoragally, Baiame has Tundun, or in places Daramulun; Nyankupon, in West Africa, has Bobowissi. Sometimes, as in the Australian Noorele's case, these active deputies are sons of the supreme being. No borrowing is needed to explain ideas so natural to early men, believing in a supreme being remote and retired, little concerned with mundane affairs, and acting through a deputy or deputies. In other cases, as of the Finnish Num, or the Zulu Unkulunkulu, or the Algonquin Atahocan, the being is quite neglected in favour of spirits who receive sacrifices of meat or grease. Human minds work on similar lines, without borrowing, which is only alleged in the case of Christianity to account for the beliefs which do not fit the 'ghost theory' of modern speculators.

The essential point of Mr. Manning's report, injured as it is by his impossible terminology, is the extreme secrecy maintained on these points by his savage informants. They used to believe that the world would perish if the women heard of their dogmas. Thus a man said to Mr. Howitt (whose competence as a witness is indisputable) : ' If a woman were to hear these things, or hear what we tell the boys, I would kill her.' [1] One of Mr. Manning's witnesses slunk ' into a wooden fireplace,'

[1] *J. A. I.* vol. xiv. p. 310.

whence he whispered his beliefs. He had previously examined doors and windows in search of listeners. A man who reported these creeds would, if they became divulged among the women, be obliged to kill his wife.

If the religious ideas were borrowed from missionaries, the women would know them as well as the men. They would not be reserved for initiates at the mysteries, through which Mr. Howitt derived his most esoteric knowledge of creeds, whereof, in 1881, he was absolutely ignorant.[1]

If the beliefs were of missionary origin, the young men, not the old men, would know most about Baiame. For similar beliefs in North-West Central Queensland I may cite Mr. Roth.[2] The being Mulkari is described by Mr. Roth as 'a benevolent, omnipresent, supernatural being; anything incomprehensible.' 'Mulkari is the supernatural power who makes everything which the blacks cannot otherwise account for; he is a good, beneficent person, and never kills any one.' His home is in the skies. He was also a medicine-man, has the usual low myths about him, and invented magic. So writes Dr. Roth, who knows the local Pitta Pitta language—and is not a missionary. Dr. Roth is pursuing his researches, and his remarks are only cited provisionally, awaiting confirmation.

Sometimes European observers do not see the trend of their own reports. In 1845 Mr. Eyre described 'the origin of creation' as narrated to him by Australian blacks on the Murring River. A being, Noorele, with three unbegotten sons, lives up among the clouds. He is 'all

---

[1] See his and Mr. Fison's *Kamilaroi and Kurnai*, 1881.

[2] *North-West Central Queensland Aborigines*, pp. 14, 36, 116, 153, 158, 165.

powerful and of benevolent nature.   He made the earth, trees, water, &c.   He receives the souls (*ladko*=shades, *umbræ*) of the natives, who join him in the skies and will never die again.'   Yet Mr. Eyre adds : ' A Deity, a Great First Cause, can hardly be said to be acknowledged.' [1] What is Noorele if not a ' Great First Cause ' ?

Among some tribes Bunjil, merely a title of authority, meaning master, lord, headman, is a name of the superior being.   Abundance of the mythology of Bunjil, often ludicrous or degrading, the being showing as a super-normal medicine-man, may be found in Mr. Brough Smyth's great collections.[2]   But no evidence can be better than that of native poetry, which proves a higher aspect of Bunjil.

A Woiworung bard of old made a song which moved an aged singer to tears by ' the melancholy which the words conveyed to him.'   It was an ' inspired ' song, for the natives, like ourselves, would think Tennyson inspired and Tupper not so.   Usually ' the spirits ' inspire singers ; this song was inspired by Bunjil himself, who ' " rushes down " into the heart of the singer,' just as Apollo did of old.   It is a dirge of the native race :

> We go all !
> The bones of all
> Are shining white.
> In this Dulur land !
> The rushing noise
> Of Bunjil, our Father,
> Sings in my breast,
> This breast of mine ! [3]

The missionaries do not inspire these songs.   They put them down.   ' The white man,' says Mr. Howitt, ' knows

[2] Eyre, vol. ii. pp. 355–357.
[3] *Aborigines of Victoria.*
[4] Arranged in lines from the literal translation, preserving the native idiom.   Howitt, *J. A. I.* vol. xvi. pp. 330, 331.

little or nothing of the black fellows' songs.' One of Mr. Manning's informants (1845) was angry when asked for the Hymn to Baiame (Boyma). He said that Mr. Manning knew too much already.

I have dwelt specially on Australia, because there, as the natives do not worship ancestral spirits (the names of the dead are tabooed), their superior being cannot have been evolved out of ghost worship. I have expressly avoided the evidence of missionaries, except the early Jesuits, because missionaries are believed by some writers to be biassed on this point, though, in fact, on other points they are copiously cited by anthropologists. As Mr. Tylor finds the saintly and often martyred Jesuits of 1620–1660 worth quoting, I have therefore admitted Father Le Jeune's testimony to the existence of Atahocan before their arrival in America, with Father Brébeuf's Oki, or ' un Oki,' whose anger is feared and who sanctions treaties. It is impossible to me to understand how the savages could borrow from Europeans the beliefs which the Europeans found extant when they arrived. I have not touched the case of Africa. In ' The Making of Religion ' (pp. 222–228), I argued against Sir A. B. Ellis's elaborate theory of borrowing a god, in the case of the Tshi-speaking races. I did not know that this exact writer had repudiated his theory, which was also rejected by Miss Mary Kingsley.

As to Australia, in face of the evidence (which settled Mr. Howitt's doubts as to the borrowing of these ideas) can any one bring a native of age and credit who has said that Baiame, under any name, was borrowed from the whites ? Mr. Palmer is ' perfectly satisfied ' that ' none of these ideas were derived from the whites.' He is speaking of the tribes of the Gulf of Carpentaria, far away indeed from Victoria and New South Wales. There is no greater authority among anthropologists than Waitz, and Waitz rejects the hypothesis that the higher Australian religious beliefs were borrowed from Christians.[1]

To sum up, we have proved, by evidence of 1558, 1586, 1612–16, and 1633, that a sort of supreme creative being was known in North America before any missionary influence reached the regions where he prevailed. As to the Australian god Baiame, we have shown out of the mouth of Mr. Tylor's own witness, Mr. Hale, that Baiame preceded the missionaries in the region where literary evidence of his creed first occurs. We have given Mr. Hale's opinion as to the improbability of borrowing. We have left it to Mr. Tylor to find the missionary who, before 1840, translated ' Creator ' by the Kamilaroi word ' Baiame ' while showing the difficulty—I think the impossibility — of discovering any Kamilaroi philologist before Mr. Threlkeld. And Mr. Threlkeld certainly did not introduce Baiame ! We have proved that, contrary to Mr. Tylor's theory of what a missionary can do, Mr. Threlkeld could not introduce his own names for God, Eloi and Jehovah-ka, into Kamilaroi practice. We note the improbability that highly conservative medicine-men would unanimously thrust a European idea into their ancient mysteries. We have observed that by the nature of Mr. Tylor's theory, the hypothetically borrowed divine names and attributes must (if taken over from missionaries) have been well known to the women and children from whom they are concealed under dreadful penalties. We have demonstrated the worthlessness of negative evidence by proving that the facts were discovered, on initiation, by a student (Mr. Howitt), confessedly in the first rank, though he, during many years, had been ignorant of their existence. We show that the ideas of age and

[1] *Anthropologie*, vi. p. 798.

paternity, in an object of reverence, are natural and habitual to Australian natives, and stood in no need of being borrowed. We suggest that the absence of prayer to a powerful being is fatal to the theory of borrowing. We show that direct native evidence utterly denies the borrowing of divine names and attributes, and strenuously asserts that before Europeans came to Melbourne (1835) they were revealed in the secret doctrine of ancient initiatory rites. This evidence again removed the doubts which Mr. Howitt had entertained on the point, and Mr. Palmer and Mr. Dawson agree with Mr. Howitt, Mr. Ridley, Mr. Günther, and Mr. Greenway, all experts, all studying the blacks on the spot. In the study, Waitz is of the same opinion. Australian religion is unborrowed.

It is rare, in anthropological speculations, to light on a topic in which verifiable dates occur. The dates of the arrivals of missionaries and other Europeans, the dates of Mr. Hale's book, of Mr. Threlkeld's books, of Mr. Ridley's primer, are definite facts, not conjectures in the air. While this array of facts remains undemolished, science cannot logically argue that the superior beings of low savage belief are borrowed from Christian teachers and travellers. That idea is disproved also by the esoteric and hidden nature of the beliefs, and by the usual, though not universal, absence of prayer. The absence of prayer again, and of sacrifice, proves that gods not bribed or implored were not invented as powerful givers of good things, because good things were found not to be procurable by magic.

This condition of belief is not what a European, whatever his bias, expects to find. He does not import this kind of ideas. If they are all misreports, due to misunderstandings in America and Australia from 1558 to 1898, what is the value of anthropological evidence?

It ought to be needless to add that when good observers like Miss Kingsley find traces of Jesuit or other missionary teaching in regions, as Africa or Canada, where Jesuits actually taught in the past, I accept their decision.[1] My arguments against the theory of borrowing apply chiefly to cases where the beliefs reported were found already extant by the first white observers, to tribes where missionaries like Mr. Threlkeld could not introduce their names for deity, and to tribes which jealously conceal their theology from the whites.

[1] Miss Kingsley, 'African Religion and Law,' *National Review*, September 1897, p. 132.

III

MAGIC AND RELIGION

' THE sin of witchcraft is as the sin of rebellion.' The idea which inspires this text probably is that a person who seeks to obtain his ends by witchcraft is rebelling against the deity or deities through whom alone these ends should be sought. Witchcraft is also an insult and injury to the official priests, who regard the witch as the surgeon regards the bone-setter, or as the geologist regards the ' dowser ' or water-finder who uses the divining-rod.

Magic or witchcraft falls into two main classes. The former is magic of the sort used by people who think that things accidentally like each other influence each other. You find a stone shaped like a yam, and you sow it in the yam plot. You find a stone like a duck, and expect to have good duck-shooting while you carry the stone about in a bag. In the same way the part influences the whole ; you burn some of a man's hair, and so he catches a fever. Imitation works in the same manner ; you imitate the emergence of grubs from the larvæ, and you expect grubs to emerge.

All magic of this kind is wrought by material objects, sticks, stones, hair, and so forth, which sometimes have been ' charmed ' by songs chanted over them. Among the Arunta of Central Australia, in many respects a backward people, we do hear of an ' evil spirit' influencing the material object which has been charmed.[1] We also hear

[1] Spencer and Gillen, p. 549.

of spirits which instruct men in medical magic. But, as a rule, the magic is materialistic. It really does produce effects, by suggestion : a man dies and a woman is won, if they know that magic is being worked to kill or woo.

The second sort of magic acts by spells which constrain spirits or gods to do the will of the magician. This magic involves itself in religion when the magical ceremonies are, so to speak, only symbolic prayers expressed in a kind of sign-language. But if the idea is to put constraint by spells on a god or spirit, then the intention is magical and rebellious. Though the official priest of a savage god may use magic in his appeal to that deity, he is not a wizard. It is the unofficial practitioner who is a witch, just as the unqualified medical practitioner is a quack. In the same way if a minister of the kirk was clairvoyant or second-sighted that was a proof of godliness and inspiration. But if a lay parishioner was second-sighted, he or she was in danger of the stake as a witch or wizard.

These, briefly stated, are the points of contrast and points of contact between magic and religion. The question has recently been raised by Mr. Frazer, in the new edition of his ' Golden Bough,' whether magic has not everywhere preceded religion. Have men not attempted to secure weather and everything else to their desire by magic, before they invented gods, and prayed to them for what magic, as they learned by experience, failed to provide ?

This question cannot be historically determined. If we find a race which has magic but no religion, we cannot be certain that it did not once possess a religion of which it has despaired. I once knew a man who, as a child, suffered from toothache. He prayed for relief : it did not come. He at once, about the age of eight, abandoned

religion.   What a child may do, in the way of despair of
religion, a childlike race may do. Therefore, if we find a race
with magic but without religion, we cannot scientifically
say that the race has never possessed a religion.   Thus the
relative priority of religion or magic cannot be ascertained
historically.

Again, all depends on our definition of religion, if we
are to pursue a speculation rather airy and unbottomed
on facts.   Mr. Frazer defines religion as ' a propitiation or
conciliation of powers superior to man which are believed
to direct and control the course of nature and of human
life.' [1]   But clearly this definition does not include all
that we usually mean by religion.   If men believe in a
potent being who originally made or manufactured the
nature of things or most things (I am warned not to use
the word ' creator '), that is an idea so far religious
that it satisfies, by the figment of a supernatural agent,
the speculative faculty.   Clearly the belief in such a
being is a germ whence may spring the ideas of duty
towards, and an affection for, the being.   Nobody can deny
that these are religious ideas, though they do not appear
in Mr. Frazer's definition.   The believers in such a
being, even if they never ask him for anything, cannot be
called irreligious.   At a period of his life when Coleridge
never prayed, he would have been much and not unjustly
annoyed if Mr. Frazer had called him irreligious.   A man
may believe in God, and yet trust him too utterly to
address him in petitions for earthly goods and gear.
' Thy Will be Done ' may be his only prayer ; yet he does
not lack religion.   He only lacks it in the sense of Mr.
Frazer's definition.

If that definition is granted, Mr. Frazer is prepared
to produce a backward race, houseless, without agriculture,

[1] *G. B.* i. p. 63.

metals, domestic animals, and without religion in Mr. Frazer's sense. They have magic, but they have no religion, says Mr. Frazer, who presently informs us that 'the first-born child of every woman was eaten by the tribe as part of a religious ceremony.'[1] So they have a religion, and a bloody religion it is.

That people is the Australian, among whom, 'while magic is universally practised, religion in the sense of a propitiation or conciliation of the higher powers seems to be nearly unknown.'[2] 'Nobody dreams of propitiating gods or spirits by prayer or sacrifice.'

We are presently to see that Mr. Frazer gives facts which contradict his own statement. But first I must cite all that he says about Australian religion. 'In the south-eastern parts of Australia, where the conditions of life in respect of climate, water, and vegetation are more favourable than elsewhere, some faint beginnings of religion appear in the shape of a slight regard for the comfort of departed friends. Thus some Victorian tribes are said to have kindled fires near the bodies of their dead in order to warm the ghost, but " the recent custom of providing food for it is derided by the intelligent old aborigines as 'white fellows'' gammon."'[3] Some tribes in this south-eastern region are further reported to believe in a supreme spirit, who is regarded sometimes as a benevolent, but more frequently as a malevolent, being.[4] Brewin, the supreme being of the Kurnai, was at first identified by two intelligent members of the tribe with Jesus Christ, but on further reflection they thought he must be the devil.[5] But whether viewed as gods or devils

---

[1] *G. B.* ii. p. 51.   [2] *G. B.* i. p. 71.

[3] J. Dawson, *Australian Aborigines*, pp. 50, *sq.*

[4] A. W. Howitt in *Journal of the Anthropological Institute*, xiii. (1884), . 191.

[5] L. Fison and A. W. Howitt, *Kamilaroi and Kurnai*, p. 255.

it does not seem that these spirits were ever worshipped.[1]
It is worth observing that in the same districts which
thus exhibit the germs of religion, the organisation
of society and the family has also made the greatest
advance.   The cause is probably the same in both cases—
namely, a more plentiful supply of food due to the greater
fertility of the soil.[2]   On the other hand, in the parched
and barren regions of Central Australia, where magic
attains its highest importance, religion seems to be
entirely wanting.[3]   The traces of a higher faith in
Australia, where they occur, are probably sometimes due
to European influence.   'I am strongly of opinion,' says
one who knew the aborigines well, 'that those who have
written to show that the blacks had some knowledge
of God, practised prayer, and believed in places of reward
and punishment beyond the grave, have been imposed
upon, and that until they had learned something of
Christianity from missionaries and others the blacks had
no beliefs or practices of the sort.   Having heard the
missionaries, however, they were not slow to invent what
I may call kindred statements with aboriginal accessories
with a view to please and surprise the whites.'[4]   Sometimes, too, the reported belief of the natives in a great or
good spirit may rest merely on a misunderstanding.
Mr. Lorimer Fison informs me (in a letter dated June 3,
1899) that a German missionary, Mr. Siebert, resident in
the Dieri tribe of Central Australia, has ascertained that
their Mura Mura, which Mr. Gason explained to be the
Good Spirit,[5] is nothing more or less than the ancestors in

[1] See A. W. Howitt in *Journal of the Anthropological Institute*, xiii.
(1884), p. 459.
[2] See A. W. Howitt in *Journal of the Anthropological Institute*, xviii.
(1889), pp. 32, *sq.*   Religion is not mentioned here.
[3] See Spencer and Gillen, *Native Tribes of Central Australia*.
[4] E. M. Curr, *The Australian Race*, i. 45.
[5] *Native Tribes of South Australia*, p. 260.

the 'dream times.' There are male and female Mura
Mura—husbands, wives, and children—just as among the
Dieri at the present day. Mr. Fison adds : ' The more
I learn about savage tribes, the more I am convinced that
among them the ancestors grow into gods.'

This is all that Mr. Frazer has here to say about the
religious belief of the Australians. He has found, in ' the
museum of the past,' a people with abundance of magic,
yet with no religion, or not enough to affect his theory that
religion was everywhere second in order of time to magic.
I am very content to meet him on Australian ground.
There we find abundance of testimony to the existence of
a belief speculative, moral, and emotional, but not practical.
The beings of this belief are not propitiated by sacrifice,
and very seldom by prayer, but they are makers, friends,
and judges. Mr. Tylor accepts (I think) the evidence for
the beliefs as at present found, but presumes many of their
characteristics to be of European importation. Against
that theory I have argued in the preceding essay, giving
historical dates. Mr. Frazer omits and ignores the
evidence for the beliefs. He denies to the Australians
more than ' some faint beginnings of religion,' and puts
down ' traces of a higher faith ' as ' probably sometimes
due ' (and perhaps it sometimes is) ' to European influence. ' For this theory Mr. Curr is cited : ' Having heard
the missionaries, they were not slow to invent what I call
kindred statements with aboriginal accessories, with a view
to please and surprise the whites.' [1]

To please and surprise the whites the natives concealed
their adaptations of Christian ideas in the mysteries, to
which white men are very seldom, or were very seldom,
admitted ! Is this likely ? I believe that the exclusive
rule is now relaxed where the natives are practically paid

[1] E. M. Curr, *The Australian Race*, i. 45.

to exhibit.[1]   One Bora was under European patronage, and
the old men and children were fed on European supplies.
But when Mr. Howitt was initiated by the Kurnai, and so
first learned the secret of their religion, ' the old men. . . .
desired to be satisfied that I had in very deed been fully
initiated by the Brajerak black fellows in their Kuringal.'
He therefore retired to a lonely spot, ' far from the possibility of a woman's presence,' and exhibited the token of his
previous initiation by the Murrings. Hitherto ' long as the
Kurnai had known me, these special secrets of the tribe had
been kept carefully from me by all but two,' one of whom
was now dead. The inmost secret was the belief in Mungan-
ngaur, ' the Great Father of the tribe, who was once on
earth, and now lives in the sky, [he] is rather the beneficent
father, and the kindly though severe headman of the
whole tribe, than the malevolent wizard, such as are other
of the supernatural beings believed in by the Australian
blacks.' [2]

Mr. Frazer cites Mr. Howitt thus : ' Some tribes in this
south-eastern region are further reported to believe in a
supreme spirit, who is regarded sometimes as a benevolent
but more frequently as a malevolent being.' [3]   What has
become of Mr. Howitt's evidence *after* initiation by the
Kurnai, evidence published in 1885 ?   How can the
blacks invent beliefs to please the whites when they only
reveal them to Mr. Howitt, after he has produced a bull
roarer as a token of initiation ?   Mr. Frazer then writes :
' Brewin, the supreme being of the Kurnai, was at first
identified by two intelligent members of the tribe with
Jesus Christ, but on further reflection they thought he
must be the devil.'   This is cited from a work of 1881,

---

[1] Cf. Mr. Matthews and Mr. Crawley, *J. A. I.* xxiv. 413.
[2] *J. A. I.* xiv. 1885, p. 521.
[3] *G. B.* i. 72, note ; *J. A. I.* xiii. p. 191 (1884).

Messrs. Fison and Howitt's 'Kamilaroi and Kurnai'
(p. 255). It must have escaped even Mr. Frazer's erudition that Mr. Howitt says : 'When I wrote of Brewin in
my paper on " Some Australian Beliefs " I was not aware
of the doctrines as to Mungan-ngaur. These the Kurnai
carefully concealed from me until I learned them at the
Jeraeil, or mysteries.' [1]

Had Mr. Frazer observed this remark of Mr. Howitt's,
he could not have cited, without comment or correction,
Mr. Howitt's earlier and confessedly erroneous opinion
that 'Brewin' is 'the supreme being of the Kurnai.' [2]
To Mr. Howitt's correction in 1885 of his mistake of
1881 Mr. Frazer, as far as I observe, makes no allu-
sion.

Mr. Frazer must either have overlooked all the evidence
for an Australian belief ruinous to his theory of the origin
of religion (ruinous if Australia represents the earliest
known stages of religion), or he must have reasons, not
produced, for thinking all that evidence too worthless to
deserve confutation or even mention. We are anxious to
know his reasons, for, on other matters, he freely quotes
our witnesses. Yet I cannot think Mr. Frazer consistently so severe as to Australian evidence. He has a
picturesque theory that the origin of the Passover was
a rite in which masked men ran about through Hebrew
towns in the night, butchering all the first born of Israel.[3]
No people, we exclaim, ever did such a thing ! In proof
of the existence of the custom Mr. Frazer adduces an
Australian parallel : ' In some tribes of New South Wales
the first-born child of every woman was eaten by the

[1] *J. A. I.*, 1885, p. 321, note 2.
[2] *G. B.* i. 72, note 1. In the first edition of *Myth, Ritual, and Religion*
I quoted Mr. Howitt's evidence of 1881. In the second edition I naturally
cited his later testimony.
[3] *G. B.* ii. 49, 50.

tribe as part of a religious ceremony.' [1]   Mr. Frazer's
authority is a communication by Mr. John Moore Davis,
and was published in 1878, twenty-three years ago, by
Mr. Brough Smyth.   Here is what Mr. Davis says : ' In
parts of N. S. W., such as Bathurst, Goulburn, the
Lachlan, or Macquarie, it was customary *long ago* for the
first-born of every lubra to be eaten by the tribe, as part
of a religious ceremony, and I recollect a black fellow
who had, in compliance with the custom, been thrown
when an infant on the fire, but was rescued and brought
up by some stock-keepers who happened accidentally to be
passing at the time.   The marks of the burns were
distinctly visible on the man when I saw him. . . . '

The evidence is what the Society for Psychical Research calls ' remote.'   In 1878 the event was already
' long ago.'   The testimony is from we know not how
remote a hand.   The black sufferer, as a baby at the
time, could not remember the facts.   The stock-keepers
who were present are not named, nor do we even know
whether Mr. Davis was informed by them, or heard their
story at third or fourth hand.   We do not know whether
they correctly interpreted the alleged sacrifice, in a
religious ceremony (by a people said to be almost or quite
irreligious), of all the first-born children of women.   Mr.
Frazer has circulated inquiries as to Australian customs,
and has published the results in the ' Journal of the
Anthropological Institute.' [2]   He does not appeal to the
answers in corroboration of Mr. Davis's remarkable story.[3]

Imbued with the superstition of psychical research,
I once investigated the famous Australian tale of Fisher's
ghost (1826).   I sent for the Court archives (the ghost led
to a trial for murder), and I received these and a contem-

[1] *G. B.* ii. 51, citing Brough Smyth's *Aborigines of Victoria*, ii. 311.
[2] November 1894, pp. 158–198.   [3] *G. B.* ii. 51–53.

porary plan of the scene of the murder and the apparition.
These documents left me doubtful about the ghost of
Fisher.[1]   May I not say that similar researches and good
corroborative evidence are needed before we accept a
settler's tale of an Australian *sacrifice*, ' long ago,' as
confirming a theory of a Hebrew *yearly massacre* of all the
first-born ?   Moreover, if Mr. Moore's evidence is good as
to a sacrifice, why is the latest evidence of Mr. Howitt and
all my other witnesses as to Australian religion not worth
mentioning ?   Why is it so bad that Mr. Frazer goes back
to Mr. Howitt's evidence of 1881, before he knew the
secret, and is silent about Mr. Howitt's evidence of 1885 ?

We may quote Sir Alfred Lyall : ' One effect of the
accumulation of materials has been to encourage speculative generalisations, because it has provided a repertory
out of which one may make arbitrary selection of examples
and precedents to suit any theory.'   Has Mr. Frazer
escaped this error ?

I cannot think that he has escaped, and the error is
fatal.   He cites Mr. Howitt, Mr. Palmer, Mr. Oldfield,
Mr. Dawson, and Mr. Cameron (whom I am about to
quote), all of whom speak to a native religion of the kind
for which I contend.   Their witness is enough for him
in other matters, but as to this matter these witnesses,
for some reason, are absolutely ignored.   I myself have
omitted the affirmative evidence of Mr. Oldfield and Mr.
Foelsche as to religion, because I think it contaminated,
although in part corroborated.   But my witnesses, all
cited for other points by Mr. Frazer, are not even mentioned
on the point where, if their reports be correct, they seem
rather to invalidate his central theory—that religion was
invented in the despair of magic.

[1] For ' Fisher's Ghost ' see *Blackwood's Magazine*, August 1897, p. 78
et seq.

As to that despair, it does not exist. The religions of Babylon, Greece, and Egypt lived side by side with superabundant magic. The Australians, when their magic fails, merely say that some other black fellow is working stronger counter-magic.[1]

However, that is a different question. The question at present is, Why does Mr. Frazer not cite and confute the evidence of witnesses, whom he quotes on other points, evidence fatal to his theory? Why does he ignore it? Among so many witnesses, distrustful of facts that surprise them, anxious to explain by borrowing, all cannot be biassed. If they were, why is not the testimony of witnesses with the opposite bias also discredited or ignored? Why is it welcomed? Mr. Frazer prefers the opinion of Mr. Siebert, a German missionary, that the Dieri propitiate ancestral spirits, to the opinion of Mr. Gason, that the being of their belief is a good spirit who made them. I do not know which of these gentlemen is right; possibly both views are held by different native informants. But Mr. Siebert's ancestral spirits come through Mr. Fison, who says: 'The more I learn about savage tribes, the more I am convinced that among them ancestors grow into Gods '—so natural a process where the names of the dead are tabooed !

'Oh no, we never mention them,
Their names are never heard.'

So they grow into gods ! Mr. Fison is a Spencerian; so, for all that I know, may Mr. Siebert be. If so, both have a theory and a bias, yet they are cited. It is only witnesses who hold that the Australians, certainly not, as a rule, ancestor worshippers, believe in a kind of god, who are not deemed worthy of mention on this point, though quite trustworthy on other points.

[1] *J. A. I.* xv. 4.

I cannot understand this method. The historian has a theory. He searches for contradictory facts. The chemist or biologist does not fail to mention facts hostile to his theory.

We are not asking Mr. Frazer to accept the testimony of Mr. Howitt, Mr. Cameron, Mr. Ridley, Mr. Greenway, Mr. Gason, Mr. Hale, Archdeacon Günther, the Benedictines of Nursia, Mr. Dawson, Mr. Eyre, Mr. Roth, Mrs. Langloh Parker; or to accept the opinion of Waitz, Mr. Howitt, and others as to unborrowed Australian religion. Their testimony may be erroneous; when it is proved erroneous I shall abandon it. But perhaps anthropologists may be allowed to be curious as to the reasons for which this and similar testimony is ignored. The reason cannot be that there is contradictory evidence, for some observers deny magic to the tribes whom they know.[1] Yet Mr.

---

[1] To be true to my own principles, I note a few points in Mr. Frazer's Australian evidence, published by him in *J. A. I.*, November 1894.

Mr. Gason, an excellent witness, says that the Dieri think some souls turn into old trees or rocks, or 'as breath ascend to the heavens,' to 'Purriewillpanina.' The Dieri believe the Mooramoora created them and will look after their spirits (*op. cit.* p. 175). Mr. Frazer, however, calls the Mura Mura 'remote ancestral spirits,' who would have a difficulty, one thinks, in creating the Dieri. The names of the dead may not be mentioned (p. 176).

The station master at Powell's Creek denies that magic 'exists in any shape or form.' There are no religious dances, no belief in a future life (p. 180). Mr. Lindsay Crawford says 'nothing is known of the nature of souls.' For the last ten years this gentleman 'had held no communication with the natives at all, except with the rifle.' Perhaps his negative evidence is not very valuable, as he does not appear to have won the friendly confidence of the blacks. Mr. Matthews says: 'Many tribes believe future existence is regulated by due observances at burial according to the rites of the tribe' (p. 190). Mr. Foelsche, described by Dr. Stirling as 'a most intelligent and *accurate* observer, who knows the natives well,' contributes a belief in a benevolent creator, with a demiurge who made the blacks. He inhabits Teelahdlah, among the stars. 'He never dies.' He is 'a very good man,' not a 'spirit.' A subterranean being 'can read and write, and keeps a book' of men's actions. This is so manifestly due to European influence that I have not cited Mr. Foelsche's evidence.

Frazer has no doubt as to the prevalence of magic, though one of his witnesses, Mr. Foelsche, gives no magic, but gives religion. 'Whether viewed as gods or devils,' Mr. Frazer says of South-East Australian beings, 'it does not seem that these spirits were ever worshipped.' He has ignored the evidence that they are worshipped (if the rights of the Bora are worship), but, if they are not worshipped, so much the worse for his theory. Gods, in his theory, were invented just to be worshipped. 'To these mighty beings . . . . man now addressed himself . . . . beseeching them of their mercy to furnish him with all good things . . . .' [1]

As against the correctness of my witnesses I only know the mass of evidence by white observers who have detected no religion among these savages. But I do not necessarily accept the negative evidence, because the beliefs are reported, by the affirmative witnesses, to be guarded with the utmost secrecy.[2] It is not every inquirer who has the power of eliciting beliefs which, for many reasons, are jealously guarded. Many Englishmen or Lowlanders are unable to extract legends of fairies, ghosts, and second-sight from Gaelic Highlanders. On the other hand, they are kind enough to communicate to me plenty of their folk-lore. 'The Urkus were very shy and frightened when asked about their religion,' says Mr. Pope Hennessy in his 'Notes on the Jukos and other Tribes of the Middle Benæ' (1898).[3]

Thus I prefer the affirmative evidence of Europeans who have won the confidence of the Australians, and have been initiated, to the denials of observers less

Mr. Foelsche 'knows of no magic or witchcraft being practised' (p. 197). The blacks believe that after death their souls 'go up'; they then point skywards (p. 198).

[1] *G. B.* i. 72, note i. 77.
[2] See 'The Theory of Loan Gods.'
[3] *J. A. I.* January to June, 1900, No. 31, p. 27.

fortunate. As for their theory that the religious practices, if they exist, are borrowed from Christians, I have stated my case in the preceding essay. There could be no stronger evidence than the absence of prayer that the Australian religion is not borrowed.

This argument ought especially to appeal to Mr. Frazer. His definition of religion is that of Euthyphro, in the Platonic Dialogue of that name.

> *Socrates.* Sacrificing is giving to the Gods, and piety is asking from them?
> *Euthyphro.* Yes, Socrates.
> *Socrates.* Upon this view, then, piety is a science of asking and giving?
> *Euthyphro.* You understand me capitally, Socrates.

Mr. Frazer agrees with Euthyphro. But if we find that the most backward race known to us believes in a power, yet propitiates him neither by prayer nor sacrifice, and if we find, as we do, that in many more advanced races in Africa and America it is precisely the highest power which is left unpropitiated, then we really cannot argue that gods were first invented as powers who could give good things, on receipt of other good things, sacrifice and prayer.

Sir Alfred Lyall here agrees with Mr. Frazer. 'The foundation of natural religion is . . . . the principle of *Do ut des* ' (' I give that you may give '), ' and the most ingenious researches into the evolution of primitive ideas will hardly take us beyond or behind it.' [1] My ' researches ' do not pretend to be ' ingenious.' It is a mere question of facts. Have Mr. Howitt's tribes the idea of a power, a very great power, which is interested in conduct, sanctions conduct, but is not asked for material benefits? Have, or had, all the American and African peoples whom I have

[1] *Asiatic Studies*, ii. 172.

cited a highest power often unconciliated ?   If so, why did
they invent these beings ?   Certainly not to play with them
at the game of *Do ut des*.   Yet that game was the origin of
religion, according to Sir Alfred and Mr. Frazer.   The facts
must be mentioned, must be disproved, before the theory
of *Do ut des* can be established.

Even if we accepted the theory of Euthyphro and of
Mr. Frazer it is beset by difficulties.   Religion is the
despair of magic, says the theory.   Magic is found by the
higher minds to be a failure.   Rain is not produced, nor
sunshine, nor food, as a result of magic.   Consequently
invisible powers, 'like himself, but far stronger,' are
invented by man.   They are immortal, and are asked to
take man's immortal spirit home to them.[1]   Yet they are
mortal themselves.[2]   They are so dependent on man, these
beings which are far stronger, that man actually has to
sacrifice his kings to them annually to keep these far
stronger beings in vigour.[3]   I am willing to suppose, with
Mr. Frazer, a very gradual process of evolution in religious
thought.   Man began by thinking his own magic all
powerful.   He found that a failure, ' and came to rest, as
in a quiet haven after a tempestuous voyage, in a new
system of faith and practice. . . . a substitute, however
precarious, for that ' (magical) ' sovereignty over nature
which he had reluctantly abdicated.'   To be sure he had
not abdicated, Greek and Babylonic magic are especially
notorious.   But let us fancy that man at large but
gradually reached the conception of powers far higher
than himself.   They were very limited powers at first :
they helped him, but he had to help them, to the extent,
sometimes, of killing his kings annually to keep them in
health.   This is Mr. Frazer's position.[4]   But if our

[1] *G. B.* i. 77.
[2] *G. B.* ii. 1.
[3] *G. B.* ii. 1–59, and *passim*, almost.
[4] *G. B.* i. 78, 79.

Australian evidence is correct, this theory is baseless. That is why our evidence cannot be neglected.

It is another difficulty that the more man ought to be finding out the fallacy of magic, the less does he find it out. Mr. Frazer chooses the Arunta of Central Australia as a people wholly without religion, but universally magicians. I have frequently read the account of Arunta magic by Messrs. Spencer and Gillen, but I never found that it included a belief like this: 'A man god . . . . draws his extraordinary power from a certain sympathy with nature.' He is defined not as an incarnation of a god ' of an order different from and superior to man,' but as only a superior sorcerer where most men are sorcerers. ' He is not merely the receptacle of a divine spirit.' We have just been told that he is not the receptacle of a divine spirit at all, and we shall take it to be so. ' His whole being, body and soul, is so attuned to the harmony of the world, that a touch of his hand or a turn of his head may send a thrill vibrating through the universal framework of things.[1] . . . .'

But you will look in vain for this portentous belief among the Arunta, who, not having found out the fallacy of magic, have not invented beings superior to man. For this sorcerer of the very highest magic you have to go to the civilisation of Japan, or to the peoples on the Congo, much more civilised than the Arunta.[2] These peoples, by Mr. Frazer's theory, had experience and intelligence enough to find out the fallacy of magic, and had gods in great plenty. But they have carried the belief in magic, in a magician much superior to his neighbours, to a pitch infinitely beyond the Arunta. Yet the Arunta have no gods with whom to draw comparisons invidious and

[1] *G. B.* i. 81.   [2] *G. B.* ii. 8; i. 232, 233.

unfavourable to magicians ; they have, it is said, no gods at all.

Just as magic thus reaches its highest power, according to Mr. Frazer, where there is most religious competition (while the reverse should be the case by his theory), so religion flourishes most in Australia, exactly where, by Mr. Frazer's theory, the circumstances are most unfavourable to religion and most favourable to magic. Magic, by the hypothesis, must prosper most, its fallacy must be latest discovered, it must latest give place to religion, where it appears to be most successful, and *vice versâ*. Yet Mr. Frazer assures us that in Australia magic flourishes alone, where every circumstance demonstrates its failure ; and religion begins to blossom precisely where magic must seem to its devotees a relative success.

Before examining this apparent inconsistency, let us note Mr. Frazer's inadvertent proof that his irreligious Australians are religious. One part of the business of magic is to produce rain in season, sun in season, and consequently an abundant food supply.[1] The Dieri of Central Australia need especially excellent magic. ' In a dry season their lot is a hard one.' Having no religion, they ought, of course, to work by mere materialistic magic, like the Arunta.[2] But they, oddly enough, ' call upon the spirits of their remote ancestors, which they call Mura Mura, to grant them power to make a heavy rain,' and then men inspired by the Mura Mura work magic, or pray in sign-language, as you please.[3] Now the Mura Mura, the rain-givers, by evidence which Mr. Frazer himself has published, is ' a Good Spirit,' not a set of remote ancestral spirits. The witness is Mr. Gason, ' than whom ' (says Mr. Frazer's authority, Dr. Stirling) ' no man living has been more among blacks or knows

[1] *G. B.* i. 81–114.   [2] *G. B.* i. 88, 89.   [3] *G. B.* i. 86.

more of their ways.' If on this excellent evidence the
Australian Dieri call for rain to a good spirit, then they
have religion, which Mr. Frazer denies. But if Mr.
Siebert, a German missionary, is right (and Mr. Frazer,
as we saw, prefers his view to that of Mr. Gason), then
the Mura Mura are only ancestral spirits.

Yet to demand the aid of remote ancestral spirits by
prayer is religion. In fact Mr. Frazer had said of the
powerful beings of the Southern Australians ' it does not
seem that these spirits are ever worshipped.' [1] But prayer
is worship, and the Dieri pray, whether to a good spirit
or to ancestral spirits, potent over the sky, and dwelling
therein. If this is not religion, by Mr. Frazer's own
definition, namely ' a propitiation or conciliation of
powers superior to man, which are believed to direct and
control the course of nature,' what is religion ? [2] Yet in
Australia ' nobody dreams of propitiating gods or spirits
by prayer and sacrifice,' says our author.[3] None the less
they ' call upon the spirits of their remote ancestors,
which they call Mura Mura, to grant them power to
make a heavy rain.' After ceremonies magical, or more
prayers in sign-language, the Mura Mura ' at once cause
clouds to appear in the sky.' [4] They see the signs which
their worshippers are making. Here then we have
prayer to ' powers superior to man ' (whether to the
Good Spirit or to ancestral spirits), and that, on evidence
collected by Mr. Frazer, occurs in a country where,
fourteen pages earlier, he had assured us that ' nobody
thinks of propitiating gods or spirits by prayer and sacrifice.'
Sacrifice, happily, there is none ; the Dieri have not
degenerated to sacrificing human victims like the Greeks.

[1] G. B. i. 72, note 1.
[2] G. B., i. 86, 87.
[3] G. B. i. 72.   [4] G. B. i. 87.

The scene is Central Australia, where 'the pitiless sun beats down for months together out of a blue and cloudless sky on the parched and gaping earth.' Consequently rain-making magic must perpetually prove a failure. Therefore, I presume, the Dieri have been driven into religion by discovering the fallacy of magic. This would be a logical argument, but Mr. Frazer's argument is the converse of what I suggest and contradicts his theory. He dubiously grants the existence of possible faint 'germs of religion' 'in the south-eastern parts of Australia, where the conditions of life in respect of climate, water, and vegetation are more favourable than elsewhere . . . . It is worth observing that in the same regions which thus exhibit the germs of religion, the organisation of society and the family has also made the greatest advance. The cause is probably the same in both cases—namely, a more plentiful supply of food due to the greater fertility of the soil.'[1] Now, according to Mr. Frazer's whole argument, the confessed failure of magic is the origin of religion.[2] But in Central Australia, where magic notoriously fails most conspicuously to supply water and vegetation, magic flourishes to the entire exclusion of religion, except among the Dieri. On the other hand, in South-Eastern Australia, where magic, if practised, is abundantly rewarded by more water and more vegetation, there these proofs of the success of magic are 'probably the cause' of the germs of religion. But, by Mr. Frazer's hypothesis, what must be the apparent success of magic in securing 'a more plentiful supply of food' ought to encourage the belief in magic, and prevent religion from even germinating. On the other hand, the successful result of magic (for to what else can a people

---

[1] *G. B.* i. 72, note.
[2] *G. B.* ii. 75-80. The hypothesis is ' offered with all due diffidence.

of sorcerers attribute the better food supply ?) has been 'probably the cause' of the first germs of religion. How can these things be ?

All this time one tribe of Central Australia, the Arunta, remains resolutely godless 'in spite of all temptations to join denominations' of a religious character. For the Arunta live in the worst country, the most rainless, and therefore their magic is most manifestly a failure. Yet, unlike the natives of South-Eastern Australia (where magic is most successful), the Arunta cling to magic, and have developed no religion. If so, as of all rain-making magic theirs is about the most unsuccessful, they must be very stupid, or they would detect the failure, and fly to religion, 'a quiet haven after a tempestuous voyage.' The Arunta are very far from stupid ; they have the most complete and adequate of savage metaphysics. If, then, they have not approached superior powers, in face of the failure of their magic, it may be that they have tried and discarded religion. 'Religion for the women and the children, magic for men' appears to be the Arunta motto : not so very uncivilised ! This I suggest because Mr. Frazer tells us that at the initiatory rites of the Arunta 'the women and children believe that the roaring noise' of the wooden slat, tied to a string and swung about, is 'the voice of the great spirit Twanyirika.'[1] A great spirit (above all if spelled with capital letters) is rather a religious conception. 'This spirit, the women are told, lives in wild and inaccessible regions. . . . Both uninitiated youths and women are taught to believe in the existence of Twanyirika.' So write Messrs. Spencer and Gillen, our only sources.[2]

A brief note is all that these inquirers give in their copious book to the great spirit. 'This belief,' they say,

---

[1] *G. B.* iii. 424.   [2] *Natives of Central Australia*, p. 246, note 1.

' is fundamentally the same as that found in all Australian tribes.' Now in the tribes reported on by Mr. Howitt, the spirit whose voice is the sound of the slat or bull roarer called the *tundun*, and by other names, is the son or other deputy of Baiame, or some such powerful good being, Mungan-ngaur, Pirmeheal, Bunjil, Noorele, or by whatever style he may be called. One of his duties is to superintend the Bora, or mysteries of the tribes. The Wiraijuri believe that their type of Twanyirika was destroyed, for misconduct, by his superior, Baiame. This sinful great spirit was called Daramulun, but in other tribes Daramulun is apparently the superior, and goes on existing. He is, says Mr. Howitt, ' the Great Master,' ' the Father,' the sky dweller, the institutor of society, the power whose voice ' calls to the rain to fall and make the grass green.' He is the moral being for whom ' the boys are made so that Daramulun likes them '—a process involving cries of *nga* (' good '), so says Mr. Howitt. His attributes and powers (where he is supreme) ' are precisely those of Baiame,' who, by Mr. Ridley and many others, is spoken of as a maker, if I may not say creator. It was in 1854, two years before publishing his ' Gurre Kamilaroi ' (in which ' Baiame ' was used for ' God '), that Mr. Ridley asked a Kamilaroi man, ' Do you know Baiame ? ' He said, *Kamil zaia zummi Baiame, zaia winuzgulda* (' I have not seen Baiame ; I have heard, or perceived him. They hear him in the thunder'). Among this tribe Daramulun was not the superior ; he was ' author of disease and medical skill, of mischief and wisdom also ; he appears in the form of a serpent at their assemblies,' like Asclepius and the American Hobamok.[1] Though Mr. Ridley is a missionary, I venture to cite him, because

---

[1] *J. A. I.*, 1872, pp. 268, 269. Lang's *Queensland*, pp. 444, 445. Winslow, in Arber's *Captain Smith*, p. 768.

his evidence goes back nearly fifty years, to a time when the blacks had less contact with Europeans. Moreover, Mr. Ridley is corroborated by Mr. Howitt and other laymen, while Mr. Frazer even prefers the evidence of a German missionary to that of Mr. Gason, a lay Englishman of the greatest experience. Mr. Howitt finds, among the Kurnai, Tundun as the patron of the mysteries and the bull roarer, like Twanyirika. In Mr. Manning's tribe[1] the same *rôle* is taken by Moodgeegally, under the control of Boyma.

We have thus five or six parallels to the Twanyirika of the godless Arunta, and all are subordinate to a higher power. If then, as Messrs. Spencer and Gillen tell us, the belief in the Arunta Twanyirika, the great spirit, ' is fundamentally the same as that found in all the Australian tribes,' Twanyirika ought to have a much more powerful benevolent superior. In that case the Arunta would

> Incline to think there is a god,
> Or something very like one,

as Clough says. If so, as they do not propitiate him, they did not conceive him as a partner in the game of *Do ut des*. But our only witnesses, Messrs. Spencer and Gillen, are extremely reticent about Twanyirika. Nothing is said about his having a superior, and I assume that he has none. It seems to follow that he is a mere Mumbo Jumbo, or bogle, devised by the men to keep the women and children in order.

But in South-Eastern Australia (if I may trust Mr. Howitt's evidence, to which Mr. Frazer does not here allude) the counterpart of Twanyirika is a mere servant of a much higher being, everywhere called by names meaning ' our father.' Therefore either ' our father ' Baiame,

---

[1] See ' The Theory of Loan-Gods,' *supra*.

Mungan-ngaur, and the rest, have been developed out of a sportive bugbear like Twanyirika, or Twanyirika (if he really has no superior) is a rudimentary survival of a belief like that in Mungan-ngaur, and his subordinate, Tundun.   In the former case Twanyirika, a germ of the more advanced religion of South-Eastern Australia, was not invented as a power behind nature, who might be useful if propitiated, as in Mr. Frazer's theory.   In the latter case the Arunta do not represent man prior to religion (as Mr. Frazer holds), but man who has cast off religion.   But Mr. Frazer does not seem to notice this dilemma.

The evidence for what most people call 'religion' among the Australian natives is so far from scanty that one finds it when looking for other matters, as I am going to show.   True, in the following report the religion does not answer to Mr. Frazer's definition, no powerful being is here said to be conciliated or propitiated : he is only said to exist and favour morality.   But Mr. Frazer's definition, if pressed, produces the effect of arguing in a vicious circle.   His theory asserts that powerful beings are only invented by man, in view of man's tardy discovery that his own magic is powerless.   The invented beings are then propitiated, for selfish ends, and that, by the definition, is religion.

If we produce, as we do, evidence that the belief in powerful beings has been evolved, and yet that these beings are certainly not propitiated by sacrifice, and seldom if ever by prayer, that they are only won by conduct, and by rites not involving sacrifice, Mr. Frazer can reply, ' Perhaps ; but by my definition that kind of belief is not religion.'   Then what is it ?   ' What else can you call it ? '   Its existence, if proved, is fatal to Mr. Frazer's theory of the origin of religion in the despair of magic, because the faithful of the belief of which I speak do not usually implore the god to do for them what magic has failed to do. Their belief satisfies their speculative and moral needs : it does not exist to supply their temporal wants. Yet it is none the less, but much the more, a religion on that account, except by Mr. Frazer's definition. If religion is to be defined as he defines it, ' a propitiation or conciliation of powers superior to man,' and so on, religion can only have arisen as it does in his theory, setting aside a supernormal revelation. But if we do not deny the name of religion to the speculative belief in a power superior to man, and to the moral belief that he lends a supernormal sanction to conduct, and to the emotional belief that he loves his children, then the belief is religion, but something other than religion as defined by Mr. Frazer. Nobody will deny the name of religion to such a belief. Mr. Frazer says : ' I would ask those who dissent from my conclusions to make sure that they mean the same thing by religion that I do ; for otherwise the difference between us may be more apparent than real.' [1]

I mean by religion what Mr. Frazer means—and more. The conciliation of higher powers by prayer and sacrifice is religion, but it need not be the whole of religion. The belief in a higher power who sanctions conduct, and is a father and a loving one to mankind, is also religion ; few, if any, will dispute the fact. But this belief, if unaccompanied, as in Australia, by prayer and sacrifice, cannot be accounted for on Mr. Frazer's theory : that religion was invented, for worldly ends, after the recognised failure of magic, which aimed at the same ends fruitlessly. It is only by limiting his definition of religion, as he does, that he can establish his theory of the origin of religion.

[1] *G. B.* i. xvii.

It is only by omitting mention of the evidence for what nobody else can deny to be religion, that he can secure his theory.

I return to my additional evidence for Australian religion. As will be seen, it does not come within Mr. Frazer's definition, but will anybody deny that the belief is religious? The evidence is that of Mr. A. L. P. Cameron,[1] and contains a brief comparative glossary of words used by different tribes of New South Wales to indicate the same objects. Mr. Cameron had been interested in the black fellows since 1868 at least, when their numbers were much larger than at present. He had seen gatherings of from 800 to 1,000. The tribes chiefly in question dwelt along the Murrumbidgee and Murray rivers, and do not include the Kamilaroi, the Kurnai, and Coast Murring of whom Mr. Howitt speaks.

As to religion, ghosts of the dead are believed to visit the earth, and to be frequently seen. The blacks ' will often resort to peculiar devices to avoid mentioning the names of the dead,' a practice hostile to the development of ancestor worship. No ghost of a man can grow into a god if his name is tabooed and therefore forgotten. ' The people of all these tribes appear to have a belief in a Deity, and in a future state of some kind.' The Wathi Wathi call this being Tha-tha-pali ; the Ta-ta-thi call him Tulong. Mr. Cameron could not obtain translations of these names, any more than we know the meaning of the names Apollo or Artemis. The being ' is regarded as a powerful spirit, or perhaps a supreme supernatural being. They say that he came from the far north, and now lives in the sky. He told each tribe what language they were to speak. He made men, women, and dogs, and the latter used to talk, but he took the power of

[1] *J. A. I.*, 1885, pp. 344–370.

speech from them. The Ta-ta-thi do not care to speak much of Tulong, and say that he does not often come to the earth. Although it seems that in many of the Australian tribes there is only a very dim idea as to the attributes of the Supreme Being and of a future state, yet in the Ta-ta-thi and its allied tribes there is certainly a belief not only in a future state of existence, but also in a system of rewards and punishments. My Ta-ta-thi informant stated that one of the doctors ascended long ago through the sky, and there saw a place where wicked men were roasted.'

Mr. Cameron, of course, had the strongest suspicions of a ' place ' so ostensibly Christian. To this we return.[1]

These tribes practise the Bora rites or initiatory mysteries. If women witness them ' the penalty is death. The penalty for revealing the secrets is probably the same.' Mr. Cameron, unlike Mr. Howitt, has not been initiated, and does not know the full secret. The presiding being (like the Twanyirika of the Arunta) is called Thuremlin, who, I conjecture, is Daramulun in his subordinate capacity. ' Their belief in the power of Thuremlin is undoubted, whereas the Arunta adults do not appear to believe in Twanyirika, a mere bugbear of the women and children. The bull roarer is Kalari, or among the Ta-ta-thi Kalk [or Kallak]—that is to say, "word." ' Concerning the instruction given to the boys, and described by Mr. Howitt, Mr. Cameron, not being initiated, gives no information.

---

[1] Parenthetically, I may remark that many beliefs as to the future state originate in, or are confirmed by, visions of ' doctors ' who visit the Hades or Paradise of a tribe, and by reports of men given up for dead, who recover and narrate their experiences. The case of Montezuma's aunt is familiar to readers of Mr. Prescott's *Conquest of Mexico*. The new religion of the Sioux is based on a similar vision. Anthropologists have given slight attention to these circumstances.

As to the future life, Mr. Cameron received his account from a tribesman named Makogo, ' an intelligent member of the Wathi Wathi tribe.' The belief was that current ' before his people came into contact with Europeans, and Makogo expressed an opinion that, whether right or wrong, they would have been better off now had their beliefs never been disturbed.' Probably Makogo was right. The beliefs were in a future state of reward or punishment. European contact does not import but destroy the native form of this creed.

The Wathi Wathi belief answers in character to the creeds expressed in the Egyptian Book of the Dead, the Fijian hymns, the famous Orphic gold talisman of Petilia, the Red Indian belief published by Kohl, and to many other examples.[1] The Way of Souls, as in these ancient or savage beliefs, is beset by dangers and temptations, to which the Egyptian Book of the Dead is a guide-book. If any one desires to maintain that this Australian idea, held before contact with Europeans, and now to some extent abandoned after that contact, is of Christian origin (we know this argument), he must suppose that the Wathi Wathi adapted the idea from our old ' Lyke Wake Dirge : '

> When Brig o' Dread is over and past,
>   Every night and all,
> To Whinny Muir thou comest at last,
>   And Christ receive thy saul.

A weak point there is. The soul of the Wathi Wathi, after death, is met by another soul, ' who directs him to the road for good men.'

But the natives had no roads, the opponent will reply. They have trade routes and markets, however, and barter of articles made in special localities goes on across

---

[1] See my *Modern Mythology*, and introduction to my *Homeric Hymns*.

hundreds of miles of country.[1] Let us allow that the Wathi Wathi may know a clean path or track from a dirty one.

The soul meets a dirty and a clean path. The good soul, being instructed, chooses the dirty path : the other path is kept clean by bad spirits ' in order to induce the unthinking to follow it,' as Bunyan's Mr. Ignorance unwarily chose a by-path into hell. The soul next meets a woman who tries to seduce him. He escapes her lures, and comes to two women who try to trip him by whirling a rope. One of them is blind, and the soul evades her. Next comes a deep narrow gap, in which flames rise and fall. The good soul watches the fall of the flames, and leaps across ; there is no Brig o' Dread. Red Indian souls cross by a log which nearly spans the abyss. Two old women meet the good soul, and take him ' to the Deity, Tha-Tha-Puli.' He tests the soul's strength and skill by making him throw a nulla-nulla. 'When the Wathi Wathi see a shooting star, they believe it to be the passage of such a nulla-nulla through space, and say : " Tha-Tha-Puli is trying the strength of some new spirit." The soul of a bad man, if it escapes the traps set for it, is sure to fall into the hell of fire. Many of the natives have had their beliefs modified by contact with the whites,' and I ' feel doubtful,' says Mr. Cameron, ' whether the pit of fire was not of this kind, and questioned my informant very closely on the subject, but he assured me that there was no doubt whatever that the above was the exact belief before the settlement of the country by the white men.'

It is the standing reply of believers in the borrowing theory that a native, cross-examined, will always agree with whatever the European inquirer wishes him to say.

[1] Roth, *North-West Queensland Central Aborigines*, p. 132. Spencer and Gillen, 575.

The natives examined by Mr. Cameron, Mrs. Langloh
Parker, Mr. Howitt, Mr. Manning, and others were
exceptions. They would not allow that their beliefs were
borrowed.

This particular form of native belief is exactly
analogous to that of ancient Egypt, of Greece, of Fiji, and
so on : not to the doctrine of our missionaries. The
believers in borrowing must therefore say that the Wathi
Wathi stole heaven, hell, and the ways thither from
missionaries, and adapted them, accidentally coinciding
with Egyptians, Greeks, Red Indians, Fijians, Aztecs, and
the rest, as to a gulf to be crossed, and temptations on the
way to the abode of the powerful being and the souls of
the good. The native proverbial explanation of a shooting star establishes, as historical fact, their belief in
Tha-Tha-Puli and his home for good spirits. Mr. Frazer
has six pages on beliefs about shooting stars.[1] One case
is to our point. The Yerrunthally of Queensland think
that the souls of the dead climb to a place among the
stars by a rope ; when they let the rope fall, it ' appeared
to people on earth as a shooting star.' [2]

Now if the evidence of Mr. Palmer, in the ' Journal of
the Anthropological Institute,' is good evidence for this
Australian belief, why is the evidence of Mr. Howitt and
Mr. Cameron, in the same serial, to an unborrowed
Australian religion (in this case with Tha-Tha-Puli and
his home for good souls) unworthy even of mention ?

We fall back on Sir Alfred Lyall: ' I think that one effect
of the accumulation of materials has been to encourage
speculative generalisation, because it has provided a
repertory out of which one may make arbitrary selection
of examples and precedents to suit any theory.' [3]

---

[1] *G. B.* ii. 18–24.   [2] *G. B.* ii. 21.   E. Palmer, *J. A. I.* xiii. p. 292.
[3] *Asiatic Studies*, i. ix.

Here I have the pleasure of agreeing with this great authority. Mr. Frazer has chosen Australia as the home of magic, as a land where magic is, but religion has not yet been evolved. As I have shown, in this and the preceding paper, there is abundance of evidence for an unborrowed Australian religion. I shall abandon the evidence so soon as it is confuted, but I cannot reject it while the witnesses are treated as good on many other points, but are unmentioned just when their testimony, if true, seems inconsistent with a theory of the priority of magic to religion.

' By the concurring testimony of a crowd of observers,' writes Mr. Tylor, 'it is known that the natives of Australia were at their discovery, and have ever since remained, a race with minds saturated with the most vivid belief in souls, demons, and deities.'[1] What can a young student commencing anthropologist think, when he compares Mr. Tylor's ' concurring testimony of a crowd of observers ' of Australian religion with Mr. Frazer's remark that there are ' some faint beginnings of religion' in Southern Australia, but that ' traces of a higher faith, where they occur, are probably sometimes due to European influence,' though the people, Mr. Tylor says, were in all things so ' saturated with the most vivid belief in souls, demons, and deities '—' at their discovery ' ? There is no use in building a theory of the origin of religion on the case of Australia till we are at least told about the ' concurring testimony of a crowd of observers.' That Mr. Frazer has some reason for disregarding the testimonies which I have cited, that he must have grounds for doubting their validity, I feel assured. But the grounds for the doubt are not apparent, and to state them would make Mr. Frazer's abstention intelligible.

---

[1] *Primitive Culture*, i. 379, 1871.

IV

THE ORIGIN OF THE CHRISTIAN FAITH

AMONG the many recent theories concerning the origin of religion, certainly the most impressive is Mr. Frazer's hypothesis as to the origin of the belief in the divinity of Christ. Unlike several modern speculations, Mr. Frazer's is based on an extraordinary mass of erudition. We are not put off with vague and unvouched-for statements, or with familiar facts extracted from the collections of Mr. Tylor, Lord Avebury, and Mr. Herbert Spencer. Mr. Frazer does not collect knowledge, as his Babylonian kings are supposed by him to have been sacrificed—by proxy. No writer is so erudite, and few are so exact in their references. While venturing to differ from Mr. Frazer, I must often, as it were, make use of his own ammunition in this war. Let me say sincerely that I am not pitting my knowledge or industry against his. I rather represent the student who has an interest in these subjects, and peruses ' The Golden Bough,' not as ' the general reader ' does, but with some care, and with some verification of the citations and sources.

It is first necessary to state, as briefly as possible, Mr. Frazer's hypothesis as to the origin of the belief in the Divinity of our Lord, or, at least, as to what he thinks a very powerful factor in the evolution of that creed.

The Babylonians, he holds, and their Persian conquerors were wont yearly, at a vernal feast, to dress a condemned criminal in the royal robes, to enthrone him, to obey him, to grant him access to the ladies of the royal harem, and then, at the end of five days, to strip, whip, and hang him. The reason why they acted thus, Mr. Frazer guesses, was that the condemned man acted as proxy for the divine King of Babylon, who, in an age less civilised, had been sacrificed annually : so Mr. Frazer conjectures. The King was thus sacrificed as a being of divine or magical nature, a man-god, and the object, according to Mr. Frazer, was to keep providing the god or magical influence resident in him with a series of fresh human vehicles. It appears, or may appear, to be Mr. Frazer's opinion, though the point is stated rather casually and late in the long argument, that the King himself was believed to incarnate a known and recognised god of vegetation, a personal principle of vegetable life. The King's proxy, therefore, the condemned criminal, is sacrificed (by hanging) in a character at once royal (as representing the King) and divine (since the King incarnates a god). All this occurs, by one of the theories advanced, at about the time of year in which our Easter falls, at a feast called Zakmuk in Babylonian, in Persian (by the theory) Sacæa : a period of hard drinking and singular licence.

The Jews, by the theory, or by one of the theories, had probably no such feast or custom before they were carried into exile in Babylonia. But from the Babylonians and Persians Mr. Frazer holds that they probably borrowed the festival, which they styled Purim, and also borrowed the custom (historically unheard of among them) of crowning, stripping, flogging, and hanging a mock-king, a condemned criminal, in March. It does not appear that this man, in Judæa, was allowed to invade the harem, for example, of Herod, as in the case of the Persian royal

harem.   The Jews also are conjectured to have borrowed
a practice, presumed by Mr. Frazer to have perhaps
prevailed at Babylon, of keeping a pair of condemned
criminals.   One of them was hanged ; the other was set
free for the year.   The first died as an incarnation of the
god of vegetable life.   The second, set free, represented in a
pseudo-resurrection the first, and also represented, I understand, the revival of the god of vegetable life.   The first
man was called Haman, probably in origin Humman, a
deity of the vanquished foes of Babylon, the Elamites.   The
second man, in Hebrew Mordecai, probably represented
Merodach, or Marduk, the supreme god of the victorious
Babylonians.   Each man had a female consort, probably
in Babylon a sacred harlot : Haman had Vashti, probably
an Elamite goddess ; Mordecai had Esther, doubtless
Ishtar, the Venus of the Babylonian creed.   These ladies
do not occur in any account of the Babylonian or Persian
feasts, nor in the Gospels : their existence is a conjecture.

The victims, as descending from the Babylonian and
Persian criminals, who stood both for the king and also,
at least in some parts of the theory, for a god of vegetation,
were conceived of as divine.   Since Christ, by what looks
like a chapter of accidents, was put to death as one of
these mock-kings, He inherited their recognised divinity,
and His mission, which had been mainly that of a moral
lecturer, at once was surrounded by a halo of divinity.

Such, in brief, if I follow Mr. Frazer, is the contention,
which, I must repeat, is presented as the combination
of many hypotheses into a single theory, offered for
criticism.

To myself, after studying Mr. Frazer's theory with
such care as it deserves, an hypothesis of its evolution
presents itself.   Before writing the first edition of ' The
Golden Bough ' (1890), Mr. Frazer had become acquainted

with a statement which Dio Chrysostom, a Greek rhetorician of the first century, puts into the mouth of Diogenes the Cynic, in an imaginary dialogue with Alexander the Great. In this essay Diogenes is made to tell Alexander about the Persian custom of yearly dressing up a condemned criminal in royal robes, at the feast called Sacæa, allowing him to live ' like a king ' for five days, giving him the *entrée* of the royal harem, and then stripping, scourging, and hanging or crucifying him. The resemblance of Dio's words to the account of the Mockery of Christ is very remarkable.

Mr. Frazer tells us that he saw this resemblance in 1890, but could not explain it. In 1897 he became acquainted with a legend, written in Greek, of the martyrdom of St. Dasius, a Roman Christian soldier, in Mœsia (303 A.D.). According to this legend, Dasius was drawn by lot as the yearly victim who, the story says, was made to represent King Saturnus, for a month of military revelry, and then was sacrificed, or obliged to slay himself, beside Saturn's altar, at the close of the Saturnalia. Dasius declined the part, and was put to death.

Here, then, in Mœsia, if we believe the legend of St. Dasius, was a mock-king, personating a god, sacrificed to a god, and therefore himself, it may be, regarded as divine. At the other extreme, in Jerusalem, was Christ, who, after mock royal honours, was scourged, crucified, and acquired a halo of divinity. The middle term was the criminal, who, in the character of a mock-king, was stripped, scourged, and hanged in the Persian feast. There was no trace in Persia of sacrifice, of a victim in the technical sense, or of any halo of divinity. But Mr. Frazer was familiar with barbaric kings who are or were put to death, to save them from dying naturally, or after a fixed term of years. In his opinion they are killed to provide the god whom they incarnate with a fresh vehicle. Combining all these facts, and strongly drawn by the resemblance of Dio's anecdote to the narratives of the Crucifixion, Mr. Frazer adopted the argument that the criminal executed at the Sacæa, in Babylon, had once been, like the Saturn sufferer in Mœsia, a divine victim, not at first hanged, but sacrificed yearly, to redeem the life of the Persian king, who in earlier ages must himself have been a yearly sacrifice. The divinity inherited by the criminal from that divine King was transmitted by a succession of executed malefactors to the victim of Calvary.

The ingenuity of the idea is undeniable. But it appears to me that the author's mind was throughout unconsciously drawn to the Crucifixion. This attraction became a 'mental prepossession.' In a recent work, 'Fact and Fable in Psychology' (Boston, U.S., 1900), Professor Jastrow has illustrated 'mental prepossession' by a common and trivial experience. A beginner in the art of bicycling is unconsciously drawn into collision with every obstacle on the road which his conscious self is doing its best to avoid.

In the same way, I fancy, our author's mind was led straight to an explanation of the halo of divinity round the Cross, instead of to what was needed first, an explanation of the Persian custom, isolated, and examined only in the light of its attendant circumstances, as described in our very scanty information. Had our author examined the circumstances of the Persian custom with an intellect unattracted by the hope of throwing new light on the Crucifixion, and uninfluenced by a tendency to find gods of vegetation almost everywhere, he would have found, I think, that they admit of being accounted for in a simple manner, granting that our information is true.   There was, as far as we are informed, no sacrifice at the Sacæa, and in that Persian festival nothing religious.   The religious element has to be imported by aid of remote inference, daring conjecture, and even, I venture to say, some disregard of documentary history.

The consequence, as I shall try to show, is that the theory has, in the Regent Moray's words, 'to pass over the bellies' of innumerable obstacles, by aid of a series of conjectures increasing in difficulty.   Thus the reader's powers of acquiescence are strained afresh at the introduction of each new trial of his faith.   If one stage out of so many stages of remote inference and bold presumption is unstable, the whole edifice falls to the ground. Meanwhile we shall have to offer a simple explanation of the circumstances of the Sacæan victim, only in a single instance demanding the use of one of Mr. Frazer's own conjectures, itself a legitimate hypothesis.   The remainder of this essay is concerned with an examination of the difficulties of his theory, and of the ' bridges of hypothesis,' by which the ' yawning chasms ' are to be crossed.

V

THE APPROACHES TO MR. FRAZER'S THEORY

I. THE EVOLUTION OF GODS

RITES so remarkable as those of the pair of criminals, supposed to have played their parts in Babylon and Jerusalem, each with his female mate, are not historically known, but are part of Mr. Frazer's theory, and have analogies in folklore. Institutions so unparalleled as a whole, in our knowledge of human religion, cannot have been evolved except through a long series of grades of development. Mr. Frazer traces these grades throughout the 1,500 pages of his book. There are, in accordance with the method, large sections of the work devoted to illustrative examples of matters which do not bear directly on the main stream of the argument, and these are apt, by the very abundance of their erudition, to distract attention from the central hypothesis. To that I try to adhere through its numerous ramifications.

To account, then, for these hypothetical rites of the double pairs of divinised human beings, we are to suppose that, before attaining the earliest germs of religion, men were addicted to magic, a theory which we have already examined in the essay 'Magic and Religion.' They believed that by imitating the cosmic processes, they could control or assist them. Thus the Arunta of Central Australia have magical rites, by which they assist the development of larvæ into grubs, increase and improve the breed and reproductive energies of kangaroos, foster the growth of edible tubers, and bring down rain. These rites are harmless, and involve no sacrifices, human or animal, for the Arunta, we are to believe, have no god to accept offerings.[1] But as men advanced from almost the lowest savagery, they gradually attained to higher material culture, developing the hitherto unknown arts of agriculture, developing also religion, in the despair of magic, developing gods, and evolving social and political rank, with kings at the head of society. In disgust with their old original magic (by which they had supposed that they controlled cosmic forces and animal and vegetable life), they invented gods and spirits who, as they fancied, did really exercise cosmic control. These gods they propitiated by prayer and sacrifice. But though it was in the despair of magic that men invented gods and religion, yet, as men will, they continued to exercise the magic of which they despaired. They persisted, like the godless Arunta, in imitating the processes of nature, in the belief (which, after all, they had not abandoned) that such imitation magically aided the efforts of nature or of the gods of nature.

Men now evolved three species of god, from one or other of which descends the godhead of the Persian criminal, whipped and hanged, and the Divinity of Christ. First, there were gods ' of an order different from and superior to man.' Second, there were men in whom these superior gods became incarnate. Third, there were men who were merely better magicians than their neighbours, ' sensitives ' who trembled at a touch of nature, and at whose touch nature trembled.[2] It is not, in thought, difficult to draw a firm line between these two kinds of

---

[1] Spencer and Gillen, *Natives of Central Australia.*
[2] *G. B.* i. 80, 81.

man-gods, though magic and religion overlap and shade
into each other. The distinction of the two types, the
man incarnating god, and the sorcerer with no god to
incarnate, is absolutely essential, and must be kept firmly
in mind. Mr. Frazer says ' In what follows I shall
not insist on it,' on this essential distinction.[1] Essential
it is : for the second sort, the magical sort, of man-god,
may, by Mr. Frazer's theory, be prior to all religion. He
is only a high kind of sorcerer, ' a dealer in magic and
spells.' The other kind of man-god comes in after magic
is despaired of and gods are invented. I shall insist on
the distinction.

The growth of society was advancing and developing
at the same time as religion and agriculture. The original
sorcerer or medicine-man, or magic-worker, through his
influence on his neighbours, was apt to acquire leadership,
and to accumulate property, as, indeed, I myself remarked
long ago in an essay on the ' Origin of Rank.'[2] In Mr.
Frazer's theory these magic-men finally develop into
both kings or chiefs and man-gods. I have observed
that there is often a lay or secular king or chief, a war-
leader, beside them. His position, if it becomes hereditary, is apt to end in leaving the man-god-king on one
side in a partly magical, partly religious, but not secular
kingship, whence it may evolve into a priesthood, carrying
the royal title. The man is more or less a man-god,
more or less a priest, more or less a controller of cosmic
processes, but is still a titular king. Of course all sorts
of varieties occur in these institutions. The general
result is the divinity of kings, and their responsibility for
the luck of the state, and for the weather and crops. If
the luck, the weather, and the crops are bad, the public
asks ' Who is to be punished for this ? ' Under a constitu-

---

[1] *G. B.* ii. 81.   [2] *Etudes Traditionistes.* A. L.

tion such as our own, the public notoriously makes the Government responsible for the luck; a general election dismisses the representatives of the party in power. But, four hundred years ago, and previously, executions took the place of mere loss of office : the heads of the Boyds, of Morton, or of Gowrie fell when these nobles lost office.

In the earlier society with which we are dealing, the king, as responsible for the weather and crops, is sometimes punished in bad times. The Banjars 'beat the king till the weather changes,' elsewhere the king is imprisoned, or, in a more constitutional manner, merely deposed.[1] There are traces of actually killing the unlucky and responsible monarch. In Sweden he is said, in a time of public distress, to have been not only killed, but sacrificed to Odin. This is not, however, an historical statement.

II. THE ALLEGED MORTALITY OF GODS

There were other magico-religious reasons for killing kings. Mr. Frazer writes :[2] 'Lacking the idea of eternal duration, primitive man naturally supposes the gods to be mortal like himself.'

Here is, I venture to think, a notable fault in the argument. Early men, contrary to Mr. Frazer's account, suppose themselves to be *naturally* immortal. The myths of perhaps all races tell of a time when death had not yet entered the world. Man was born deathless. Death came in by an accident, or in consequence of an error, or an infraction of a divine command. To this effect we have Zulu, Australian, Maori, Melanesian, Central African, Vedic Aryan, Kamschadal, and countless

[1] *G. B.* i. 157.   [2] *G. B.* ii. 1–5.

other myths ; not to speak of the first chapters of
Genesis.[1] 'In the thought of immortality' early man is
cradled.   His divine beings are usually regarded as prior
to and unaffected by the coming of death, which invades
men, but not these beings, or not most of them.

Indeed, some low savages have not yet persuaded
themselves that death is natural.   'Amongst the Central
Australian natives,' say Spencer and Gillen, 'there is no
such thing as belief in natural death ; however old or
decrepit a man or woman may be when this takes place,
it is at once supposed that it has been brought about by
the magic influence of some enemy,' and it is avenged on
the enemy, as in the blood-feud.[2]   These Australians in
Mr. Frazer's opinion (though not in mine) are 'primitive.'

Thus, far from lacking the idea of eternal duration of
life, 'primitive man' has no other idea.   Not that he
formulates his idea in such a term as 'eternal.'   Mariner
says, indeed, concerning the Tongan supreme being
Tá-li-y-Tooboo, 'Of his origin they had no idea, rather
supposing him to be eternal.'   But, in Tongan, the
metaphysical idea of eternity is only expressed in the
meaning of the god's name, 'wait-there-Tooboo.'   This
god occasionally inspires the How, or elective king, but
the How was never sacrificed to provide the god with a
sturdier incarnation, a process which Mr. Frazer's theory
of the Divinity of Christ demands as customary.   Being
'eternal' Tá-li-y-Tooboo was independent of a human
vehicle.[3]

These facts must be remembered, for it is indispensable to Mr. Frazer's theory to prove that the
immortals are believed, to a sufficient extent, to be

---

[1] *Modern Mythology*, ' Myths of the Origin of Death.'
[2] Spencer and Gillen, p. 476.   [3] Mariner, ii. 127.

mortal. Hence the supposed need of killing divine kings, their vehicles. Primitive man, according to Mr. Frazer, thinks his gods mortal. But primitive man by his initial hypothesis had no gods at all. Mr. Frazer clearly means that when man was no longer primitive, he conceived the gods to be mortal like himself. I have elsewhere given many examples of the opposite belief among races of many grades of culture, from the Australian blacks to the immortal gods of Homer.[1] The point will be found to be important later, and I must firmly express my opinion that, so long as people believe their gods to be alive, and testify that belief by prayers, hymns, and sacrifices, it is impossible to argue from a few local, and contradictory, and easily explicable myths, that these peoples believe their gods to be dead, or in danger of dying. Here, I think, the common sense of students will agree with me.

However, as this general and pervading belief in the mortality of the gods is absolutely essential to Mr. Frazer's argument, perhaps the point had better be settled. As examples of belief in the fact that the god is dead, we have the Greenlanders.[2]

The Greenlanders believed that a wind could kill their most powerful god, and that he would certainly die if he touched a dog. Mr. Tylor, on the other hand, tells us that to 'the summerland' of the Greenland deity, 'beneath the sea, Greenland souls hope to descend at death.' Let us trust that 'No Dogs are Admitted.' This Greenland divine being, Torngarsuk, 'so clearly held his place as supreme deity in the native mind that,' as Cranz the missionary relates, 'many Greenlanders hearing of God and His almighty power were apt to fall on the idea that it was their Torngarsuk who was meant.' The Greenland

[1] *Making of Religion*, chapters xi.–xiii.   [2] *G. B.* ii. 1.

deity was unborrowed; he 'seems no figure derived from the religion of Scandinavian colonists, ancient or modern.' [1]

From Cranz's evidence (and much more might be cited) the most powerful god of the Greenlanders was not dead, nor likely to die, in spite of the apprehensions of certain Greenlanders, communicated to a person not named by Mr. Frazer, but quoted in a work of 1806.[2] At the best the Greenland evidence is contradictory; all Greenlanders did not agree with Mr. Frazer's Greenland authority. Nor was the Accuser of the Brethren currently believed to be deceased, when the ancient folk-song assures us that

> Some say the Deil's deid,
> The Deil's deid, the Deil's deid,
> Some say the Deil's deid,
> And buried in Kirkcaldy:
> Some say he's risen again,
> Risen again, risen again,
> Some say he's risen again,
> To dance the Hieland Laddie.

'Risen again' he was, and did dance the Hieland Laddie at Gledsmuir and Falkirk. The 'Volkslied' scientifically represents the conflict of opinion as unsettled, despite the testimony of the grave of Satan at the lang toun of Kirkcaldy; like the grave of Zeus in Crete.

Mr. Frazer, then, ought not, I think, to assume a general belief in the mortality of Greenland gods in face of contradictory but uncited evidence.

1. A North American Indian told Colonel Dodge that 'the Great Spirit that made the world is dead long ago.

---

[1] *Prim. Cult.* ii. 308, 1871; ii. 340, 1873. In the edition of 1891, Mr. Tylor, in accordance with his altered ideas, dropped his denial of borrowing, and said that Torngarsuk was later identified with the devil—a common result of missionary teaching, just as Saints under Protestantism became, or their statues became, 'idols.'

[2] *G. B.* ii. 1. Meiners, *Geschichte der Religionen*, Hanover, 1806, 1807, i. p. 48.

He could not possibly have lived so long as this.' [1]   Now this was the *ipse dixit* and personal inference of a vague modern 'North American Indian,' living in an age which, as Mr. Frazer remarks, must 'breach those venerable walls' of belief.   To prove his case, Mr. Frazer needs to find examples of the opinion that the 'Great Spirit' was believed to be dead (if he grants that there ever existed an American belief in a Great Spirit) among the American Indians as first studied by Europeans.   I have elsewhere argued that the supreme being of most barbaric races is regarded as otiose, inactive, and so may come to be a mere name and by-word, like the Huron Atahocan, [2] 'who made everything,' and the Unkulunkulu of the Zulus, who has been so thrust into the background by the competition of ancestral spirits that his very existence is doubted. 'In process of time we have come to worship the spirits only, because we know not what to say about Unkulunkulu.'   'We seek out for ourselves the spirits that we may not always be thinking about Unkulunkulu.' [3]   In the same way, throughout the beliefs of barbaric races, the competition of friendly and helpful spirits pushes back such beings as the Australian Baiame and Mungan-ngaur, who exist where sacrifice to ancestral spirits has not yet been developed ; and the Canadian Andouagni of 1558. [4]   Thus a modern North American Indian may infer, and may tell Colonel Dodge, that the creator is dead, because he is not in receipt of sacrifice or prayer.   But the cult of such high beings, where it existed and still exists, in North America, the cult of Ti-ra-wá with whom the Pawnees

---

[1] R. I. Dodge, *Our Wild Indians*, p. 112.

[2] Le Jeune, *Relations des Jesuites*, 1633, p. 16 ; 1634, p. 13.

[3] Callaway, *Religion of the Amazulu*, pp. 26, 27.

[4] Thevet, *Singularitez de la France Antarctique*, ch. 77.   Paris, 1855. Andouagni is a creator, not addressed in prayer.   See 'Science and Superstition,' pp. 10, 11.

expect to live after death, of the Blackfoot Nà-pi of Ahone, Okeus, Kiehtan, and the rest, proves belief in gods who are alive, and who are not said to be in any danger of death.

2. A tribe of Philippine Islanders told the Spanish conquerors that the grave of the Creator was on the top of Mount Cabunian. So the Philippine Islanders did believe in a Creator. The grave may have been the result of the usual neglect of the supreme being already explained, or may have meant no more than the grave of Zeus in Crete, while Zeus was being worshipped all over the Greek world.

3. Heitsi Eibib, of the Hottentots, had a number of graves, accounted for by the theory of successive lives and deaths. But so had Tammuz and Adonis yearly lives and deaths, yet the god was *en permanence*.

The graves of Greek gods may be due to Euhemerism, a theory much more ancient than Euhemerus. People who worship ancestral spirits sometimes argue, like Mr. Herbert Spencer, that the gods were once spirits of living men, and show the men's graves as proofs ; ' the bricks are alive to testify to it.' But that the Greeks regarded their gods as mortal cannot be seriously argued, while they are always styled ' the immortals ' in contrast to mortal men ; and while Apollo (who had a grave) daily inspired the Pythia. Her death did not hurt Apollo. She was not sacrificed for the benefit of Apollo. The grave of Zeus ' was shown to visitors in Crete as late as about the beginning of our era.' But was it shown as early as the time of Homer ? Euhemerus was prior to our era.

4. The Egyptian gods were kings over death and the dead, with tombs and mummies in every province. But they were also deathless rulers of the world and of men.

' If Ra rises in the heavens it is by the will of Osiris ; if he sets it is at the sight of his glory.' ' King of eternity, great god . . . whoso knoweth humility and reckoneth deeds of righteousness, thereby knows he Osiris.' [1]

This is a living god, and Seb and Nut can scarcely die. Despite myth and ritual the gods of Egypt lived till they ' fled from the folding star of Bethlehem.'

5. As to the legend of ' great Pan is dead,' in the reign of Tiberius, Mr. Frazer mentions a theory that not Pan, but Adonis or Tammuz was dead ; he was always dying. The story is pretty, but is not evidence.

6. About 1064 A.D. there was a Turkish story of the death of the King of the Jinn. The Jinn are not gods but fairies, and we have heard of fairy funerals.

7. Concerning ' the high gods of Babylon ' it is especially needful for Mr. Frazer to prove that they were believed to be mortal and in danger of death, for Dr. Jastrow denies that they are mortal. ' The privilege of the gods' is ' immortality.' [2] But Mr. Frazer's hypothesis derives the doctrine of the Divinity of Christ from the opinion that he represented, in death, a long line of victims to a barbarous superstition.[3] And that superstition was, in Mr. Frazer's conjecture, that a substitute died for the King of Babylon, and that the King of Babylon died to reinforce the vitality of a mortal god of Babylon, whose life required a fresh human incarnation annually.

To prove the Babylonian belief in the mortality of the deities, Mr. Frazer writes : ' The high gods of Babylon also, though they appeared to their worshippers only in dreams and visions, were conceived to be human in their bodily shape, human in their passions, and human in their

---

[1] Hymns in Maspero, *Musée de Boulaq*, pp. 49, 50.
[2] *Religion of Babylon and Assyria*, p. 483.   [3] *G. B.* iii. 198.

fate; for like men they were born into the world, and
like men they loved and fought and even died.'¹ How
many of them died? If they were dead in religious
belief, how did they manage to attend 'the great
assembly of the gods which, as we have seen, formed
a chief feature of the feast of Zakmuk, and was held
annually in the temple of Marduk at Babylon?'² Did
Marduk die? If so, why is he addressed as

> O merciful one who lovest to give life to the dead!
> Marduk, King of heaven and earth,
> The spell affording life is thine,
> The breath of life is thine.
> Thou restorest the dead to life, thou bringest things to completeness (?)³

Supposing, again, that the King was really sacrificed
to keep a god in good condition—why only one sacrifice?
There were at least scores of gods, all of them, if I understand Mr. Frazer, in the same precarious condition of
health. They appear, he might argue, to have been
especially subject to hepatic diseases.

> O supreme mistress of heaven, may thy liver be pacified,

says a hymn to Ishtar.⁴

Of course every one sees that 'thy liver' is only a
phrase for 'thy wrath;' the liver (as in our phrases
'pluck' and 'lily-livered') being taken for the seat of the
'pluck' of men. It is manifest that the Babylonian gods
are not dead but living, otherwise they could not attend
the yearly divine assembly, nor could they be addressed in
prayer. Moreover, if they could only be kept alive by
yearly sacrificing their human vehicles, great holocausts
of human vehicles would have been needed every year:
one man for one god, and their name was legion.

---

¹ *G. B.* ii. 3, 4, citing L. W. King, *Babylonian Religion and Mythology*,
p. 8 (1899).   ² *G. B.* iii. 154.
³ Jastrow, *The Religion of Babylonia and Assyria*, p. 307. Boston, U.S.,
1898.   ⁴ Jastrow, p. 311.

Once more, if men believed that gods could die, unless kept alive by sacrifices of their human vehicles, we must say of the Greeks that they

did not strive
Officiously to keep alive

their deities. Had the Greeks known that this was in their power to do, then Apollo, Dionysus, Cronos, Zeus, Hermes, Aphrodite, Ares had not died. Yet die they did, if the graves of each of these mortals prove the prevailing belief in their decease.[1] Mankind, according to Mr. Frazer, believed in 'mighty beings,' 'who breathed into man's nostrils and made him live.' He implored them 'to bring his immortal spirit . . . to some happier world . . . where he might rest with them,' and so on.[2] Yet, 'lacking the idea of eternal duration, primitive man naturally supposed the gods to be mortal like himself.' Mr. Frazer has, we see, also told us that they did not believe their gods to be mortal. Probably, then, the belief in their immortality was a late stage in a gradual process.[3] Yet it had not prevailed when the grave of Zeus was shown 'about the beginning of our era.'[4] Man, then, believed that he could keep one out of the crowd of gods alive (though he implored them to keep *him* alive) by sacrificing his rightful king once a year, thereby overthrowing dynasty after dynasty, and upsetting the whole organisation of the state. All this we must steadfastly believe, before we can accept Mr. Frazer's theory of the origin of the Nicene Creed. It is a large preliminary demand.

The gods keep on being 'immortals,' and this we must insist on, in view of Mr. Frazer's theory that man-gods who are slain are slain to keep alive the god who

---

[1] *G. B.* ii. 2.
[2] *G. B.* i. 77.
[3] *G. B.* i. 77, 78.
[4] *G. B.* ii. 1.

is incarnate in them, of which he does not give one
example. His instances of beliefs that the high gods are
dead notoriously contradict the prevalent belief that
they are deathless. And the prevalent belief regulates
religion.

However, man-gods certainly die, and some South Sea
Islanders—by a scientific experiment—demonstrated
that Captain Cook was no god, because he died when
stabbed, which a genuine god would not have done.
This, of course, proves that these benighted heathen knew
the difference between an immortal god and a deathly
man as well as did Anchises in the Homeric hymn to
Aphrodite.

III. RELIGIOUS REGICIDE

Peoples who think that all the luck depends on their
king-man-god (the second sort, the superior sorcerer,
with no god in him) hold, we are to believe, that his luck
and cosmic influence wane with his waning forces.
Therefore they kill him, and get a more vigorous recipient
of his *soul* (not of a god) and of his luck.[1] Of king-killing
for this reason Mr. Fraser gives, I think, one adequate
example. Of the transmission of the soul of the slain
divinity to his successor he 'has no direct proof,' though
souls of incarnating gods are transmitted after natural
deaths.[2]

Now this is a very important part of the long-drawn
argument which is to suggest that Christ died as a mock-
king, who also represented a god. First, we have seen
that there are two kinds of man-god. In one kind a real
god, ' of an order different from and superior to man,' is
supposed to become incarnate. The other kind of man-
god is only a superior ' sensitive ' and sorcerer.[3]

---

[1] *G. B.* ii. 6.   [2] *G. B.* ii. 56 ; i. 151 *et. seq.*   [3] *G. B.* i. 80–82.

Now Jesus, by Mr. Frazer's theory, died as representative of a god, therefore as one of the first two kinds of man-gods. But Mr. Frazer does not here, as I said, produce one solitary example of a man-god proved to be of the first class—a king in whom an acknowledged god is incarnate—being slain to prevent his inspiring god from waning with the man's waning energies.[1] Many examples of that practice are needed by the argument. I repeat that not one example is produced in this place. Mr. Frazer's entire argument depends on his announced failure to 'insist on' the distinction between two sorts of man-gods which he himself has drawn.[2] So I keep on insisting.

Again, it can hardly be said that any examples are produced of a king of the second sort (a man-god who is really no god at all, but a 'sensitive,' sorcerer, or magic-man) being slain to preserve the vigour of his magic. The examples to be cited all but universally give no proof of the idea of preserving man's *magical* vigour from the decay of old age.

The cases given, as a rule, are mere instances of superannuation. It is possible (would that it were easy) to pension off aged professors in the Scottish Universities. But to pension off a king merely means a series of civil wars. The early middle ages 'tonsured' weak kings. How tempting to represent this dedication of them to God as a mitigation of sacrifice! Kings, in fact, among some barbaric races, are slain merely by way of superannuation. Nay, the practice is not confined to kings. It is usual among elderly subjects.[3]

Let us take Mr. Frazer's examples.[4]

---

[1] The mortals who incarnate gods are catalogued in *G. B.* vol. i. pp. 139-157. Not one is said to be put to death.

[2] *G. B.* i. 80, 81.   [3] *G. B.* ii. 6-8.   [4] *G. B.* ii. 8-57.

1. A Congo people believe that the world would perish if their chitome, or pontiff, died a natural death. So he was clubbed or strangled by his successor. But what god is incarnate in the chitome? None is mentioned.[1] The king himself ' is regarded as a god in earth, and all powerful in heaven.'

2. The Ethiopian kings of Meroe were worshipped as gods, but were ordered to die by the priests, on the authority of an alleged oracle of the gods, ' whenever the priests chose.' That they first showed any signs of decay ' we may conjecture.' [2] We have no evidence except that the priests put an end to the king ' whenever they chose. And, far from alleging the king's decay or bad crops as the regular recognised reason, they alleged a special oracle of the gods.

3. When the King of Unyoro, in Central Africa, is old, or very ill, his *wives* kill him (an obvious reason readily occurs : it is the wives, not a god, who need a more spirited person), alleging an old prophecy that the throne will pass from the dynasty if the king dies a natural death. But it is not here shown that this king is a man-god of either species; and the prophecy does not concern injury to a god, or to magical *rapport*.[3]

4. The King of Kibanga, on the upper Congo, is killed by sorcerers when he ' seems near his end.' So are old dogs and cats and horses in this country, and peasants are even thought to provide euthanasia for kinsfolk 'near their end.' If the King of Kibanga is a man-god, Mr. Frazer does not say so.

5. If wounded in war the King of Gingero is killed by his comrades or kinsfolk, even if he be reluctant. The reason alleged is ' that he may not die by the hands of his

---

[1] *G. B.* i. 236.　　　　　[2] *G. B.* ii. 11.
[3] *Emin Pasha in Central Africa*, p. 91.

enemies.' Did Saul, Brutus, and many other warriors who refuse to survive wounds and defeat die as man-gods? Is the King of Gingero a man-god?

6. Chaka, King of the Zulus, used hair-dye, having a great aversion to grey hairs. The Zulus, a warlike people, would not elect, or accept, a greyhaired king, and, though I know no instance of slaying a Zulu king because he was old, Mr. Isaacs (1836) says that grey hair is 'always followed by the death of the monarch.' Even if an historical example were given, a warlike race merely superannuates a disabled war-leader in the only safe way.

7. At last we reach a king-man-god in Sofala, who, according to Dos Santos, was the only god of the Caffres, and was implored to give good weather.[1] A modern Zulu told Dr. Callaway that 'when people say the heaven is the chief's they do not believe what they say.'[2] The Sofalese, or rather their neighbours, were perhaps more credulous ; and it appears to have been a custom or law among them that a blemished king should kill himself, though a reforming prince denounced this as insanity, and altered the law. We are told that the king-god of the Sofalese was under this law, and a neighbouring king (who is nowhere said to have been a man-god) was. But what god, if any, was incarnate in this man-god, if he *was* a man-god, like his neighbour?[3]

[1] *G. B.* i. 155; compare ii. 10.

[2] Callaway, *Religion of the Amazulu*, p. 122.

[3] Here the facts of Dos Santos are confused. In volume i. p. 155 we read: 'The King of Quiteva, in Eastern Africa, ranks with the deity;' 'indeed, the Caffres acknowledge no other gods than their monarch, and to him they address those prayers which other nations are wont to prefer to heaven' (Dos Santos, Pinkerton, xvi. 682, 687, *seq*.). If the Caffres have no gods, a god cannot be incarnate in their king. But, elsewhere in Dos Santos (ii. p. 10), there is no 'King of Quiteva' (as in i. p. 155). Quiteva is no longer a district, but we read 'contiguous to the domains of the Quiteva ; ' a title like 'the Inca,' in fact, as Dos Santos tells us the Quiteva is 'the King of Sofala.' Is Sofala also known as Quiteva, and

8. The Spartans were warned by an oracle against a lame king, as the Mackenzies were warned by the Brahan seer against a set of physically blemished lairds. The seer's prophecy was fulfilled.[1] We do not hear that the Spartans killed any lame king.

9. The King of the Eyeos is warned to kill himself, warned by a gift of parrot's eggs, ' when the people have conceived an opinion of his ill-government.' His wives strangle him, and his son succeeds, or did so before 1774, when the King refused to die at the request of his ministers. To make a case, it must be shown that the king was a man-god of one or other variety. He is, in fact, merely king while popular, ' holding the reins of government no longer than whilst he merits the approval of his people.'

10. The old Prussians were governed by a king called God's Mouth. ' If he wanted to leave a good name behind,' when weak and ill he burned himself to death, in front of a holy oak.

11. In Quilacare, in Southern India, the king cut himself to pieces, before an idol, after a twelve years' reign. We are not told that he was an incarnation of the god, if any, incorporated in, or represented by, the idol.

12. The King of Calicut, on the Malabar coast, used to cut his throat in public after a twelve years' reign. About 1680–1700 this was commuted. If any man could cut his way through 30,000 or 40,000 guardsmen, to kill the king, he succeeded. Three men tried, but numbers overpowered them. Other examples are given in which every

the King of Sofala as ' the Quiteva ' ? The King of Quiteva ' ranks with the deity '—though the Caffres have no deity for him to rank with (ii. 155). But when the Quiteva becomes ' King of Sofala ' (ii. 10), the neighbouring prince who kills himself is ' the Sedanda,' who is not said to ' rank with the deity.' And Dos Santos assures us that the Caffres *have* a God, unworshipped !

[1] *Prophecies of the Brahan Seer*, Mackay, Stirling, 1900.

regicide might become king, if he could, like Macbeth. It was held, at Passier, that God would not allow the king to be killed if he did not richly deserve it. These kings are not said to incarnate gods.

13. Ibn Batuta once saw a man throw a rope into the air, and climb up it. Another man followed and cut the first to pieces, which fell on the ground, were reunited, and no harm done. This veracious traveller also saw a man, at Java, kill himself for love of the Sultan, thereby securing liberal pensions for his family, as his father and grandfather had done before him. 'We may conjecture that formerly the Sultans of Java, like the Kings of Quilacare and Calicut, were bound to cut their own throats at the end of a fixed term of years,' [1] but that they deputed the duty to one certain family. We *may* conjecture, but, considering the lack of evidence, and the stories that Ibn Batuta freely tells, I doubt! Ibn, at the Court of Delhi, saw cups and dishes 'at a wish appear, and at a wish retire.' Did the Sultan of Java incarnate a god?

14. This case is so extremely involved and hypothetical (it concerns Sparta, where I never heard that the king was a man-god) that the reader must be referred to the original. [2]

Meanwhile the list of instances is numerically respectable. But are the instances to the point? Do they prove a practice of killing a royal man-god, for the purpose of helping a god incarnate in him, or even of preventing his magical power (or *mana*, in New Zealand) from waning? They rather prove regicide as a form of superannuation, or as the result of the machinations of priests, or of public discontent. Above all, they do not demonstrate that the king is ever killed as an incarnation of a deity who needs a sturdier person to be incarnate in.

[1] *G. B.* ii. 18.   [2] *G. B.* ii. 18–24.

So recalcitrant is the evidence, that of all Mr. Frazer's kings who are here said to be gods, or to incarnate gods, not one is here said to be put to death by his worshippers.[1] And of all his kings who are here said to be put to death, not one is here said to incarnate a god.[2] Such are the initial difficulties of the theory: to which we may add that elderly men are notoriously killed by many savages just because they are elderly, whether they are kings or commoners.

Mr. Frazer's point is that Christ died in 'a halo of divinity,' visible 'wherever men had heard the old, old story of the dying and rising god.'[3] But, apart from other objections already urged, Mr. Frazer's present instances do not contain one example of a 'dying and rising god,' stated to be represented by a living man who is therefore killed; even if there are one or two cases of a slain king who is a medicine-man, sorcerer, or cosmic sensitive. Thus the argument fails from the first. Christ is to be reckoned divine as representing a king who was killed as an incarnation of a god. But of regicide for this reason no proof is afforded, as far as I can see.

IV. ANNUAL RELIGIOUS REGICIDE

Next we arrive at an absolutely necessary hypothesis, which I find it difficult to accept. ' In some places it appears that the people could not trust the king to remain in full mental and bodily vigour for more than a year; hence at the end of a year's reign he was put to death, and a new king appointed to reign in his turn a year, and suffer death at the end of it. . . . When the time drew near for the king to be put to death (in Babylon this appears to have been at the end of a single year's

---

[1] *G. B.* i. 139–157.   [2] *G. B.* ii. 8–24.   [3] *G. B.* iii. 197.

reign), he abdicated for a few days, during which a temporary king reigned and suffered in his stead.' [1]

Later we read of 'the time when the real king used to redeem his own life by deputing his son to reign for a short time and die in his stead.' [2]

The hypothesis is, then, that at Babylon the king used to be sacrificed once a year. Later he appointed a son, or some other member of the royal family, or some one else, to die for him, while, last of all, a criminal was chosen.

Is not this a startling hypothesis? Yet on it the whole argument about the Divinity of Christ depends. Mr. Frazer overestimates human ambition. We wonder that Moray, Lennox, and Morton pined to be Regents of Scotland. Yet at least they had a faint chance of escaping death within the year. But the kings of Babylon had no chance: they were sacrificed annually. Mr. Frazer asks us to suppose that any men of royal race, anywhere, men free and noble, not captives, not condemned criminals, would accept a crown, followed, in 365 days, by a death of fire! A child knows that no men have ever acted in this way. Even if they were so incredibly unlike all other human beings as to choose a year's royalty, followed by burning to death, how was the succession regulated? Even the primitive Arunta, naked savages in Central Australia, have a kind of magistrate, merely a convener, called the Alatunja, 'the head man of a local totemic group.' He is an hereditary official, inheriting in the male line.[3] Does any one believe that a poor black man would accept the Alatunjaship if he knew he was to be roasted, and so die, at the end of a year? Now the Babylonians (or

---

[1] *G. B.* ii. 24, 26.   [2] *G. B.* iii. 194.
[3] Spencer and Gillen, Glossary, *s.v. Alatuja* and pp. 9–11.

rather the Persians) were infinitely more civilised than the Arunta. Their kings were hereditary kings. How, then, would Mr. Frazer's system work ? The king is sacrificed ; his eldest son succeeds ; is sacrificed next year ; they soon work through the royal family. Thus, in Scotland, Darnley is sacrificed (1567). Next year you sacrifice the baby, James VI. Next year you begin on the Hamiltons. Châtelherault lasts a year : then Arran, then Lord John, then Lord Claude. Beginning in 1567 you work out that result in 1572. Then you start on the Lennox Stewarts. You have Lennox offered up in 1573, his son Charles in 1574, and by the end of the century you have exhausted the female and illegitimate branches of the royal family. You can only sacrifice males, and these must be adults, for each sacrificed man, by Mr. Frazer's theory, has to consort before his death with a lady, probably ' a sacred harlot.' [1]

Mr. Frazer perhaps will say ' these Babylonian kings were polygamous, and had large families of sons.' But think of the situation ! When the king comes to providing a son as a substitute, to reign for a few days and be sacrificed in his stead, he may be a young king, just married. Even if he could count on a male baby, or a score of them, annually, they would be of no use : they could not consort with the sacred harlot, which is indispensable.[2] So, after the young king is sacrificed, we are in a quandary. We must overlook primogeniture, and begin sacrificing the king's brothers ; they will not last long ; we fall back on the cousins. Soon we need a new dynasty. Now no government could be carried on in the circumstances imagined by Mr. Frazer. The country would not stand it. No individual king would ever accept the crown. Human beings never had such a pre-

[1] *G. B.* iii. 178.   [2] *Ibid.*

posterous institution. But, if they had not, Mr. Frazer's whole theory of the Crucifixion is baseless, for it all hangs on the yearly sacrifice of the divine king in Babylon. Where there is no historical evidence of annual regicide, we must appeal to our general knowledge of human nature. The reply is that the thing is impossible. Moreover, that sacrifice is wholly without evidence.

The only reason for believing that the kings of the great Babylonian Empire, or even the kings of Babylon when it may have been a small autonomous town, were sacrificed once a year, is the faint testimony existing to show that once a year at a Persian feast a mock-king was hanged. To account for that *hanging* Mr. Frazer has to invent the hypothesis that real kings, in olden times, were annually *sacrificed*. The only corroboration of actual fact is in the savage instances of king killing, *not* annual, which we have explained as, in most cases, a rude form of superannuation ; in no case as certainly the deliverance of a recognised god incarnate in the king There are also instances in folklore of yearly mock executions of a king of the May, or the like, and a dubious case in Lower Mœsia. These do not prove annual sacrifices of actual kings in the past, if they prove any sacrifice at all. In these circumstances, I venture to hold, science requires us, if we must explain the alleged yearly hanging of a mock-king at Babylon, to look for a theory, an hypothesis, which does not contradict all that we know of human nature. For all of human nature that we know is contradicted by the fancy that the kings of Babylon were once sacrificed annually. I shall later produce a theory which, at least, does not run counter to the very nature of man, and so far is legitimate and scientific.

Mr. Frazer says that his theory 'will hardly appear extravagant or improbable' when we remember that, in Ngoio, the chief who puts on the cap of royalty one day is, by the rule, killed the next day.[1] So nobody puts on the cap. And nobody would have put on the Babylonian crown under the condition of being roasted to death at the end of the year.

If the theory were correct, the king incarnating a god would be slain yearly. But he would not like that, and would procure a substitute, who would yearly be slain (a) as a proxy of the king, or (b) as the god of vegetation, incarnate in the king, or as both. Yet, I repeat, not a single instance has been given of a king who is slain for magico-religious reasons, and who is also the incarnation of any god whatever. The slain kings in the instances produced were, as a rule, superannuated because they were old, or got rid of because they were unpopular, or because a clerical cabal desired their destruction, or for some other reason : at most, and rarely, because they were outworn 'sensitives.' We know scores of cases of god-possessed men, but none are killed because they are god-possessed.

The argument has thus made no approach to Mr. Frazer's theory of the origin of the belief in the divine character of Christ and of his doctrine.

At this point Mr. Frazer's theory turns from god-man-kings slain to preserve their *mana*, or cosmic *rapport*, to persons who suffer for these kings. Not one single historical proof that there ever was such a custom is adduced. All is a matter of inference and conjecture. There is, we saw, a region Ngoio, in Congo, where the throne is perpetually vacant, because whoever occupied it was killed the day after coronation day—no substitute

[1] *G. B.* ii. 26.

is suggested, and no one sits in the Siege Perilous.[1]
There are cases of 'temporary kings,' as King February,
for three days in Cambodia—the temporary king being of
a cadet branch of the royal family. Hs is not killed. In
Siam a temporary king for three days conducted a *quête*,
or jocular pillaging, like our Robin Hood in Scotland.
This is an example of the *Period of Licence* when law is
in abeyance, and the importance of this period we shall
later prove. The mock-king also ploughed nine furrows,
and stood later with his right foot on his left knee. He
did the same thing on a later occasion, and omens were
drawn from his steadiness; he was supposed, if firm, to
conquer evil spirits, and had another *quête*. In Upper
Egypt a king of unreason for three days holds mock
tribunals, then is condemned, and his 'shell' is burned;
probably, as I shall show, to mean that 'the gambol has
been shown' and is over.[2] There are two or three similar
cases, and Mr. Frazer suggests that the mock-king is
invested with the 'divine or magical functions' of the real
king. But the local Pacha, on the Nile, has no such functions, and his august representative wears 'a tall fool's
cap.' None are put to death: the Upper Egyptian case
alone and dimly, if at all, suggests the proxy supposed (as
in Ibn Batuta's tale interpreted by Mr. Frazer) to die for
the king.

Next we approach instances of sons of kings who are
sacrificed, but these are cases of sin offerings (as when the
King of Moab sacrificed his son on the wall), and, even if
the lads were substitutes for their royal fathers, there is
no presumption raised that the fathers were habitually
killed year by year. to keep their cosmic *rapport* unimpaired, or to release the god incarnate within them, a
custom of which I find no example at all.

[1] *G. B.* ii. 26.   [2] *G. B.* ii. 30.

One instance of what he conjectures to be a proxy
sacrifice for a king Mr. Frazer finds in a festival at
Babylon called the Sacæa.[1] To this we return in due order.
We must first examine cases of similar customs, or inferred
customs, in Greece and Rome.

Meanwhile we hope to have shown that Mr. Frazer's
theory of the origin of the belief in the Divinity of Christ
already rests on three scarcely legitimate hypotheses.
First, there is the hypothesis that kings were slain to
release a known deity, incarnate in them, and to provide a
better human vehicle. Of this rite no instances were given.
Next, there is the hypothesis that the King of Babylon
was annually sacrificed, and succeeded by a new king, who
was sacrificed at the end of the year. Historical evidence
does not exist, and the supposed custom is beyond belief.
Thirdly, we are to believe in proxies or substitutes who
die annually for the king. Of this practice no actual
example is adduced.

Here, perhaps, the reader may be invited to ask
himself whether he believes that there ever was, anywhere,
a custom of yearly killing the king, the head of the
state. If he cannot believe this, in the entire lack of
proof, he may admire the faith which can move this
mountain in the interests of Mr. Frazer's conclusions.
For my part I may say that I was so hypnotised, after
first reading through the long roll of Mr. Frazer's 'sad
stories of the deaths of kings,' that I could only murmur
'But there is no historical evidence for the yearly
Babylonian, or rather Persian, regicides.' Then I woke
out of the hypnotic trance ; I shook off the drowsy spell
of suggestion, and exclaimed ' The king is killed
annually ! ' Next, I asked myself whether mortal men
would take the crown, and how the arrangement would

[1] *G. B.* ii. 24.

work, and, alas! it was my belief in Mr. Frazer's theory that was shattered.

But the 'general reader,' perusing an argument of 1,400 pages, may fall under the hypnotic spell of numerous 'cases,' though none are to the point, and may accept an hypothesis, however violently opposed to his knowledge of human nature. To that test we are, in a case like this, compelled to appeal, however little we may value 'common sense' in other fields of speculation. Ours is the field of normal human nature, motive, and action, in which every man may be a judge. I cannot but think that the author of the theory would have been stopped by considerations so obvious and obstacles so insuperable. But first he had the remote analogy of the Aztec war-prisoner who personated a god, and to a god was sacrificed. That example is of no real service: the man was a captive and could not help himself; he was not King of Anahuac. Moreover, he was sacrificed: he was not put to a death of special shame. Again, there was the Saturnian victim, if we believe the legend about to be narrated. But he too was sacrificed: he was not stripped, scourged, and hanged. Our author, however, was fascinated by the Cross at the end of the long vista of the argument. In place, therefore, of seeking, or at least in place of finding, a simple explanation of the Persian custom, or leaving it unexplained, he accepted the impossibility of the annual regicide at Babylon, and was launched into a new wilderness of conjectures and inferences to explain the absence, in the Persian case, of sacrifice and religion, the presence of a merrymaking and a hanging.

V. THE SATURNALIA

We are next to look for an historical case of the yearly
sacrifice, not of a king, but of a mock-king. The argument thus carries us to the Roman feast of the Saturnalia.
This festival (in late times held in December, 16–23) so
closely resembled our Christmas in jollity, that Pliny (like
some of us) used to withdraw to the most retired room in
his Laurentine villa to escape the noise. Mr. Frazer
does not remark the circumstance, but in Rome before
the Empire, or earlier, the Saturnalia seem to have been
a feast of one day only. 'Among our ancestors,' says
Macrobius, 'the Saturnalia were completed in a single
day,' though he does not seem very certain of his fact. Livy
says : 'The Saturnalia were instituted as a festal day.'[1]
After the time of Caligula, the Saturnalia endured for five
days, 'precisely like the feast of the Sacæa at Babylon,'
of which we are fated to hear a great deal.[2]

It would thus appear that the Saturnalia were
originally a feast of one day, later lengthened to five days,
and again to seven days. By the time of writers like
Lucian and Martial the feast continued for a week, and
Lucian represents Cronos (Saturn) as a jolly old king of
unreason.[3] The rich helped the poor, people made
presents to each other, 'a Christmas carol philosophy,' as
Dickens calls it, prevailed. The masters served the slaves
at table ; all was licence and riot. Wax candles were
given as presents (*cerea*), like those on our Christmas
trees. These *cerea*, according to Macrobius, were thought

---

[1] Macrobius himself is an author of the fourth or fifth century of our
era.   Macrobius, i. x. 2 ; Livy, ii. xxi. 2.

[2] Cumont, *Revue de Philologie*, July 1897, vol. xxi. p. 149, citing
Mommsen, C.I.L. 1² p. 337, and Marquhardt, *Staatsverw*. iii.² 587.

[3] Lucian, *Saturnalia*, 2.

by some antiquaries to be substitutes for human sacrifices.
Originally, it was said, the Pelasgi, before migrating to
Italy, received an oracle from Dodona :

Τῷ πατρὶ πέμπετε φῶτα :

' Send a man to the Father,' that is, to the god Cronos or,
in Italy, Saturn.   But, by a pun on the Greek φῶτα, they
were induced to substitute lights, the wax candles.[1]

Now it is a really astonishing thing that, if actual
human sacrifices were offered after our era, at the
Saturnalia, no Roman antiquary (and there were plenty
of antiquaries) should mention the fact, while discussing
the theory that *cerea* were commutations of sacrifice.   If,
now and then, under the Empire a survival or recrudescence of human sacrifice was heard of in a rural
district, the antiquaries would catch at it greedily, as a
proof that wax tapers really were commutations of human
sacrifice, which some doubted.   That rural recrudescences
do occur we know from the recent case of burning an
Irish peasant woman to death, to deliver her from a fairy.[2]

Mr. Frazer, however, believes that survivals of human
sacrifices at the Saturnalia did really occur.   He is
' tempted to surmise ' that the king of the revels (who
answered to our ' Twelfth Night ' ' King ' or ' Queen of the
Bean ') ' may have originally personated Saturn himself.'[3]
In the following page we read that the victim ' cut his
own throat on the altar of the god whom he personated.'
The only known or alleged instance of human sacrifice at
the Saturnalia follows.

In A.D. 303, when the persecution under Diocletian
began, one Dasius, a Christian soldier, in Lower Mœsia,
is said to have been the victim whom the soldiers yearly

---

[1] Macrobius, i. vii. 31–33.
[2] The reason was probably a mere ' blind ' for wife-murder.
[3] *G. B.* iii. p. 140.

chose for the mock-king of a *month*, not a week, the
Saturn of the occasion. Why a month, if the ancient
feast lasted but a day, and, later, but a week? After
being a merry monarch for thirty days, he should have
cut his own throat at the altar of Saturn (Κρόνος, in the
Greek MSS.).[1] Dasius declined the crown and was
knocked on the head, on November 20, by a soldier,
apparently a christened man, named John. The
Saturnalia at Rome lasted (at least under the Empire)
from December 16 to December 23. Dasius must have
been executed for his refusal, announced before his *month's*
reign (only a week is elsewhere known) should have begun
—on November 23; if the regnal month ended on
December 23. Thus the festive Saturnalian kings at
Rome may be guessed to descend from a custom, at Rome
unknown, but surviving among the soldiers, of killing a
mock-king Saturnus. Dasius was no slave or criminal, but
himself a soldier. The revels of a month, in place of a day
or a week, must also, one presumes, be a survival, though
a day was the early limit. The date of the MSS. about
Dasius Mr. Frazer does not give, but he thinks that
the longest MS. is ' probably based on official documents.'
To the MSS. I shall return.

The grotesque figure of Carnival, destroyed at the end
of a modern Roman feast which does not fall in December,
is also a survival of a slain mock-king ' who personated
Saturn,' so Mr. Frazer suggests, though in ancient Rome
even this carnival practice is to us unknown.[2]

It will already have been observed that even if the
Romans were, in some remote age, wont yearly to sacrifice
a mock-king who represented a god, they did not do so at
Easter, as in the case of Christ, did not do so in spring,
and did not scourge the victim. Their rite, if it really

---

[1] *Analecta Bollandiana*, xvi. pp. 5-16.   [2] *G. B.* iii. p. 143.

corresponded to that of the soldiers who slew Dasius, began in November, and ended in December, lasting thirty days, or, *teste Macrobio*, originally lasting one day. If the slaying of Dasius really occurred, and was a survival of a custom once prevalent (as in ancient Anahuac), then the early Saturnalia lasted for a month, from November 23 to December 23 ; but Roman antiquaries knew nothing of this. The month date is remote indeed from Easter, so Mr. Frazer must try to show that originally the Saturnalia were a spring festival, like carnival.

To make the carnival and Saturnalia coincide, Mr. Frazer points out that ' if the Saturnalia, like many other seasons of licence, was always observed at the end of the old year or the beginning of the new one, it must, like the carnival, have been originally held in February or March, at the time when March was the first month of the Roman year.' [1] Thus, in conservative rural districts, the Saturnalia would continue to be held in February, not, as at Rome, in December, though Roman writers do not tell us so, and though non-Roman pagan peoples held festival at the winter solstice. The soldiers who killed poor Dasius were ultra-conservative, but they killed him in November, when their month of Saturnalia began, not in February, when, as they held by old usage, their Saturnalia should have been kept. The hypothesis may be stated thus :

1. In rural districts ' the older and sterner practice ' of murder may long have survived.[2]

2. In rural districts the Saturnalia continued to be held in February–March, not in December.[3]

3. Therefore the soldiers, who kept up ' the older and sterner practice ' of remote districts where the Saturnalia fell in February–March, killed Dasius—in November !

---

[1] *G. B.* iii. p. 144.   [2] *G. B.* iii. p. 142.   [3] *G. B.* ii. p. 144.

4. Meanwhile, so wedded were the rural districts to Saturnalia in February–March, that the feast continued in these months under the Church and became our carnival.

5. The eclectic soldiers in Lower Mœsia kept up the *old* killing and full month of revelry (though we never hear of a full month in older or later Rome), but they accepted the *new* date, November (not kept in Rome) and December ; though in their remote rural homes the Saturnalia were in February–March. Doubtless their officers insisted on the new official date, while permitting the old month of revel and the human sacrifice. Yet, apparently, of old there was but one day of revel.

But is the story of St. Dasius a true story ? The editor and discoverer of the Greek text in which the legend occurs at full length, Professor Franz Cumont of Ghent, at first held that as far as the sacrifice of the military mock-king goes the story is false. I have already observed that Mr. Frazer says nothing about the date of the Greek MS. containing the longest legend of Dasius. M. Cumont does. The MS. is of the eleventh century of our era, and the original narrative, he thinks, was done into Greek out of the Latin, which may have been based on official documents, before the end of the seventh century [1] A.D., by some one who knew Latin ill, wrote execrable Greek, did not understand his subject, and was far from scrupulous. These sentiments of M. Cumont ‘ set in a new and lurid light ’—as Mr. Frazer says of something else—the only evidence for the yearly military sacrifice of a mock-king of the Saturnalia. Our author was unscrupulous, for he makes Dasius profess the Nicene Creed

[1] Later (*Rev. de Philol.*, xxi. 3, pp. 152, 153), M. Cumont dates the Greek at about 500–600 A.D., because there were then apprehensions, as in the MS., of the end of the world. But so there were in 1000 A.D.

before it was made. As to the thirty days' revel, M. Cumont supposes *that* to be a blunder of our author, who did not know that the Saturnalia only occupied a week.[1] M. Cumont held that the king of the feast had not to slay himself, but only to sacrifice to Saturn ; in fact, Bassus, his commanding officer, does ask him, in the legend, to 'sacrifice to our gods, whom even the barbarians worship.' Dasius, the MS. says, refused, and was knocked on the head by a soldier named John. 'John' was likely to be a Christian, and M. Cumont suggests that the ignorant translator of the Latin took 'sepultus est' ('he was buried' by a soldier named John) for 'pulsus,' or 'depulsus est,' 'he was knocked on the head' ($\dot{\epsilon}\kappa\rho o\dot{\upsilon}\sigma\theta\eta$). In fact the Greek translator of the seventh century retouched his Latin original *à plaisir*. Human sacrifices, says M. Cumont, had been abolished since Hadrian's time. The soldiers, if they sacrificed a mock-king, broke an imperial edict.[2]

Our evidence then would seem, if M. Cumont is right, to be that of an unfaithful and not very scrupulous translator and embellisher of a Latin text. He informs us by the way that similar noisy performances went on in his own Christian period, not in December, but on New Year's Day. The Saturnalia were thus pushed on a week from December 23 ; we do not learn that they were transferred to, or retained at, February–March. The moral lesson of the legend is that we must not be noisy on New Year's Day.

Thus M. Cumont did not at first accept the evidence

---

[1] December 16–23. So also thinks M. Parmentier, *Rev. Phil.* xxi. p. 143, note 1. M. Parmentier says that we must either suppose the victim to have been selected by lot a whole month in advance (of which practice I think we have no evidence), or else cast doubt on the whole story, except the mere martyrdom of Dasius. But the latter measure M. Parmentier thinks too sceptical.

[2] Porphyry, *De Abstinentia*, ii. 56 ; Lactantius, i. 21.

for the annual sacrifice of a mock-king representing the god Saturn. But M. Parmentier suggested that an old cruel rite might have been introduced by Oriental soldiers into Mœsia (303 A.D.) thanks to the licensed ferocity of the persecutions under Diocletian. The victim, Dasius, was a Christian, and the author of his legend told the tale to illustrate the sin of revelry on New Year's Day. But what led to the revival of the cruelty? M. Parmentier quoted the story of our Babylonian festival, the Sacæa, in which a mock-king was scourged and slain. This or a similar rite the Roman legions finally confused with their own Saturnalia, both as to date and as to characteristics. The Oriental soldiers of the Roman Empire imported into the army this Oriental feast and sacrifice : just as they brought monuments of Mithra-worship into Mœsia. In an hour of military licence and of persecution, the cohorts in Mœsia may actually have tried to sacrifice a Christian private as a representative of King Saturn.

So far the sacrifice is an Asiatic importation, not a Roman survival. But M. Cumont, after reading M. Parmentier, returned from his disbelief in the veracity of the Dasius legend. He thought that the extension of the Saturnalia from one day to five days, after Caligula, might be due to an imitation introduced by Eastern slaves in Rome (an influential class) of the five days' feast of the Babylonian Sacæa. But thirty days, as in Mœsia, are not five days. He also inclined to accept the recently proposed identification of the Sacæa with a really old Babylonian feast called *Zagmuk*, or Zakmuk, and with the Jewish Purim, an identification which we shall later criticise. As to the imperial edict forbidding human sacrifice, M. Cumont now suggested that it had become a dead letter and impotent. In the general decadence of 303 monstrous cruelties flourished, and the Saturnalia were marked by gladiatorial combats. Thus, in remote Mœsia, the half Oriental soldiery might really sacrifice a Christian ' for the safety of his comrades under arms.'

So far the sacrifice of Dasius looks rather like a cruelty introduced into decadent Rome, and at the good-humoured Saturnalia, by Oriental legionaries, than like a Roman survival or recrudescence of a regular original feature of the Saturnalia. In any case the stripping and scourging of the Sacæan mock-king, his hanging, and his simulated resurrection (at which we shall find Mr. Frazer making a guess) are absent, while the date of the alleged trans- action (November–December) does not tally with Purim, or Eastertide, or the date of the Sacæa. The duration of the Dasius feast, thirty days, is neither Roman nor Oriental. Thus, far from illuminating the Oriental practice, the rite reported in Mœsia does but make the problem more perplexing. The evidence has all the faults possible, and the conjecture that the Greek writer in- vented the sacrifice, to throw discredit on the New Year revels of his contemporaries, may be worth considering.

Perhaps I may hint that I think the historical evidence of the author of the Dasius legend so extremely dubious that I might have expected Mr. Frazer to offer a criticism of its character. The general reader can gather from the ' Golden Bough ' no idea of the tenuity of the testimony, which, of course, is at once visible to readers of French and Greek. We address ourselves to scholars, and for scholars Mr. Frazer has provided the necessary citations, but my heart inclines to regard the needs of the general reader. (Cf. ' Man,' May 1901, No. 53.)

VI. THE GREEK CRONIA

From Rome we turn to Greece. Cronos, in Greece, answered, more or less, to Saturn in Rome, though how

much of the resemblance is due to Roman varnishing with
Greek myth I need not here discuss.   Now the Athenian
festival of Cronos fell neither in November, December,
February, nor March, but in July.[1] Therefore Mr. Frazer
needs to guess that the July feasts of Cronos were once,
or may have been, a spring festival, like the carnival and
like the Saturnalia, which (by another hypothesis) were
originally in February or March, though of this we have
no proof. Indeed, it is contrary to use and wont for a populace to alter a venerable folk-festival because of an official
change in the calendar. If the Romans for unknown
ages had kept the Saturnalia in spring they would not
move the date of their gaieties, and cut off three weeks
(or twenty-nine days) of their duration, because the new
year was shifted from March to January. In Scotland,
all through the Middle Ages and much later, the year
began in March. But Yule was not shifted into March :
it remained, and remains, like the Saturnalia, at the
winter solstice.

As proof that the Attic feast of Cronos (supposed to
answer to the Saturnalia) was originally in spring, not in
July, Mr. Frazer writes: 'A cake with twelve knobs,
which perhaps referred to the twelve months of the year,
was offered to Cronos by the Athenians on the fifteenth
day of the month Elaphebolion, which corresponded
roughly to March, and there are traces of a licence
accorded to slaves at the Dionysiac festival of the opening
of the wine jars,' in the month of flowers preceding.[2] It
was a proper season for licence.

The possible meaning of the cake does not go for
much, and Cronos is not Dionysus. There was a spring
festival of Cronos at Olympia, and Aug. Mommsen thinks
that the Athenian Cronos feast was originally vernal,

[1] *G. B.* iii. 147.   [2] *G. B.* iii. 148.

though Athenian tradition thought it was a harvest feast.[1]

The Attic customs, then, do not suit Mr. Frazer's argument. But he has another Greek instance. Sacrificers called 'kings' offered to Cronos, at Olympia, in spring, and why should they not once have been sacrificed like Dasius, only in spring, not in November? This evidence is an inference from a presumed survival of human sacrifice to Cronos, who certainly received many such offerings.

We are not told, we do not know why the Athenian Cronia were shifted from March to July, or when, but let no arbitrary proceedings of the kind prevent them from being equated with the Saturnalia, only known to us, in fact, as a December festival, not as a vernal rejoicing. It is singularly unlucky that the July date of the Athenian Cronia does tally with the June–July date of the Persian Sacæa, as given by Mr. Frazer (and probably given correctly) in his second volume.[2] But in his third volume he awakes to the desirableness of placing the Sacæa about Eastertide, not in July, and so loses any benefit which his argument might have acquired from the coincidence in date of the Attic harvest feast (Cronia) and the Persian Sacæa as that date is originally established.[3]

How deeply this is to be regretted we shall see later, for periods of licence like the Sacæa usually occur just after harvest, the real time of the Cronia. Liberty to slaves of feasting with their masters was a feature of the harvest Cronia, as of many other harvest rejoicings.[4] But the conjecture that the Cronia originally were a vernal feast removes them from such merrymakings of harvest licence as the Sacæa in June–July. On the other hand,

---

[1] *G. B.* iii. 147, note 2 ; 148, note 2.
[2] *G. B.* ii. 253, 254.   [3] *G. B.* ii. 254.   [4] *G. B.* ii. 147.

the conjecture that the Sacæa were vernal brings them
into touch with Eastertide, and with the other conjecture
that kings were once sacrificed at the conjecturally vernal
Cronia, and so has its value for Mr. Frazer's argument.

VII. THE SACÆA

We are still trying to find an historical case of a man
who is sacrificed in the character of a god and a king.
The argument next introduces us to the Sacæa at Babylon, when the mock-king was hanged, the Persian feast,
which, as we saw, M. Parmentier, following Herr Meissner, is inclined to identify with the ancient Babylonian
Zagmuk, or Zakmuk, and with the Jewish Purim.

This identification, this theory that Zakmuk, Sacæa,
and the Jewish Purim are all the same feast, is essential
to Mr. Frazer's theory. But, before his theory was published, Meyer, in the new volume of his 'History of
Antiquity,' had declared that the identification is impossible, philologically and as a matter of fact (*Geschichte des
Alterthums*). It would be interesting to know the meaning
of the word Sacæa, or *Sacea*, or *Sakia*, which Hyde trans-
lates 'convivial drinking, drinking healths' (*compotatio,
propinatio*).[1] We remember the Persian butler, called a
Sáki, in Omar Khayyam :

> The eternal *Sáki* from the bowl has poured
> Myriads of other bubbles, and will pour.

If the wine-pourer, the *Sáki*, of Omar is etymologically
connected with the Sakæa, or Sacæa, then the feast means
a wine-party. The Greeks, however, connected the
Sacæa with the Sacæ, an Oriental tribe of the great race
stretching from the Black Sea to Dacia. Indeed, in
Strabo's time, the feasters at the Sacæa dressed as Scythians

---

[1] Hyde, *De Rel. Pers.* p. 267.

(Sacæ) and drank, as Horace tells us that the Scythians were used to drink. This occurred at Zela, a town of Pontus, where a love goddess, in Persian Anaitis, of the type of the Babylonian Ishtar, was adored. Mr. Frazer even conjectures that her high priest, or a substitute, ' who played the King of the Sacæa,' was yearly sacrificed here, perhaps as Tammuz.[1] No record of the fact has reached us.

The interesting point about this derivation of Sacæa from the tribe of the Sacæ is that the festival was believed, says Strabo, to commemorate a great victory of the Persians over the Sacæ. In precisely the same way the Persian feast of the Magophonia was supposed to commemorate a victory over and massacre of the Magi.[2] Purim, again, was held to commemorate a triumph of the Jews over the Persians and a massacre of the Persians. In three cases, then, Sacæa, Magophonia, and Purim, a feast which was a secular drinking bout, preserve the memory of a bloody victory. I do not observe that Mr. Frazer notices this coincidence.

But manifestly this kind of feast is not a feast of the death of a mock-king, still less, if possible, a religious festival of the death and resurrection of a vernal god.[3] Yet there really was (if we accept rather poor evidence) *not* a sacrifice but an execution of a mock-king, a criminal, at the Sacæa, as held in Babylon. I quote our authorities. First comes Athenæus, who is writing about feasts of unreason, at which, in various regions, the slaves are waited upon by their masters.[4] He says nothing of the execution of a mock-king. He remarks : ' Berosus, in the first book of his " History of Babylon," says that on the sixteenth day of the month Lous there is a great festival celebrated at Babylon, which is called *Sakeas*, and it lasts five days ;

---

[1] *G. B.* iii. 163, 164.
[2] Herodotus, iii. 79.
[3] Strabo, p. 512.
[4] Athenæus, xiv. p. 639, c.

and during these days it is the custom for the masters to be under the orders of their slaves, and one of the slaves puts on a robe like the king's, being called *Zoganes*, and is master of the house. And Ctesias also mentions this festival in the second book of his " History of Persia." ' (Ctesias flourished rather earlier than Berosus, who is about 200 B.C.)

Thus Athenæus is silent about the execution of a mock-king, though doubtless he had the book of Berosus before him. And Dio Chrysostom, who does speak of the execution, and he alone does so, says nothing about Berosus, or any other authority. I cite the observations of Dio Chrysostom. He puts them into the mouth of the cynic, Diogenes, who is lecturing Alexander the Great, to tame his pride ; and who tells illustrative anecdotes, some of them absurd, much as Mr. Barlow was used to instruct Masters Harry Sandford and Tommy Merton. Dio, then, makes Diogenes say that at the Sacæa 'they take one of the prisoners condemned to death and seat him upon the king's throne, and give him the king's raiment, and let him lord it and drink, and run riot and use the king's concubines during these days, and no man prevents him from doing just what he likes. But afterwards they strip, and scourge, and crucify (or hang, ἐκρέμασαν) him.' [1] He dies, not as a victim, by sacrifice, but as a criminal, by a cruel and degrading form of capital punishment.[2]

---

[1] Dio, *Oratio* iv., vol. i. p. 76, Dindorf.

[2] Mr. Frazer, in his text, attributes the statement to Berosus, a Babylonian priest of about 200 B.C. In fact, we do not know Dio's authority for the tale (*G. B.* ii. 24, note 1). Mr. Frazer admits this in his note. Ctesias may be Dio's source, or he may be inventing. On the other hand, Macrobius, a late Roman writer, says that the Persians used to regard ' as due to the gods the lives of consecrated men whom the Greeks call Zanas ' (Macrobius, *Saturnalia*, iii. 7, 6). But what Zanæ are the learned do not know : whether the word means ζωγάνας, or the Zanes at Olympia (Pausanias, v. xxi. 2 ; *G. B.* ii. 24, note 1). Moreover, Macrobius may have drawn his facts from Dio. But Dio says nothing about ' consecrated men.'

According to Dio any condemned criminal would serve the turn. But Mr. Frazer suggests that perhaps the profession of victim was hereditary.[1]

Such is the story which Dio makes Diogenes tell Alexander, in a humorous apologue against royal pride. ' You will soon be growing a crest like a cock,' says Diogenes in Dio's essay. I cannot think that evidence found only in a literary *tour de force*, and put into the mouth of a professed humourist, proves historically that the mock-king was actually hanged once a year, at a feast described by Athenæus, Strabo, and Hesychius, who never mention so strange an affair as the hanging. The reader will not find that Mr. Frazer suggests all these doubts. Indeed, the student who avoids foot-notes will believe that the tale of the hanging is ' according to the historian Berosus, who, as a Babylonian priest, spoke with ample knowledge.' [2]

Now, granting that there really was a yearly execution at Babylon of a criminal, a mock-king, why was he put to death ? We know what Mr. Frazer's theory needs. It needs historical examples of men who, by being sacrificed as victims, obtain a divine character, as representing the god to whom they are sacrificed. The theory also demands that these victims shall be arrayed and crowned as kings. It is desirable, too, that they should perish about our Eastertide, and that they should be supposed to rise again. The solitary example of a Saturnalian victim in Mœsia did not fulfil these conditions. He was arrayed as a king, indeed, and was sacrificed, if we believe the legend of St. Dasius; but he was not stripped and scourged, and he died, not at Easter, but in November : if he had not refused the part thrust on him he would have died in December. There was no word about his resurrection. It was found necessary to suggest

<hr>

[1] *G. B.* iii. 186.   [2] *G. B.* ii. 24.

that originally the Saturnalian victim died in February–March, but this was not proved.

The other historical case, the mock-king of the Sacæa, also does not fulfil the conditions required. He is robed, and crowned, and scourged, but he is not sacrificed. We have no hint of a resurrection ; none of a religious character attaching to the feast ; none of a divine character attaching to the victim. The feast is traditionally a revel commemorative of a victory : the victim is a condemned criminal. As to the date of the death, Mr. Frazer has two contradictory theories. By the first (which is correct) the victim died probably in June–July (if not, certainly in September). By the second, the month date of the death is fixed (provisionally) in March–April. Let me add that, to suit Mr. Frazer's theory, the victim must not only have been divine at the origin of the institution, but must have been recognised as divine at the time of the Crucifixion of our Lord : otherwise our Lord's death, in the character of the victim, could lend him no 'halo of divinity.'

VI

ATTEMPTS TO PROVE THE SACÆAN CRIMINAL DIVINE

As our historical evidence does not meet Mr. Frazer's needs, as the Sacæan victim is not regarded as divine, as he is no 'victim' but a criminal, as he is not sacrificed, as the feast is not religious but a secular merrymaking, as no resurrection is mentioned, as the historical date does not fit Eastertide, Mr. Frazer has to invent theories which will prove far more than the facts alleged by Dio Chrysostom, Berosus in Athenæus, Strabo, and Hesychius; or will prove that originally the facts were the opposite of those historically recorded.

Through his whole argument Mr. Frazer seems to me to present two distinct theories alternately, and only at the close can I detect any attempt at reconciliation. A third theory, distinct from either, appears to be rejected. Indeed, Mr. Frazer's task is not easy. He may say that the Sacæan victim represents the king, and that the king being, by the hypothesis, divine, the victim is divine also. But he needs, moreover, a resurrection of the dead man, hence the theory that the victim represents not only the king, but a god of the type of Tammuz or Adonis. At the feasts of that god, a god of vegetable life, there was wailing for his death, rejoicing for his resurrection. At Babylon this occurred in June–July. But there is no evidence that a human victim was slain for Tammuz:

none that he was scourged and hanged. How are the two theories, the victim as divine king, the victim as Tammuz, to be combined ? Their combination is necessary, for the king is needed to yield the royal robes ; while Tammuz is needed to yield the resurrection, and the fast preceding the feast before Purim, a fast of wailing for Tammuz. We hear of no fast before the Sacæa, but if Purim be borrowed from the Sacæa (which is indispensable to the theory), the Sacæa too must have been preceded by a fast, though it is unrecorded.

Clearly the king theory alone, or the Tammuz theory alone, will not yield the facts necessary to the hypothesis. Consequently the two theories must be combined. The king must not only be divine, be a god ; he must also be a god of vegetation, a god of the Tammuz type, who has a resurrection. Now we have no evidence, or none is adduced, to prove that the king, whether Babylonian or Persian, was ever deemed to be an incarnation of Tammuz or any such vegetable deity. Without sound evidence to that effect the theory cannot move a step. We have abundance of Babylonian sacred and secular texts : not one is adduced to prove that the king incarnated any god, especially Tammuz.

Mr. Frazer then, after putting forward alternately the king theory and the Tammuz theory, does finally, if I understand him, combine them. He talks of ' the human god, the Saturn, Zoganes, Tammuz, or whatever he was called.' [1] Thus the victim is the king, and we get the royal robes, and the five days of royalty. The king is also Tammuz (unless I fail to grasp the meaning), the victim too is Tammuz, and we get the fast (though we hear of none before the Sacæa), the feast, and the resurrection. But this is a late and rather casually

[1] *G. B.* iii. 185.

introduced theory, quite destitute of evidence as regards the king's being recognised for Tammuz.

Previously, throughout two volumes, the victim had *alternately* derived his necessary divinity from the king and from the Tammuz god.   He derived more : as king he had the *entrée* of the royal harem ; as Tammuz he was the consort of a woman, ' probably a sacred harlot, who represented the great Semitic goddess Ishtar or Astarte.' His union with her magically fertilised the crops.[1] A similar duty, in the dream-time of Mr. Frazer's hypotheses, had been that of the majesty of Babylon. ' Originally, we may conjecture, such couples exercised their function for a whole year, on the conclusion of which the male partner—the divine king—was put to death ; but in historical times it seems that, as a rule, the human god—the Saturn, Zoganes, Tammuz, or whatever he was called— enjoyed his divine privileges, and discharged his divine duties, only for a short part of the year,' namely five days, at the Sacæa.[2]

The divine duties of the early kings of Babylon (if I understand Mr. Frazer) were ' to stand for the powers that make for the fertility of plants and perhaps also of animals.'   Are we to conceive that these pleasing exercises with the lady of the divine pair were all the duties of the early kings of Babylon ? In that case, who carried on the civil and military control of the Empire ? Of course, if the early king did nothing at all but associate with ' the human goddess who shared his bed and transmitted his beneficent energies to the rest of nature,'[3] then he may have been a man-god, a Tammuz, if the texts say so, and his substitute might die at once as royal proxy, to save the king's life, and also as Tammuz.   Moreover, it

---

[1] *G. B.* iii. 178.   [2] *G. B.* iii. 185.   [3] *G. B.* iii. 186.

would not matter a pin's fee whether such a king died or not. Only, no man could take the billet of king.

Thus it may be Mr. Frazer's intention to combine in one the two theories of the victim as Tammuz and as royal proxy. In that case his two apparently inconsistent theories are one theory.

But, if I apprehend it correctly, it is a very audacious theory. Where have we a proven case of a king who incarnates a god of vegetation, plays the part of ' making for the fertility of plants ' by the assistance of ' the human goddess who shares his bed, and transmits his beneficent energies to the rest of nature,' and who is sacrificed annually ? Does this divine voluptuary also keep a royal harem, or is that essential and more or less attested part of the Sacæa a later excrescence ?

Without some historical evidence for such a strange array of facts, including the yearly sacrifice of the monarch, I must hesitate to think that Mr. Frazer's theory of a king who is both king and Tammuz, and has, later, a substitute who is both Tammuz and king, is a practical hypothesis explanatory of ' the halo of divinity which was shed around the cross of Calvary.' I cannot accept as evidence for a combination of facts separately so extraordinary, a series of inferences and presumptions from rural or barbaric revels in spring or at harvest. The existence of a King or Queen of the May, or of the Bean on Twelfth Night, with occasional or even frequent mock destructions of the monarch of a playful day, cannot be used as proof that early Babylonian kings consorted for a year with a human goddess, and then were burned to death as gods of vegetable produce ; especially when there is no historical testimony, and only inference from myth, in favour of any human goddess or of a burned king.

We have not, meanwhile, even any testimony to show

that, in any time, in any place, any human victim was
ever slain, let alone a king (and a king annually), as
Tammuz.   We have only a guess, founded on the weakest
possible basis, that of analogy,   ‘ The analogy,’ says Mr.
Frazer, ‘ of Lityerses and of folk-custom, both European
and savage, suggests that in Phœnicia the corn-spirit—
the dead Adonis—may formerly have been represented by
a human victim.’ [1] . . . . This can hardly persuade me
that the kings of Babylon were annually sacrificed as
Tammuz or as Adonis.

While admitting that Mr. Frazer may really mean to
combine his two theories (the victim as king, the victim
as Tammuz), and while he certainly makes his victim both
a king and a god, I shall take the freedom to examine his
theory in the sequence of the passages wherein it is proposed, and request the reader to decide whether there be
one theory or two theories.

But first, have we any examples of a sacrifice by hanging, not by burning, the human victim?   For the Sacæan
victim, though confessedly hanged, is said, by Mr. Frazer,
to be ‘ sacrificed.’

I.   SACRIFICE BY HANGING.   DOES IT EXIST?

Let us look at actual human victims, actually known
to have been slain in the interests of agriculture.   Are, or
were, these human victims put to the infamous death of
malefactors, like the mock-king of the Sacæa?   They
were not.   Cases are given in vol. ii. p. 238 *et seq.*

1. The Indians of Guyaquar used to sacrifice human
blood and the hearts of men when they sowed their
fields.[2]

2. In the Aztec harvest festival a victim was crushed

---

[1] *G. B.* ii. 253.   [2] *Cieza de Leon*, p. 203.

between two great stones (perhaps to represent the grinding of the maize ?).

3. The Mexicans sacrificed young children, older children, and old men for each stage of the maize's growth. We are not told *how* they were sacrificed.[1]

4. The Egyptians *burned* red-haired men, and scattered their ashes with winnowing fans. This burning is a usual feature of sacrifice, and is not hanging or cruci-fying.

5. The Skidi, or Wolf Pawnees, *burned* a victim to Ti-ra-wá, ' the power above that moves the universe, and controls all things,' but the victim was a deer or a buffalo. There were also occasional human sacrifices before sowing ; the victim had his head cleft with a tomahawk, and was then riddled with arrows, and afterwards *burned*.[2] In some cases he was tied to a cross, before being slain with an axe.[3]

6. A Sioux girl was *burned* over a slow fire, and then shot with arrows. Her flesh, for magical purposes, was squeezed over the newly sown fields.

7. West African victims were killed with spades and hoes, and *burned* in newly tilled fields.

8. At Lagos a girl was impaled among sacrificed sheep, goats, yams, heads of maize, and plantains hung on stakes. Though impalement is a form of capital pun-ishment, probably the girl's blood was expected to fertilise the earth. We have no proof that crucifixion was used in Babylon, or the same motive might be alleged for the mock-king at the Sacæa. ' It may be doubted whether crucifixion was an Oriental mode of punishment,' says Mr. Frazer. He does not say that it was an Oriental form of sacrifice.[4]

---

[1] *G. B.* i. 143.   [2] Grinnell, *Pawnee Hero Stories*, pp. 362–369.
     [3] *G. B.*, ii. 238.   [4] *G. B.* ii. 24, note 1.

9. The Marimos kill and *burn* a human victim, and scatter the ashes on the ground to fertilise it.

10. The Bagolos hew a slave to pieces.

11. Some tribes in India chop victims up.

12. The Kudulu allow to a victim all the revels, women and all, of the Sacæan mock-king, and then cut a hole in him, and smear his blood over an idol. This is sacrifice, not capital punishment.

13. The Khonds slew their revered and god-like victim in a variety of ways, strangling him in a tree, *burning*, and chopping up, that his flesh might be sown on the fields. The head, bowels, and bones were *burned*.

Such are the examples of a real human victim slain for the good of the crops. In six out of fourteen cases the victim's ashes, blood, or flesh is used magically to fertilise the fields, and probably this is done in several other instances. In seven cases burning occurs. In two sacrifice to a god or idol occurs. In one only is the mode of death a recognised form of capital punishment.

Therefore Mr. Frazer does not seem to me to be justified in taking for and describing as ' sacrifice ' the capital punishment inflicted at the Sacæa on a mock-king who notoriously was a criminal condemned to death, and who was hanged, not sacrificed.

To be sure Mr. Frazer tries to turn this point, and how ? Perhaps ancient kings of Lydia were once burned alive on pyres, ' as living embodiments of their god.' For the Lydian, like the Macedonian and many other royal houses, claimed descent from Heracles, who, being on fire already under the shirt of Nessus, homœopathically burned himself. Crœsus, defeated, was about to die by fire, but not out of his own head. Cyrus was going to burn him alive, like Jeanne d'Arc, Cranmer, Wishart, and others. This cruel infliction by a foreign enemy hardly

proves a Lydian custom, nor are Lydians exactly Babylonians. Again, if an old Prussian king ' wished to leave
a good name behind him,' he burned himself before a
holy oak. 'Crummles is not a Prussian,' nor were the
kings of Babylon. Once more Movers thought that
the ' divine pair who figured by deputy' at the Sacæa
were Semiramis and Sandan or Sardanapalus. (Which
divine pair, the king's proxy and one of the king's concubines, or the Tammuz man and the sacred harlot ?)
Sandan was thought to be Heracles by the Greeks, and
his effigy was perhaps burned on a pyre at his festival
in Tarsus. Now the Persians, according to Agathias,
worshipped Sandes (Sandan), and perhaps the Babylonians
did so also, though really that agreeable Byzantine minor
poet, Agathias, cannot be called a good witness. Next,
K. O. Müller thinks that Sandan (Sandes) may have been
burned in a mystery play in Nineveh, Müller giving free
licence to his fancy, as he admits. Movers, too, thought
that ' at the Sacæa the Zoganes represented a god, and
paired with a woman who personated a goddess.' [1] And
Movers thinks that the Sacæan victim was originally
burned.[2]

For these ' exquisite reasons,' that the Lydian
monarchs claimed descent from Heracles, who was
burned, that Cyrus wanted to burn Crœsus alive, that
old Prussian kings who wished to leave a good name
burned themselves, that Movers thought that Sandan or
Sardanapalus might have figured at the Sacæa as
Zoganes, that Agathias mentioned Sandes as a Babylonian deity, and that Movers thinks that the man who
acted the god was burned, Mr. Frazer suggests that
perhaps the mock-king of the Sacæa *was* burned, once
upon a time.[3] But we only know that he was scourged

<hr>

[1] *G. B.* iii. 167.   [2] *G. B.* iii. 171.   [3] *G. B.* iii. 170, 171.

and hanged. So perhaps, Mr. Frazer suggests, he was *both* scourged, hanged, and burned afterwards, or perhaps hanging or crucifixion ' may have been a later mitigation of his sufferings '—a pretty mitigation ! And why was flogging added ?[1] One had liefer be burned, like a god and a king, than be first whipped and then crucified, as a malefactor of the lowest and most servile kind, losing, too, the necessary suggestion of sacrifice and divinity implied in being burned. Besides, apart from this theory of a cruel and debasing ' mitigation,' there is no evidence at all except what proves that the mock-king at the Sacæa was first stripped of his royal robes, then whipped, then hanged. If he dies as god or king, why is he stripped of his royal robes ? The man was hanged, was capitally punished (which as a condemned criminal he richly deserved), and ' there is an end on't,' as Dr. Johnson rudely remarked. Now ' we must not forget ' that Mr. Frazer has announced this ' sacrifice ' of a divine king as his theory, but we need not, I may even say must not, accept the theory. Because, first, Mr. Frazer gives many examples of persons believed each to contain a god, either temporarily or permanently.[2] But in not one single case is the person said to be killed for the benefit of the god whom he contains.

Secondly, there was historically no sacrifice in the case of the Sacæan mock-king.

The mock-king, then, if he has any divinity, has it not as a sacrifice, for he is not sacrificed; nor as representing a king who incarnates a god, for no kings or others thought to incarnate gods, whether temporarily or permanently, are proved to be slain for the benefit of that god. Nor are any kings who are actually slain, slain by hanging. The death of a man, as a god, belongs, if to

[1] *G. B.* iii. 171.　　　　[2] *G. B.* i. 131–157.

anything, to quite another festival, that of Tammuz or Adonis, and to quite another set of ideas. We have no proof indeed that a man was ever hanged or sacrificed as an embodiment of Adonis or Tammuz. But Mr. Frazer's theory of the reason for the Crucifixion on Calvary demands the *sacrifice* of a human victim, who is, *ex officio*, a god, is sacrificed in that character, and is feigned to rise again. He must also be royal, to account for the scarlet robe and crown of thorns of the great victim.

II. STAGES IN MR. FRAZER'S THEORY

Let us now trace the stages of Mr. Frazer's theory that the Sacæan victim is both god and king.

1. First in order of statement comes the description of the Sacæa, combined from Athenæus, who mentions no victim, and Dio Chrysostom, who does. We learn (from Mr. Frazer, not from Dio) [1] that the victim 'dies in the king's stead.' But ' we must not forget that the king is slain in his character of a god, his death and resurrection, as the only means of perpetuating the divine life unimpaired, being deemed necessary for the salvation of his people and the world.'

That is Mr. Frazer's theory: we have seen no proof of it, we have remarked that sacrificed victims are not hanged; that kings are not scourged; that there is no evidence beyond conjecture for an earlier Babylonian process of burning; while conjecture also explains whipping and hanging as a ' mitigation,' or alleges that possibly the victim was hanged first and burned afterwards.

Here the king is certainly not,[2] on the face of it, a god of vegetation: if anything, he is more like the

---

[1] *G. B.* ii. 24–26.   [2] *G. B.* ii. 24–26.

Chitome in Congo, who was a 'pontiff.' His credulous people believed that the world would end if the Chitome died a natural death, ' so when he seemed likely to die ' he was clubbed or strangled. He was sacrificed to no god whom he incarnated.[1] He was not clubbed once a year (like the Babylonian king of Mr. Frazer's theory) ; he was given a rude euthanasia ' when he seemed likely to die.' Does science ask us to believe that each Babylonian king had the cosmic *rapport* of a Congo savage pontiff, and was sacrificed after a year's reign, because a savage pontiff in Congo is put to death, not annually, but ' when he seems likely to die ' ?

Here, whatever science may expect us to believe, we are told by Mr. Frazer that the king in Babylon was annually sacrificed, as a god, indeed, but not explicitly as a god of vegetation, who has a resurrection.

2. A Babylonian god of vegetation, and a known god, appears in ii. 123, 124. This god is Tammuz. We hear that ' water was thrown over him at a great mourning ceremony, at which men and women stood round the funeral pyre of Tammuz lamenting. . . . *The dead Tammuz was probably represented in effigy*, water was poured over him, and he came to life again.' Mr. Frazer does not here plead for a human victim. The festival ' doubtless took place in the month Tammuz (June–July),' or in different places, at different times, from midsummer to autumn, or from June to September, as the late Mr. Robertson Smith calculated. Tammuz, so Mr. Sayce is cited, ' is originally the spring vegetation, which dies in his month, Tammuz or Du'ûzu ' (June–July).

Here, then, we have a death and resurrection of Tammuz. It occurs in June–July, or June–September, and Tammuz is undoubtedly the god of spring vegetation.

[1] *G. B.* ii. 8.

But Mr. Frazer does not here tell us that the king of
Babylon is also Tammuz. Tammuz is not whipped and
hanged at the Tammuz feast in July. His dead body is
' probably ' a dummy.

In vol. ii. 253 Mr. Frazer returns to the victim, the
mock-king, of the Sacæa. But he says nothing here about
the real king of Babylon. He wishes to show how and
why the victim is divine. Now, in ii. 26, we were told that
the victim is divine because he ' represents a dying god.'
' For we must not forget that the king dies in his character
of a god.' . . .

Was Mr. Frazer satisfied with this explanation given
in ii. 26 ?   Apparently not ; for [1] he gives a new explanation and a different one.   ' It seems worth suggesting
that the mock-king who was annually killed at the Babylonian festival of the Sacæa on the sixteenth day of the
month Lous may have represented Tammuz himself.'
Here the Tammuz dummy or effigy of ii. 123, 124, is,
perhaps, discarded. Still, if a real live Tammuz was
burned on a funeral pyre [2] his ashes might well be represented by a dummy. It has not yet occurred to Mr.
Frazer, as it does later, to have the re-arisen god personated by a living human counterpart (Mordecai in a later
page) of the dead Tammuz (Haman). The festival of
the Sacæa is now a Tammuz festival, a religious feast,
and, indeed, is identical with that of ii. 123, 124, for it
occurs in the month Lous. Now Lous, says Mr. Robertson Smith, ' answered to the lunar month Tammuz,' [3] and
the month of Tammuz [4] was June–July, or June–September.

There could not surely be *two* Tammuz feasts in the
month Tammuz ?   We are therefore confronted by the

---

[1] *G. B.* ii. 253, 254.   [2] *G. B.* ii. 123.
[3] *G. B.* ii. 254, note 1.   [4] *G. B.* ii. 123.

singular facts that Tammuz lay 'on a funeral pyre'[1] and also that, as the Sacæan victim, who, Mr. Frazer thinks it 'worth suggesting' personated Tammuz, he was at the same feast, the Sacæa, whipped and hanged.[2] Mr. Frazer goes on : ' If this conjecture is right, the view that the mock-king at the Sacæa was slain in the character of a god ' (Tammuz) 'would be established.'

But it was established already, was it not on other grounds, to Mr. Frazer's satisfaction, in ii. 26 ? There the criminal victim died as a king, and as a god, for the king was a god, and so was his proxy. Now, on the other hand, if Mr. Frazer's latest conjecture is right, the victim dies as a real known god, Tammuz. We keep asking, Was the king also an incarnation of Tammuz ? May I not be excused for surmising that we have here an hypothesis in the making, an hypothesis resting on two different theories ? If Mr. Frazer holds that the king of Babylon was also Tammuz, as the mock-king was, here was the opportunity for saying so, and proving the fact from Babylonian texts.

Mr. Frazer here gives us a Tammuz feast in which Tammuz lies on a funeral pyre, and also a Tammuz feast in which the human representative of that deity is whipped and hanged, while 'the dead Tammuz was probably represented in effigy,' water was poured over him, and he came to life again. How ? In the person of Mordecai ? These are the results of ii. 123, 124, and of ii. 253, 254.

These things are, confessedly, conjectures. But one thing is quite certain : the Sacæa, wherein Tammuz either lay on a funeral pyre, and afterwards had water poured over him, 'probably in effigy,' or was hanged, was a festival of June–July. Variations of calendars, however, might make the Sacæa fall ' from midsummer to autumn

---

[1] *G. B.* ii. 123.   [2] *G. B.* ii. 253, 254.

or from June to September ' (ii. 123, note of Mr. Robertson Smith).   These dates are remote from Eastertide.

To this point Mr. Frazer [1] promises ' to return later.' He does so in the most disconcerting manner.   For when he returns the Sacæa, which were in the month Tammuz, June–July,[2] startle us by being held in March or March–April.[3]   May I not say that I seem to detect traces of an hypothesis in the making, and of discrepant theories?   We have already been rather puzzled by the Tammuz on a funeral pyre, who has cold water poured over him, 'probably in effigy,' and also is honoured by being whipped and hanged in the person of a human representative, a mock-king, at the same festival.   But perhaps there were two Tammuz feasts in the month of Tammuz?   And possibly the victim was whipped and hanged at one of them, while his mortal remains were burned on the pyre at the other?   'It is quite possible,' says Mr. Frazer, when explaining why a victim of a sacrifice was hanged, not burned as is usual, ' that both forms of execution, or rather of sacrifice, may have been combined by hanging or crucifying the victim first and burning him afterwards; '[4] but he neglects the buxom opportunity of corroborating this conjecture, by referring to the Tammuz victim who had both a funeral pyre and a gibbet, in ii. 123, 124, 253, 254.

III. A POSSIBLE RECONCILIATION

There is, perhaps, a mode of reconciling the dates of the Tammuz festivals, at one of which Tammuz was honoured with a pyre, at the other (in the person of his representative, the Sacæan mock-king) with a gibbet.   Dr. Jastrow places a Tammuz feast in the fourth month, which, if the Babylonian year begins, as Mr. Frazer says it does, with

[1] *G. B.* ii. 254.
[3] *G. B.* iii. 152, 154.
[2] *G. B.* ii. 123, 124; ii. 253, 254.
[4] *G. B.* iii. 171.

the month Nisan, means that the fourth month and a
Tammuz feast occurred in our June–July. But Dr. Jastrow
also writes that in the sixth Babylonian month, our
August-September, 'there was celebrated a festival to
Tammuz.'[1]

Thus Tammuz might have his gibbet in June–July,
and his pyre in August–September. But alas! this
will not do, for the pyre is of June–July.[2] Nor can he
have his gibbet in August–September, as I had fondly
hopèd, for he is to be identified with the mock-king of the
Sacæa, and the month of his hanging is Tammuz,
Lous, or June–July, if Mr. Robertson Smith is right.[3]
Thus I really fail to believe that Tammuz could have
both a burning and a hanging in June–July. I hoped
that Dr. Jastrow's two Tammuz feasts had solved the
problem, but I hoped in vain.

IV. THE SACÆA SUDDENLY CHANGES ITS DATE

Meanwhile, even though we have allowed for two
Tammuz feasts, are we also to admit a third Tammuz
feast at the March festival of the Sacæa? For in vol. iii.
151–153, March has become the date of the Sacæa, rather
to our surprise, for the date had been June–July.[4] Now
three Tammuz feasts in six months seem one too many, if
not two. Consequently the arguments which in ii. 123, 124,
253, 254, show the Sacæan victim, because he died in the
month Tammuz, to represent the god Tammuz fail, perhaps, if the victim really died in March, at the Babylonian
Zakmuk, or Zagmuku, a feast in honour, not of Tammuz,
but of Bau (a goddess), and later of Marduk.[5] Neither
Bau nor Marduk is Tammuz; nor does the victim seem

---

[1] Jastrow, p. 484. [2] *G. B.* ii. 123, 124. [3] *G. B.* ii. 253, 54.
[4] *G. B.* ii. 123, 124. [5] Jastrow, 59, 127, 631, 677, 678–9.

likely to represent Tammuz, after his death is shifted from
the Tammuz feasts of May–June or June–July, July–
August, to March, when the feast was really in honour,
not of Tammuz, but of Bau, or later, of Marduk.

All our difficulties, indeed, pale before the fact that
the date of the Sacæa, when the possible Tammuz victim
was hanged, is fixed twice ; once, with much show of
reason and ' with unconcealed delight,' in June–July, in
the second volume ; while, next, it is argued from, in the
third volume, as if the date were March–April.

I conjecture, therefore, that the July date was not
inconsistent with what is now Mr. Frazer's theory when
he revised his second volume. Otherwise he would not
have said that Mr. Robertson Smith's decision as to the
July date ' supplies so welcome a confirmation of the
conjecture in the text,'[1] and then, in iii. 152, 153, have
proceeded to argue on the presumption that Mr. Robertson
Smith's calculations may be, for the purposes of the theory,
disregarded. And they are disregarded, as we shall see. If
they were dubious, they should never have been welcomed.

V. VARIOUS THEORIES OF THE VICTIM

Meanwhile, for our own argument, as to the precise
nature of the Babylonian King's divinity, vegetable or
not, I do not think that we have yet found the King of
Babylon explicitly identified with a god of vegetation.

The victim, remember, was at first divine, either as proxy
of the king, incarnating, I think, a god unknown ; or as full
of cosmic *rapport*, as a man-god of the second species.[2]
Next his divinity was established, if Mr. Frazer rightly
conjectured that he ' represented Tammuz himself.'[3]

---

[1] *G. B.* ii. 254, note 1.   [2] *G. B.* ii. 24–26 ; i. 80–82.
[3] *G. B.* ii. 253, 254.

Next he was a criminal vicariously sacrificed for 'the saving of the king's life for another year.'[1]

Next ' it would appear that the Zoganes' (the same old victim) ' during his five days of office personated not merely a king but a god, whether that god was the Elamite Humman, the Babylonian Marduk, or some other deity not yet identified.'[2] Next the victim personated ' a god or hero of the type of Tammuz or Adonis, (and) enjoyed the favours of a woman, probably a sacred harlot . . . .' in addition to the caresses of the royal seraglio.[3] Next the indefatigable victim represented the king, ' the human god, the Saturn, Zoganes, Tammuz, or whatever he was called,' though all we know of the god Zoganes is that Zoganes was the title of the slave lord of the household at the Persian Sacæa.[4]

It would thus appear almost as if all gods are one god to Mr. Frazer by a kind of scientific ' Henotheism.' Humman or Saturn, Zoganes or Tammuz, Marduk or Adonis, any one of them, or all of them, will do for the king to incarnate or personate. Any one of them, or all of them, will figure as representatives of vegetable life in company with Zeus and the horses of Virbius! ' We may conjecture that the horses by which Virbius was said to have been slain were really embodiments of him as a deity of vegetation.'[5] Now let me too say ' we may conjecture.' Mr. Frazer tells us that ' horses were excluded from the grove and sanctuary ' of Virbius.[6] Is it putting too great pressure on evidence to conjecture that the horses, while being driven out, were whipped ? Now the horses embodied, perhaps, as we are told, a deity of vegetation. They were whipped, and therefore it was usual to whip the representatives of a deity of vegetation.

---

[1] *G. B.* iii. 152.　　　[2] *G. B.* iii. 160.　　　[3] *G. B.* iii. 178.
[4] *G. B.* iii. 185.　　　[5] *G. B.* ii. 314.　　　[6] *G. B.* i. 6.

This solves our problem, why was the victim, the divine victim, whipped ?

Seriously, have we not in all this book to do with that method of arbitrary conjecture which has ruined so many laborious philosophies of religion ?

As to one essential conjecture, that the Babylonian, or rather the Persian, kings represented a deity of vegetation, I can offer only one shadowy testimony. Nebuchadnezzar for a while exhibited a caprice in favour of a purely vegetable diet. This may have been a survival of a royal taboo. As a god of vegetation, a king would not eat vegetables any more than a savage usually eats his totem. But some savages do eat their totems on certain sacred occasions, and that may be the reason why Nebuchadnezzar, for a given period, turned vegetarian.

VII

ZAKMUK, SACÆA, AND PURIM

IT is necessary to get the death of the Sacæan victim into touch with Easter. The Sacæa, when he died, had been in June–July, in vol. ii., in Mr. Frazer's first edition, before he evolved his theory. When the theory is evolved, in the second edition and third volume, the Sacæa prefer to occur in March–April, which gets the sufferings of the mock-king into touch with the Jewish Purim, and so within measurable distance of our Passion Week, though the June–July date of the first edition survives in the second volume of the new edition. The change of date of the Sacæa is arranged for by the plan, rejected by Meyer and Jastrow, of identifying the Persian Sacæa and the Jewish Purim with the ancient Babylonian Zagmuk or Zakmuk, a New Year festival of March-April.[1] To be sure, if that be the date, we seem bereft of our useful Tammuz, from whom, in ii. 254, it was conjectured that the victim mock-king derived his divinity, an old superstitious belief which ' shed the halo of divinity ' on the victim of Calvary. For the Tammuz feast was certainly in June–September. However, perhaps there were three Tammuz feasts, resurrection and all, and Mr. Frazer's last choice of a date, in March–April, has the

---

[1] ' Zimmern's view of a possible relationship between Purim and Zagmuku is untenable,' says Dr. Jastrow (*op. cit.* p. 686, note 2). This is also the opinion of Meyer.

immense advantage for his theory of getting us near Eastertide.

But did the Sacæa actually desert their old date, June–July? To prove that we must identify the Sacæa, a Persian, with Zakmuk, a Babylonian feast, which really fell in March or April. The old Babylonian feast, Zakmuk, is known to the learned through inscriptions. We have seen that M. Cumont and Herr Meissner inclined to regard Zakmuk as identical with the Sacæa, while the feast Zakmuk-Sacæa is supposed by Mr. Frazer to be the origin of the Jewish Purim. But the Sacæa fell in the Macedonian month Lous, as Athenæus tells us according to Berosus, a Babylonian priest, using the Macedonian Calendar. And Lous, as Mr. Robertson Smith proved, was our July.[1] Zakmuk, on the other hand, fell in our March–April, and Purim in our March, neither of which is July, when the Sacæa were held.

Now it is desirable for Mr. Frazer's argument that the Sacæa should fall, not in July, as it did in ii. 254, but in or about Eastertide. Mr. Frazer therefore shifts the Sacæa from July to Eastertide in face of difficulties.

All we know concerning Zakmuk is [2] that this feast, originally a feast of Bau, says Dr. Jastrow, fell about the vernal equinox (near the beginning of the old Babylonian year); that, after a certain period, it was held in honour of the chief god of Babylon, named Merodach; that a council of gods was thought to meet in Merodach's temple, under his presidency, and that they determined the fate of the year, 'especially the fate of the king's life.' The festival existed as early as 3000 B.C., whereas the Sacæa, 'so far as appears from our authorities, does not date from before the Persian conquest of Babylon' (536 B.C.).[3] But in spite of dates it is desirable for Mr. Frazer's purpose to identify

[1] *G. B.* ii. 254.　　　[2] *G. B.* iii. 151, 152.　　　[3] *G. B.* ii. 24, note 1.

the Persian Sacæa with the Babylonian Zakmuk. For,
if he succeeds in this, then Sacæa must fall when Zakmuk
fell, and nearly when Purim fell, at—or not so very far
from—Eastertide. But [1] Sacæa was eagerly welcomed by
Mr. Frazer as a July, not a spring, feast, whereas, in iii.
152, Sacæa is identified with Zakmuk, which did fall in
spring. Again, we have not even a hint that any mock-
king, or Tammuz man, or anybody, was slain at the
Babylonian feast of Zakmuk, as a man was slain, says
Dio, at the Sacæa. However, Mr. Frazer tries to show
that Sacæa and Zakmuk may be the same feast. For
Sacæa and Zakmuk are names that resemble Zakmuk
and Zoganes.[2] We may reply that the word Sacæa also
rather closely resembles the name of the tribe of Sacæ,
from whom the Perso-Greeks derived the word Sacæa,
while the Sacæa were held to commemorate a victory over
the Sacæ. Again the word Sacæa, which was a drinking
feast, resembles the word *Sáki*, Persian for a pourer
forth of wine. ' The word *Sáki* is Arabic, being the
nomen agentis of the verb *Saḳá* " to water " (*abreuver*).
This root is common to several Semitic languages—*e.g.*
Hebrew and Æthiopic—and if we could prove the word
Sacæa to be of native Babylonian origin, it might very
probably come from the same root,' Mr. Denison Ross
informs me. In any case we cannot build on resemblances
in the sound of words. That argument for the identification of Zakmuk and the Sacæa fails.

Next Mr. Frazer contends that since, at Zakmuk, the
gods determined the fate of the king's life, it was a critical
time for the king. Now ' the central feature of the
Sacæa ' appears to have been ' the hanging of the mock-
king for the saving of the real king's life.' [3] Here, then,
are two critical hours for the king : one at Zakmuk, when

<hr/>

[1] *G. B.* ii. 254.   [2] *G. B.* iii. 152.   [3] *Ibid.*

the gods settle his fate ; one at the Sacæa, when his life is saved by the execution of his proxy. Are not then these two critical periods one period, and is not Sacæa another name for Zakmuk ? [1] But Mr. Frazer has also told us that the main feature of the Sacæa was the death of a man who represented Tammuz, and was killed after doing sympathetic magic with a sacred harlot. [2] Was there, then, in connection with this Tammuz man, a third Tammuz feast in March–April, for there were two, in June–September? Thus, even if we could admit that, because two periods are critical, both are the same period, yet as the victim of the Sacæa was a Tammuz man, slain to do good to the crops, we are unable to concede that he also died ' in the king's stead,' and to save his life, unless the king was Tammuz. Besides, no authority tells us that either, or both, of this victim's deaths occurred at the Babylonian feast of Zakmuk : it occurred at the Persian feast of the Sacæa, if at all.

Indeed, even if Mr. Frazer's two arguments for the identity of Zakmuk and Sacæa were persuasive (and how persuasive they are we have seen), there would remain a difficulty. For Berosus says, as we saw, that the Sacæa fell on Lous 16, which is July, whereas Zakmuk fell in March–April.

I. HISTORICAL DIFFICULTY

This obstacle seems to be, and really is, insuperable. But Mr. Frazer, undaunted, writes : ' The identification of the months of the Syro-Macedonian Calendar is a matter of some uncertainty ; as to the month Lous in particular the evidence of ancient writers appears to be conflicting, and until we have ascertained beyond the reach of doubt

---

[1] *G. B.* iii. 152.   [2] *G. B.* iii. 178.

when Lous fell at Babylon in the time of Berosus' (say 200 B.C.) 'it would be premature to allow much weight to the seeming discrepancy in the dates of the two festivals' (namely Zakmuk and the Sacæa). Henceforth Mr. Frazer's hypothesis seems to me to proceed on the fancy that Sacæa and Zakmuk are identical, which is impossible, since the Sacæa fall in July or September, and Zakmuk in March–April.

It is absolutely certain, historically, that Sacæa and Zakmuk cannot be identical. They were as remote in date as they well could be. For the conflicting evidence of ancient writers as to the date of the month of the Sacæa, namely the Macedonian month Lous (Λῶος), Mr. Frazer gives two references. The first is to Mr. Robertson Smith's proof that Lous is July.[1] That does him no good. The second is to Smith's ' Dictionary of Greek and Roman Antiquities.'[2] In that work I read that the only doubt as to the month Lous is whether it fell in July or September. Smith's 'Dictionary' is a book so common and accessible that I need not inflict on the reader the nature of the conflicting evidence. It is enough to say that the month of the Sacæa, Lous, was almost certainly July, but, if not July, was undeniably September. Now neither July nor September is Eastertide, or near it. So that the effort to make the Sacæa identical with Zakmuk, and therefore more or less coincident with Purim, and with our Easter, is an absolute failure. The Jews, then, could not (as in Mr. Frazer's theory) borrow abroad a July or September mock-king, and attach him to a vernal festival, their Purim. Thus, as Zakmuk is several months remote from the Sacæa, it is not identical with the Sacæa. Mr. Frazer himself says: 'If the Sacæa occurred in July and the Zakmuk in

[1] *G. B.* 254, note 1.   [2] 3, i. 339.

March, the theory of their identity could not be maintained.'[1] But he loses, rather than gains, if the Sacæa were in September, and that is the only possible alternative. The game is over; the mock-king of Babylon died, if at all, in July or September, at the Sacæa; not at Zagmuk or Zakmuk, in March–April. There is not a known hint that any mock-king died in Babylon about Eastertide, or earlier, at the feast of Zakmuk.

I confess that when I found Mr. Frazer declining to 'allow much weight to the seeming discrepancy in the dates of the two festivals,' till it was 'ascertained beyond the reach of doubt when Lous fell at Babylon in the time of Berosus,' I presumed that 'the apparently conflicting evidence of ancient writers' meant a difference of opinion as to whether Lous was a spring or a midsummer month. But I looked at Smith's 'Dictionary' and found nothing of the sort! The difference of opinion, the conflict of evidence, is concerned (see Smith) with the question whether Lous was September (as it seems to have been in the time of Philip of Macedon) or whether it was July, as in the time of Plutarch. Neither opinion gives Lous the faintest chance of being a spring month. Therefore the vernal Zakmuk is not the Sacæa; therefore there is not the ghost of a reason for guessing that a mock-king was hanged at Zakmuk; therefore Zakmuk, in April, cannot lend a hanged mock-king to Purim, in March; therefore Purim, having no slain mock-king, cannot hand one on to Eastertide, which, moreover, does not occur at the same date as Purim, but some weeks later, as may happen. Therefore the mock-king, if he had been divine (which he was not), and if he had been sacrificed (which he was not), could not have lent his 'halo of divinity' to

[1] *G. B.* iii. 152.

gild the Cross at Calvary. But that he did so is Mr.
Frazer's hypothesis—sometimes.

II. PERSIANS ARE NOT BABYLONIANS

The Sacæa, according to all our authorities, was a
Persian, not a Babylonian, feast. We have not a tittle of
evidence to show that the Babylonians, with whom Zakmuk
was a feast of old standing, ever heard of the Sacæa before
they were conquered by the Persians (B.C. 536).
Mr. Frazer admits this : the Babylonian custom, ' so far as
appears from our authorities, does not date from before
the Persian conquest ; but probably it was much older.' [1]
Why 'probably'? On the strength of this 'probably'
Mr. Frazer calls the doings at the Persian Sacæa 'a
Babylonian custom.' [2]   It was a custom of the Persian
conquerors of Babylon, if we can believe Dio Chrysostom ; but we have no evidence that it was a Babylonian custom. Yet it ' has just got to be ' a Babylonian
custom that Mr. Frazer may attach it to a vernal Babylonian feast, Zakmuk, and so to Purim, and so to Eastertide.

III. ORIGIN OF PURIM

About the real origin of Purim, a purely secular
jollification, preceded, after a certain date, by a fast, we
know nothing. It is first mentioned in the Book of
Esther, which is so secular that the name of God is never
mentioned in it. Scholars have debated as to the date of
Esther, which Mr. Frazer places in the fourth or third
century B.C.; some, as Kuenen, place it later. Some
think it historical, as Mr. Sayce does ; others regard it as
a romance, composed to supply an account of the origin

[1] *G. B.* ii. 24, note 1.   [2] *G. B.* ii. 26.

of the feast of Purim, which we never hear of before the
exile.

The account in Esther is well known. Xerxes
quarrelled with his queen, Vashti, and, after a series of
experiments in wives, selected Esther, cousin of an artful
Jew named Mordecai. This man discovered, and through
Esther reported, a conspiracy. He later behaved with
insolence to Haman, the Vizier, who settled with Xerxes
a kind of St. Bartholomew's day for all the Jews. But
Xerxes was accidentally reminded of the services done by
Mordecai, and asked Haman how a grateful prince should
reward an unnamed servant. Haman suggested the ride
in royal splendour, which Mordecai enjoyed. Haman
then erected a very tall gallows whereon to hang Mordecai.
But Esther got news of the intended massacre, and, as
Xerxes had promised to give her any gift she asked for,
she demanded the death of Haman. So Haman was hanged,
and the Jews were allowed to defend themselves. They
massacred an enormous number of their enemies, and
henceforth kept Purim, a feast of two days, on Adar
(March) 14 and 15. 'Wherefore they called these days
Purim, after the name of Pur,' and ' pur, that is, the lot, was
cast before Haman for a whole year from Nisan to Adar.' [1]

The word *pur*, ' a lot,' does not occur in Hebrew, says
Mr. Frazer. However, the Assyrian *puhra* means an
assembly, and there was an assembly of the gods at the
feast of Zakmuk. Why the Jews went after an Assyrian
word we may guess; but we also learn that '*pur* or *bur*
seems to be' (one wants to know if it really *was*) 'an
old Assyrian word for 'stone,' and a stone may be used
for a lot,[2] as the Greek ψῆφος, a pebble, also means a
vote. Thus either the Assyrian *puhra* or *pur* may have
lent a name to the feast of Purim.

---

[1] Esther iii. 7.   [2] *G. B.* iii. 154, 155.

I am no friend to etymological conjecture, especially when two Assyrian words put in rival claims to be, each of them, the origin of a Jewish word. Mr. Frazer does not, I think, allude to the other guess, connecting Purim with the Persian feast, Phurdigan (Phurim ? or Purim).[1] We find Purdaghan, Purdiyan, and so forth. This Persian feast was a drinking bout and time of jollity, so that Hyde very naturally compares it to Purim and to the old Persian Sacæa, or Sakea, or *Sakia*, which means 'drinking together,' or 'drinking healths.'[2] If Sakia means a convivial feast in Persian, it fits very well the Persian Sacæa, which were a time of jollity. The learned may settle their etymological guesses among themselves, but we are not obliged, for want of another conjecture, to fly to old Assyrian for Purim : still less do we agree that Mr. Frazer has made out a fairly probable case for holding that 'the Jewish feast (Purim) is derived from the Babylonian new year festival of Zakmuk.'[3]

No case at all, I venture to think, is made out. Mr. Frazer's Assyrian etymologies are met by competing etymologies. Moreover, we know next to nothing of the Babylonian Zakmuk, but we do know that the Persian Sacæa, Sakea, or *Sakia* was, like Purim, a period of hard drinking and wild licence : which does not resemble a solemn religious festival of the supreme god, Marduk, or a period of wailing for Tammuz. There is another coincidence, unnoted, I think, by Mr. Frazer, but already noted by us. Herodotus, our oldest Greek source for the Persians, tells us that their chief feast was called *Magophonia*, and celebrated the *massacre* of the hostile Magi.[4] Strabo tells us that the Sacæa were supposed to

[1] Kuenen, *Hist. and Lit. of Israelites*, iii. 149, 150.
[2] Hyde, *Hist. Rel. Pers.* pp. 266, 267. Oxford, 1760.
[3] *G. B.* iii. 155.   [4] Herodotus, iii. 79.

commemorate a *massacre* of intoxicated Sacæ. Purim is held to celebrate a *massacre* of the foes of the Jews. Can these three feasts for a massacre coincide by accident? It is not easy to see how this tradition attached itself to the slaying of a criminal, either as king's proxy or as representative of Tammuz.

IV. IS PURIM PRE-EXILIAN OR POST-EXILIAN?

In any case Purim has not been successfully connected with Zakmuk. Mr. Frazer, however, says that 'an examination of that' (the Jewish) 'tradition, and of the manner of celebrating the feast, renders it probable that Purim is nothing but a more or less disguised form of the Babylonian feast of the Sacæa or Zakmuk.'[1] We have seen that stern dates do not allow us to identify Sacæa with Zakmuk. The month Lous is firm as the Macedonian phalanx, and will not masquerade as March–April, when Zakmuk was held. Setting that aside, 'there are good grounds for believing that Purim was unknown to the Jews until after the exile,' and yet 'that they learned to observe it during their captivity in the East.'[2] But their captivity in the East *was* the exile, so how did they know nothing of Purim at the very time when they also learned to celebrate that festival? However, it is reckoned 'fairly probable' that the Jews borrowed Purim either 'directly from the Babylonians or indirectly through the Persian conquerors of Babylon;' the only question is from which?[3] The Jews probably borrowed Purim in or after the exile. But they also kept Purim before the exile, at least Mr. Frazer thinks that 'the best solution.' It is Jensen's

[1] *G. B.* iii. 153, 154.   [2] *G. B.* iii. 153.
[3] *G. B.* iii. 155.

solution, stated, however, only 'in letters to correspondents.' [1]

It really seems hardly consistent that Mr. Frazer should both think Purim probably a feast borrowed in or *after* the exile, and also appear to approve a theory which regards the feast as familiar to the Jews *before* the exile. Yet that is what he has apparently succeeded in doing.

He prefers Jensen's solution, which is this: A fast was held before the feast of Purim.[2] Why?

'The best solution appears to be that of Jensen, that the fasting and mourning were originally for the supposed annual death of a Semitic god or hero of the type of Tammuz or Adonis, whose resurrection on the following day occasioned that outburst of joy and gladness which is characteristic of Purim.' [3] Yes; but the Jews had that institution before the exile. In the first days of his own captivity Ezekiel was carried, in the flesh, or out of the flesh, to the temple at Jerusalem. 'Then he brought me to the door of the gate of the Lord's house which was towards the north, and, behold, there sat women wailing for Tammuz.' [4]

Now Jensen's solution is that the fast at Purim represents the wailing for Tammuz, or somebody of his type. But, if the Jews did that, as they did, *before* the exile, and if that was Purim, how did they also borrow Purim *after* the exile, especially as 'there are good grounds for believing that Purim was unknown to the Jews till after the exile'?[5] How can both views be correct? Or is this March feast of the Tammuz kind an addition to the old pre-exilian Jewish Tammuz feast?

Moreover, Purim is probably, according to Mr. Frazer,

---

[1] *G. B.* iii. 177, and note 2.   [2] Esther iv. 3, 16; ix. 31.
[3] *G. B.* iii. 177.   [4] Ezekiel viii. 14.
[5] *G. B.* iii. 153.

' a mere disguised form of the Sacæa,' which, in his opinion, is the same as Zakmuk.[1] But ' the central feature of the Sacæa appears to have been the saving of the king's life for another year by the vicarious sacrifice of a criminal.' [2] Yet its central feature is also the sorrow for the death and glee for the resurrection ' of a Semitic god or hero of the type of Tammuz or Adonis,' following Jensen. How can the Sacæa have two central features? If it is only an affair of hanging a man to save the king's life, why should the Jews at Jerusalem fast before the vicarious sacrifice of a criminal for the Babylonian king? They did fast, we know. And why should the victim's resurrection (if any) on the following day ' occasion that outburst of joy and gladness which is characteristic of Purim ' ? [3] What had the Jews to make with the resurrection of a proxy of the king of Babylon ?

Mr. Frazer has not, I think, suggested that the kings of Israel or Judah were once annually sacrificed. So why were the Jewish women wailing at the north gate of the Temple? For Tammuz, as we know from Ezekiel ; but Tammuz was not a Jewish king, or, if he was, it should be stated. Also, if the Jewish ladies wailed and rejoiced for Tammuz at the Temple in Jerusalem before the exile, how can it be consistently maintained that they knew nothing of these rites till after the exile, and then borrowed them from Babylonians or Persians ? If Purim is a Tammuz rite, the Jews had it before the exile, as Ezekiel proves. If it is not a Tammuz rite, why is Jensen's the best solution? for Jensen's solution is that ' the fasting and mourning were originally for the supposed annual death of a Semitic god or hero of the type of Tammuz or Adonis, whose resurrection on the following

---

[1] *G. B.* iii. **153, 154.**   [2] *G. B.* iii. **152.**

[3] *G. B.* iii. **177.**

day occasioned that outburst of joy and gladness which is characteristic of Purim.' [1] Then, once more, that outburst of joy and gladness for the re-arisen Tammuz was [2] probably in the month Tammuz, our June–July. But now [3] it is at Purim—that is, in March.

How are Mr. Frazer's theories to be reconciled with each other and with the facts? Did the Jews wail for Tammuz, in spring, before the exile; and, after the exile, adapt their old rite of a Tammuz fast and feast to the vicarious sacrifice of a condemned criminal (whether in July or in April) in the interests of the king of Babylon? Had they been wont to hang a man, while they wailed for Tammuz, before the exile? If so, why did they hang him, and what did they borrow during the exile? Or was all that they borrowed just the habit of crowning, discrowning, whipping, and hanging a mock-king, as an addition to their pre-exilian Tammuz fast and feast? We have certainly no evidence that they did these cruel things before the exile. And there is no evidence, as we shall see, that they yearly committed the same atrocity after the exile.

V. THEORY OF A HUMAN VICTIM AT PURIM

As Mr. Frazer is to make our Lord one of the annual victims at Purim, he has to try to prove that the Jews did annually hang or crucifiy a mock-king supposed to be divine at Purim. To be sure neither prophet nor legislator, neither Ezekiel, Ezra, Nehemiah, Haggai, nor Zachariah, says one word about this heathen abomination borrowed by the Jews. Mr. Frazer therefore tries to prove that the man was hanged at Purim by the evidence of 'traces of human sacrifice lingering about

---

[1] *G. B.* iii. 177.   [2] *G. B.* ii. 254.   [3] *G. B.* iii. 177.

the feast of Purim in one or other of those mitigated forms to which I have just referred,' such as the uncertain ' burning an effigy of a man at Tarsus.' [1]

Mr. Frazer is, I think, rather easily satisfied with this kind of testimony to human sacrifice. Every fifth of November a man, called Guy by the populace, is burned in effigy. But, as we know the historical facts, we do not, though science in the distant future may, regard this rite as a trace of Druidical human sacrifice, Guy being a god of the dying foliage of November, when St. Dasius was slain. Mr. Frazer explains the old custom of burning Judas on Easter Saturday as ' all for the purpose of protecting the fields from hail,' and as ' really of pagan origin.' [2] It may be so : the ashes are used in agricultural magic. But we know that Guy Fawkes is not a relic of human sacrifice. Moreover, it is natural to destroy a foe, like Haman, or John Knox, or Mr. Kruger, in effigy : the thing is often done. The Jews undeniably regarded Haman, on the authority of Esther, as an enemy of their race. So they destroyed him in effigy. In the fifth century of our era, when the hatred between Jews and Christians had become bitter, the Jews, ' in contempt of the Christian religion,' attached the effigy of Haman to a cross. This insult was forbidden by the Codex Theodosianus.[3] Similar doings, without the cross, prevailed at Purim in the Middle Ages. But how does this prove the hanging of a real Haman victim before the rise of Christianity ? It merely proves that, after the strife between Jews and Christians began, an effigy of Haman, the national enemy, was crucified 'in contemptu Christianæ fidei,' as the edict says—to annoy the Christians.

But Mr. Frazer has ' some positive grounds ' for thinking that ' in former times the Jews, like the Baby-

[1] *G. B.* iii. 171, 172.   [2] *G. B.* iii. 246, 247, 258.   [3] *G. B.* iii. 172.

lonians from whom they appear to have derived their
Purim, may at one time have burned, hanged, or crucified
a real man in the character of Haman.' We have seen
that [1] Purim, if it is a Tammuz feast and fast, was kept
by the Jews before they went to Babylon. But, passing
that, what are the ' positive grounds ' ?

Merely that in 416 A.D. some Jews in Syria, being
heated with wine after ' certain sports,' began to deride
Christianity, and, for that purpose, bound a Christian
child to the cross. At first ' they only laughed and jeered
at him, but soon, their passions getting the better of them,
they ill-treated the child so that he died under their
hands.' Mr. Frazer ' can hardly doubt that ' the ' sports '
' were Purim, and that the boy who died on the cross
represented Haman.' Granting that the ' sports ' were
Purim, and that the Christian child did duty for Haman, the
purpose was ' to deride Christians and even Christ himself.' These motives did not exist before Christianity,
so how does the anecdote of brutal and cruel mockery,
ending in murder, afford ' positive grounds' for the
hypothesis that, ever since the exile, the Jews, in imitation of the Sacæan proceedings in July or September,
yearly hanged a mock-king in March ? [2]

VI. CONTRADICTORY CONJECTURE

Mr. Frazer is so far from holding by these arguments
for the practice of hanging a yearly victim at Purim, as
to suggest a conjecture that the victim was not killed at
Purim at all, but a month later ! [3] If he thinks this

---

[1] *G. B.* iii. 177 ; Ezekiel viii. 14.

[2] *G. B.* iii. 173, 174. The source cited for the murder of 416 A.D. is Socrates,
Hist. Eccles. vii. 16, with Theophanes, *Chronographia*, ed. Classen, vol. i.
p. 129.

[3] *G.B.* iii. 189.

possible, what becomes of his 'positive grounds' for holding that Purim was the date of the hanging? I have
shown the value of the positive grounds for maintaining
a theory that the Jews, before our era, annually hanged
a mock-king as Haman at Purim. Mr. Frazer himself
is so far from being convinced that the Jews hanged a
man at Purim[1] as to suggest the supposition that they
did not do so.[2] If they did not, it gets him out of the
difficulty caused by the unlucky circumstance that our
Lord was crucified, not at Purim, but a month after
Purim, as we read in the Gospels. But, alas! if the Jews
did not (on this theory) hang a Haman at Purim, what
becomes of all Mr. Frazer's proofs that they did hang a
Haman at Purim? In the total absence of all evidence
to that effect, we may be sure that the Jews did not
borrow (unrebuked by prophets and legislators) a heathen
brutality in March from a heathen brutality occurring, if
at all, in July or September. And if they did not, Christ
was not the Haman of a year, which it is Mr. Frazer's
contention that he may have been.

VII. A NEW THEORY OF THE VICTIM

We have seen that Purim is either an old Jewish
Tammuz feast, existing before the exile, or a post-exilian
adaptation of a Persian rite, in which a condemned
criminal died to save the king's life; or both.[3] The
victim next 'personates not merely a king but a god,
whether that god was the Elamite Humman, the Babylonian Marduk, or some other deity not yet identified.'[4]
But[5] the victim represented the king: no other god was
mentioned. Again Mr. Frazer says: 'At the Sacæan
festival, if I am right, a man who personated a god or

[1] *G. B.* iii. 172–174.   [2] *G. B.* iii. 189.   [3] *G. B.* iii. 152, 177.
[4] *G. B.* iii. 159, 160.   [5] *G. B.* iii. 152.

hero of the type of Tammuz or Adonis enjoyed the favours of a woman, probably a sacred harlot, who represented the great Semitic goddess Ishtar or Astarte. . . .'[1] But did the king also stand for 'a god or hero of the type of Tammuz or Adonis'? Did he associate with sacred harlots? And did he, and the victim also 'personate a god, whether that god was the Elamite Humman, the Babylonian Marduk, or some other deity not yet identified'?[2] Were the 'Elamite Humman and the Babylonian Marduk' (or Merodach) gods of vegetation? Marduk, or Merodach, to be sure, was the chief god of Babylon, a solar deity, says Dr. Jastrow. But as Mr. Frazer suggests that the supreme Aryan god, Zeus, may have derived his name, 'the Bright or Shining One,' from the oak tree (he being 'actually represented by an oak,' and oakwood producing *bright* sparks when used in fire-making),[3] why then another supreme god, Marduk, may also be a god of vegetable life. But, like the horses of Virbius, the Sacæan victim has been plausibly identified with Tammuz or Adonis.[4] 'It seems worth suggesting that the mock-king who was annually killed at the Babylonian festival of the Sacæa on the sixteenth day of the month Lous may have represented Tammuz himself.' He also takes that *rôle*, with his sacred harlot, in iii. 178. It is, therefore, a little bewildering to find him appearing as Humman or Marduk, or some other god unknown, in iii. 159, 160. How many single gods are rolled into one, scourged, and hanged in this most unhappy condemned criminal?

We have been told that Marduk presided over a council of the gods at the Zakmuk, which is the Sacæa.[5] But the hanged man[6] very probably personates Marduk.

[1] *G. B.* iii. 178.   [2] *G. B.* iii. 160.   [3] *G. B.* iii. 456, 457.
[4] *G. B.* ii. 253, 254.   [5] *G. B.* iii. 152.   [6] *G. B.* iii. 159, 160.

Mr. Frazer may think that, when the supreme god is presiding over the Olympian assemby in his Temple, it is a natural and pious compliment to whip and hang him in the person of his human representative. This, at least, is the result of his theory in iii. 159, 160. I do not feel sure that the supreme god, whether Marduk or Humman, would have taken the same favourable view of the tactless rite.

VIII. NEW GERMAN THEORY OF PURIM

I have hitherto but incidentally mentioned Marduk and Humman as competitors with Tammuz and the king for the glory of receiving a vicarious whipping and hanging. They are brought into this honourable position by an entirely new Teutonic theory of Purim : *not* Mr. Frazer's. It was lately an old Jewish Tammuz rite, or quite a new adaptation of the Sacæa. But ' it is possible,' says Professor Nöldeke, ' that we have here ' (in Purim) ' to do with a feast whereby the Babylonians commemorated a victory gained by their gods over the gods of their neighbours, the Elamites, against whom they had so often waged war. The Jewish feast of Purim is an annual merrymaking of a wholly secular kind, and it is known that there were similar feasts among the Babylonians.' From the Babylonians, then, the Jews borrowed Purim, a feast commemorative of a victory of the gods of Babylon over the Elamites. But, if that feast was religious, the Jews turned it into ' an annual merrymaking of a totally secular kind.' [1]

Mr. Frazer, if I do not misunderstand him, does not accept the hypothesis of Nöldeke. He says, however, ' We can hardly deny the plausibility of the theory that

---

[1] *G. B.* iii. 159 ; Nöldeke, *s.v.* ' Esther,' *Encyclopædia Biblica.*

Haman and Vashti on the one side, and Mordecai and Esther on the other, represent the antagonism between the gods of Elam and the gods of Babylon, and the final victory of the Babylonian deities in the very capital of their rivals.' But plausibility, we shall see, is remote from proof. And how can Mr. Frazer think this theory plausible if the Sacæa really is a King-Tammuz feast?

But, if Purim is now to be a rejoicing over a victory of the Babylonian gods (naturally endeared as these gods were to the Jews), why was the fast held before Purim? It was held, according to 'Jensen's solution' (which is 'the best'), 'for the supposed annual death of a hero of the type of Tammuz or Adonis, whose resurrection on the following day occasioned that outburst of joy and gladness which is characteristic of Purim.' [1] But, if 'the outburst of joy and gladness characteristic of Purim' is a jubilation over a victory of the Babylonian gods, on Nöldeke's theory, why is there a fast, 'the fast of Esther,' before Purim, which is a feast of the Tammuz type? To fast for the death of Tammuz is a comely thing, but why should Jews, of all people, fast before a feast commemorative of a victory of the Babylonian gods? And why should the Jews, of all people, scourge and hang, at the same time, the possible human representative of Marduk, the chief of the gods whose victory they for some reason are commemorating? [2]

IX. ANOTHER NEW THEORY.   HUMMAN AND THE VICTIM

To be sure we are given our choice: the victim may represent Marduk, the chief of the victorious gods; but he may also represent Humman, one of the defeated gods. In that case the vanquished hostile god's human

[1] *G. B.* iii. 177.   [2] *G. B.* iii. 159, 160.

VIII

MORDECAI, ESTHER, VASHTI, AND HAMAN

IT may be asked, How did Humman or Marduk come to appear as the god connected with the Sacæa, whereas Tammuz had previously taken that part? The answer is that Humman and Marduk came in when we were tentatively regarding Purim, not (1) as a Semitic Tammuz feast, nor yet (2) as a Persian punishment of a condemned criminal acting as king's proxy, but (3) as a festival for ' the final victory of the Babylonian deities' (Marduk and the rest) ' in the very capital of their rivals ' (Humman and his company).[1] This was a theory suggested by Professor Nöldeke. It has etymological bases.

The name Mordecai resembles Marduk, Esther is like Ishtar, Haman is like Humman, the Elamite god, and there is a divine name in the inscriptions, read as resembling ' Vashti,' and probably the name of an Elamite goddess. Thus the human characters in Esther are in peril of merging in Babylonian and Elamite gods. But, lest that should occur, we ought also to remember that Mordecai was the real name of a real historical Jew of the Captivity, one of the companions of Nehemiah in the return from exile to Jerusalem.[2] Again, Esther appears to me to be the crown-name of the Jewish wife of Xerxes, in the Book of Esther : ' Hadassah, that is Esther.' [3] In the Biblical story she conceals her Jewish descent. Hadassah, says Nöldeke, ' is no mere invention of the writer of

[1] *G. B.* iii. 159.   [2] Ezra ii. 2 ; Nehemiah vii. 7.   [3] Esther ii. 7.

'Esther.' [1] Hadassah is said to mean 'myrtle bough,' and girls are still called Myrtle. Esther appears to have been an assumed name, after a royal mixed marriage.

Now if a real historical Jew might be named Mordecai, which we know to be the case, a Jewess, whether in fact, or in this Book of Esther, which, says Dr. Jastrow, 'has of course some historical basis,' might be styled Esther.[2] Dr. Jastrow supposes from the proper names 'that there is a connection between Purim' (the Jewish feast accounted for in 'Esther') and *some* Babylonian festival, '*not* that of Zagmuku,' or Zakmuk. Nöldeke says that no Babylonian feast coinciding with Purim in date has been discovered.[3] Indeed this fact gives Mr. Frazer some reason for various conjectures, as the date of Purim is not that of Zakmuk. But, if Mordecai be, as it is, an historical name of a real Jew of the period, while Esther may be, and probably is, a name which a Jewess might bear, it is not ascertained that Vashti really is the name of an Elamite goddess. Yet Vashti is quite essential as a goddess to Mr. Frazer's argument. 'The derivation,' he says, 'of the names of Haman and Vashti is less certain, but some high authorities are disposed to accept the view of Jensen that Haman is identical with Humman or Homman, the national god of the Elamites, and that Vashti is in like manner an Elamite deity, probably a goddess whose name appears in inscriptions.'[4] Now suppose that we adopt Mr. Frazer's method about that unruly month Lous. 'The identification of the months of the Syro-Macedonian Calendar is a matter of some uncertainty; as to the month Lous in particular the evidence of ancient writers appears to be conflicting, and until we have ascertained beyond the reach of doubt when

[1] *Encyclop. Bibl. s.v.* 'Esther.'   [2] Jastrow, p. 686, note 2.
[3] *Encyclop. Bibl. s.v.* 'Esther.'   [4] *G. B.* iii. 158, 159.

Lous fell at Babylon in the time of Berosus, it would be premature to allow much weight to the seeming discrepancy in the dates of the two festivals.'

Following this method we might say ' the identificacation of Haman and Vashti with a probable Elamite god and goddess is a matter of some uncertainty ; as to Vashti in particular the opinion of modern writers seems to be conflicting, and until we have ascertained beyond the reach of doubt that Vashti was an Elamite goddess, and a goddess of what sort, it would be premature to allow much weight to the conjecture '—and then we might go on to allow none at all.   But this would be too hard a method of dealing with Mr. Frazer's hypothesis. We should merely be getting rid of his theory in the same way as his theory evades a definite historical obstacle.

It is clear, from the facts about the names Mordecai, Esther, Haman, and Vashti, that to explain these as necessarily connected with Purim, Zakmuk, and the Sacæa, as a feast of rejoicing for a Babylonian divine victory over Elamite gods, is a very perilous hypothesis, among many others as hazardous, or even more insecure. Mr. Frazer, however, is intent on connecting the characters of ' Esther ' with Babylonian and Elamite gods.   They are essential to his theory that, at the Sacæa and Purim, there were a pair of human representatives of gods : Haman, with a probable sacred harlot, Vashti, doing duty for the dying ; Mordecai with Esther, doing duty for the re-arisen god of vegetation.   To this point we return.

Now, as to this festival of a resurrection of such a god, we have seen that, in vol. ii. 122, 253, 254, it occurred in July, to Mr. Frazer's content.   But, when it had to occur in March in vol. iii., we were met by the difficulty of two, or rather three, feasts of this kind in the year.   Perhaps we get rid of this obstacle in iii. 177–179.   The

resurrection is here that not of Tammuz, but of a hero of
the same type, is fixed by Jensen at Zakmuk, and therefore by Mr. Frazer, though not by Jensen, at the Sacæa
in spring.

Jensen's theory is that the death and resurrection
' of a mythical being, who combined in himself the features
of a solar god and an ancient king of Erech, were celebrated
at the Babylonian Zakmuk or festival of the new year,
and that the transference of the drama from Erech, its
original seat, to Babylon, led naturally to the substitution
of Marduk, the great god of Babylon, for Gilgamesh or
Eabani in the part of the hero.' Jensen, fortunately for
his peace of mind, ' apparently does not identify the
Zakmuk with the Sacæa.' Jensen constructs his scheme
thus.

Gilgamesh was a hero of Erech, who repelled the amorous advances of the goddess Ishtar. Gilgamesh became
extremely unwell. His friend Eabani also aroused the fury
of Ishtar, and died. Gilgamesh procured his return from
the world of the dead to the upper world.[1] The feast celebrating this resurrection was removed from Erech to Babylon. Instead of a mortal hero, Gilgamesh or Eabani, a being
cold and chaste as Joseph Andrews, the Babylonians
now cast Marduk, their supreme god, for the part. The
feast was Zakmuk.[2]

Of course this is precisely as if we said that an old
feast of Adonis was turned into a new feast of Zeus,
whose coldness, as regards goddesses, was not proverbial,
like the frigidity of Adonis, Gilgamesh, Eabani, Mr.
Andrews, and other notable examples.

The theory seems to lack plausibility, but as Jensen

---

[1] Jastrow does not indicate that, in the ancient poem on Eabani, he *did*
' return to the upper world.' But see L. W. King, *Bab. and Ass. Rel. and
Myth.* p. 146.

[2] *G. B.* iii. 178.

'apparently does not identify Zakmuk with the Sacæa'
he escapes the curious theory of supposing that
Marduk (late Gilgamesh, or Eabani) is whipped and
hanged in the person of his human representative—an
unheard-of way of honouring the personator of the
supreme being.   However, if we accept Jensen's theory,
and also, like Mr. Frazer, identify Zakmuk with the
Sacæa, then, remembering that Eabani rose from the dead
(if he did), and that Marduk is now Eabani, and that the
Sacæan victim is or may be Marduk, and is also the
king, we get a reason for supposing that the victim, too,
was feigned to rise from the dead—in the person of
Mordecai (Marduk).   But why was the representative of
Marduk, who in Jensen's theory represented Eabani,
whipped and hanged ?   The victim, on this theory, if we
add it to Mr. Frazer's, seems to me to personate

1. The King of Babylon,
2. Marduk,
3. Eabani,
4. Or Gilgamesh,

and thus to combine a god or hero of vegetation (which
Eabani is bound to be) with a mortal king, and a supreme
god—and, oh, *why* is he whipped and hanged ?   Taking
the theory of iii. 177–179 it seems to run thus, in combination with all that has gone before : The king was
burned alive annually.   His royal substitute was next
burned alive annually.   His criminal substitute was
burned alive annually, till this was commuted for
whipping and hanging, with or without burning.   The
king (before the feast of Zakmuk was brought from
Erech to Babylon) had incarnated some god or other (I
presume of vegetation).   After the Eabani feast at Erech
became the Marduk feast at Babylon, the king, I think,
but I may be wrong, represented Eabani *plus* Marduk.   If

he did, so, too, does the victim at the Sacæa. But Eabani,
in a Babylonian poem, has a resurrection : though I cannot
find it in Jastrow's account of the poem. The victim then,
being a personation of Eabani, of Marduk, and of the king,
has a resurrection—after he has been hanged under the
name of Humman, a god of the Elamites. He owes *that*
name, Mr. Frazer thinks, to a popular misconception, for
he really is the king, *plus* Eabani, *plus* Marduk. Dying
as king, and as Marduk, under the *alias* of Humman
(Haman), he is feigned, according to the theory, to rise
under the name of Marduk (Mordecai). The Mordecai of
one year becomes the Haman of the next, is hanged, and
so on.

This is an hypothesis of some complexity. An effort is
needed to maintain the mental equilibrium as we
contemplate this hypothesis. However, by thus amalgamating the ideas of Jensen and of Mr. Frazer, one gets
in the mock royalty (from the king), the scourging and
hanging (from the mitigation of burning alive), the
divinity of vegetation (from Eabani, who lends that part
of his attributes to Marduk), and the resurrection from
Eabani, who, in the Babylonian poem, rose again : though
I own that in Dr. Jastrow's account of the poem I am
unable to discover this incident. The spirit of Eabani is
conjured up, indeed, in the poem, but ' there is a tone of
despair in the final speech of Eabani.' [1] This is hardly a
resurrection. However, I am but poorly seen in Babylon
and its poetry, and no doubt Eabani had his resurrection.
From that or a similar resurrection Mr. Frazer deduces
the probability that the Sacæan victim in his resurrection
was represented by Mordecai.[2] He, like Haman, had a
sacred bride, Esther. In the Book of Esther, to be sure, she

---

[1] Jastrow, p. 513.   [2] *G. B.* iii. 179.

is Mordecai's cousin and adopted daughter. Mr. Frazer knows better.

I. ESTHER LOVED BY MORDECAI

' A clear reminiscence ' of the time when Esther was the goddess bride of Mordecai (her cousin) appears in modern Jewish plays in which Mordecai is the lover (I hope merely platonic) of Esther.[1] And a very natural modern touch it is. The pair were cousins, and Esther was extremely pretty.   In exactly the same way two little girls of my acquaintance dramatised ' Bluebeard,' and made the *brother* (who rescues Mrs. Bluebeard in the tale) the *lover* of Mrs. Bluebeard. She had preferred to marry Bluebeard for his money, on which, in this most immoral drama, Mrs. Bluebeard and her lover, her husband's slayer, lived happily ever afterwards. This is modern ! The original tale does not run thus.

Again, Mr. Frazer says that the Rabbis maintain that Xerxes only wedded a shadow Esther, ' while the real Esther sat on the lap of Mordecai.' A most natural shift to save Esther's character in a case of mixed marriages. So Stesichorus and Euripides, long before, gave a shadow Helen into the arms of Paris. The real Helen, meanwhile, saved her character by leading a life of remarkable purity in Egypt. These late shifts and evasions have no real bearing on the question of the original relations between Esther and Mordecai.

II. THE PERSIAN BUFFOON

Mr. Frazer now harms his cause, perhaps, by proving that just as, in Esther, Mordecai had a royal ride, so, in Persia, a beardless, and if possible one-eyed buffoon rode

[1] *G. B.* iii. 180.

in mock royalty through the streets, collecting money or
goods, exactly like our Robin Hood before and even after
the Scottish Reformation.[1] It was *une quête* ; examples
are endless.   After his second round he fled, for the people
might beat him if they caught him, obviously in revenge,
I think, for his robberies. But Mr. Frazer, as usual,
supposes the right to beat the buffoon to ' point plainly
enough to the harder fate ' of the sacrificed mock-king.
No date is given for this Persian custom, but, if it existed
when the Jews were in Persia, did it coexist with sacrifice
of a mock-king ? If not, if it was a substitute for that
obsolete cruelty, why are the Jews supposed to have
borrowed the cruelty no longer practised ? This is a
question of dates, which may be implied, but are not
given, though I understand Mr. Frazer to mean that the
buffoon's ride is later than the origin of Purim.[2]

On the other hand, Lagarde, one of the most learned
of Orientalists, thinks that the ride of the beardless was
already customary at the time when the stories about
Esther and Purim were composed. The Persians, says
Lagarde, had the Feast of Farwardîgân, a feast of jollity,
the rich making presents to the poor, as at Purim. They
had also the Feast of the Massacre of the Magi
(Magophonia), and, thirdly, they had the popular diversion
of the Ride of the Beardless. Now the authors of the
Esther legend ' had these three colours on their palette,
and with these three painted, not a portrait of one feast,
but a kind of mixed caricature for the Jewish carnival.' [3]
The Magophonia lent the colours of the massacre,

---

[1] *G. B.* iii. 181–184. Laing's *Knox*, ii. 157–160.

[2] Hyde, *Hist. Rel. Pers.* (1760), p. 250, says that some call this ride an
innovation, but they are wrong, and the ride is very ancient, in his
opinion. *G. B.* iii. 183.

[3] Purim, *Ein Beitrag zur Geschichte der Religion*, p. 51. Von Paul de
Lagarde, Göttingen, 1887.

Farwardîgân lent the jollity and the presents, the ride
of the beardless lent the procession of Mordecai.

In that case, and if Lagarde is right, the Jews found
at Babylon, not a slaying of a mock-king, but the ride of
the beardless. So they did not borrow the slaying of a
mock-king, but introduced into the Esther legend an
incident of a ride suggested by the ride of Mordecai,
which Mr. Frazer calls ' a degenerate copy of the original,'
namely the reign and death of the mock-king.[1]

Whether Lagarde's view be correct or not, this part of
the evidence is far too sandy a foundation for a theory
about a matter of solemn importance. The Jews could
not borrow the hanging of a victim from the Sacæa, if in
their exile they only found the ride of the beardless one,
as in Lagarde's theory—not that he mentions the Sacæa.

Mr. Frazer, at all events, sees a connection between
Purim and the ride of the beardless. But the latter is
popular, not official, in spite of the fact that the king
takes most of the goods facetiously robbed. As popular,
the ride is more primitive, he thinks, and shows its
meaning better than the Sacæa does. So Mr. Frazer
says ' if there is any truth in the connection thus traced
between Purim and the " Ride of the Beardless One,"
we are now in a position to finally unmask the leading
personages in the Book of Esther,' and show how Marduk
and Humman got into the plot.

Purim is not only the Sacæa, sacrifice and all, but is
also connected with the ' Ride of the Beardless One,' in
which there was no sacrifice. How this, if true, enables
us ' to finally unmask ' the characters in *Esther*, is not at
first very clear. Apparently the buffoonery of the
beardless one, who complained of the heat while the
populace snowballed him in March, was a magical

[1] *G. B.* iii. 183.

ceremony, to make hot weather by pretending that the
weather, in fact, *was* hot.[1] Therefore, the hypothetical
rites of

$$\left.\begin{array}{l}\text{Haman}\\\text{Vashti}\end{array}\right\}$$
$$\left.\begin{array}{l}\text{Mordecai}\\\text{Esther}\end{array}\right\}$$

represent, in the first pair, the decaying ; in the second
pair, the reviving, energies of vegetation, past and present.
One pair mates and the male, at least, is slain ; the other
pair mates and survives, to encourage vegetable life.

By the hypothesis the first pair (Haman and Vashti)
originally lived as man and wife for a whole year, ' on the
conclusion of which the male partner ' (Haman) ' was put
to death.'   Of course, even if Haman was the mock-king
slain at the Sacæa (which we do not grant), his mock-
kingship was very brief.   However, it lasted for a year,
' originally, we may conjecture.'   The later fortunes of
Vashti are wrapped up in mystery.   But I cannot refrain
from quoting one of my author's most eloquent passages
on this obscure subject.   We do not hear that Vashti was
put to death, in fact we do not hear anything about her
at all from our one authority ; but ' the nature of
maternity suggests an obvious reason for sparing her a
little longer, till that mysterious law, which links together
woman's life with the changing aspects of the nightly sky,
had been fulfilled by the birth of an infant god, who
should in his turn, reared perhaps by her tender care,
grow up to live and die for the world.' [2]

As Vashti, except for her profession, was not an
habitual criminal, let us hope that she was spared to look
after the baby. Her issue, if any, and if male, was
apparently an hereditary criminal, for otherwise he would

[1] *G. B.* iii. 184.   [2] *G. B.* ii. 186.

not be hanged : the victims were always condemned criminals. The cruelty of thus deliberately breeding such a criminal class, for the mere purpose of hanging them, is shocking to the modern mind. We wish to know whether the Jewish Hamans were also born and bred up to the business. Mr. Frazer does not tell us that this was the case, or what became of Vashti's female issue.

The ride of Mordecai in royal raiment is connected with and explained (if I follow my author) by the ride of the Persian beardless buffoon. To be sure the buffoon rode naked on an ass ; Mordecai rode ' in royal apparel of blue and white, with a crown of gold.' But the buffoon is clearly later than the origin of Purim in Mr. Frazer's opinion, though not in that of Lagarde. ' So long as the temporary king was a real substitute for the reigning monarch, and had to die sooner or later in his stead, it was natural that he should be treated with a greater show of deference . . . .' [1]

But Mordecai, who rode royally, was the man who did *not* die : Haman died. Therefore Mr. Frazer has to guess that the Mordecai of one year died as the Haman of the next.

Ah me, there are so many guesses !

In any case, Mordecai is nothing but ' a slightly altered form of Marduk or Merodach,' as is now ' generally recognised by Biblical scholars.' Nevertheless, a real historical Jew called Mordecai occurs, as we saw, in Ezra and Nehemiah : so the name was a Jewish name, odd as it appears.[2] Now Mordecai, by the theory, has to be whipped and hanged finally ; and that seems an odd compliment to Merodach, or Marduk, who, as supreme Babylonian god, is presiding over the gods, while his human substitute is being slain infamously. But, remember, when whipped

---

[1] *G. B.* iii. 183.   [2] Nehemiah vii. 7; Ezra ii. 2.

and hanged, the Mordecai of 1900, so to speak, has
become the Haman of 1901.   And 'some high authorities
are disposed to accept the theory of Jensen that Haman
is identical with Humman or Homman, the national god
of the Elamites.'[1]

III. A HELPFUL THEORY OF MY OWN

If these high authorities are right, I at last see my way
clear ! Haman, or the victim of the Sacæa, is now neither
the representative of the King of Babylon, nor of Tammuz,
nor of both at once, nor of Marduk, nor of Eabani,
nor of Gilgamesh. He is now (if Nöldeke or Jensen is
right) the representative of a conquered and hostile god,
Humman of the Elamites. *Tout va bien !* The human
representative of a hostile and defeated god may well
have been whipped and hanged in derision.   I shall grant
that Humman was also the Elamite god of vegetation,
Tammuz or the like (what else could he be?), and so had
to fall as the leaves fall, and also had to spring up as the
flowers do ; and this both in June–July[2] and also in
March–April.[3]

If all this is the case, if the Sacæan victim is Haman,
and represents Humman, and if Humman is a defeated
Elamite god, and if Purim is adapted from a Babylonian
feast of rejoicing for ' victory gained by the Babylonian
gods over the gods of their neighbours the Elamites,' as
Nöldeke thinks possible,[4] then all is comparatively plain
sailing.   But this is only if we follow Jensen, which I do
not understand Mr. Frazer to do.   Indeed, Jensen is only
responsible for identifying Haman with Humman.
Jensen does not identify him with the Sacæan victim.
It is Mr. Frazer who does that.

[1] *G. B.* iii. 158, 159.   [2] *G. B.* ii. 123, 254.   [3] *G. B.* iii. 152.
[4] *G. B.* iii. 159.

The theory, if Haman is Humman, and is also the victim, has now put on an aspect which I can almost accept. If Haman stands for Humman, and if Humman is a vanquished god of the hostile Elamites, then we solve that hard problem, namely why the human representative of a king or friendly god was whipped and hanged, and mocked at the Sacæa. The victim, I shall show, *did* represent the rightful king, but also personated the vanquished deity of a race long inimical but now subdued. So his harsh treatment was, if vulgar, not unnatural.

But all this depends on following Jensen, which we are not to do. Mr. Frazer seems to hold that though according to ' the view of Jensen, which some high authorities are disposed to accept, Haman is identical with Humman or Homman, the national god of the Elamites,' [1] yet *originally* this was not really the case.

Let us suppose it to have been the case, and I can suggest an excellent solution. Fatigued by the task of producing sons who had to be sacrificed yearly as his sub- stitutes, the king of early Babylon at one time annually sacrificed as his proxy an Elamite captive, who, to deride Elamite religion, was also the human representative of the Elamite god, Humman, and therefore was called Humman, or Haman. Just so the Aztecs sacrificed captives as representatives of their own gods.[2] But, as relations between Elam and Babylon grew more peaceful, Elamite captives were scarce. The king of Babylon then substituted for an Elamite war-prisoner a condemned criminal, who still represented the Elamite Humman, or Haman, but also, as in the original hypothesis, represented the king of Babylon. We must next conjecture that Humman himself was a god of vegetation ; indeed, I can hardly suppose that any god whatever did not represent

[1] *G. B.* iii. 159.   [2] *G. B.* iii. 134–137.

the principle of vegetable life. So Humman must not only die but have a resurrection, as vegetable gods often do.

Now, thanks to my hypothesis, all is clear, and every difficulty is removed. We once more see that the kings of Babylon were sacrificed regularly every year. Let us say that they were burned, as victims usually were. Indeed, Movers thought that ' at the Sacæa also the man who played the god for five days was originally burnt at the end of them.' [1] Mr. Frazer himself suggests that, in the progress of philanthropy, the man who used to be burned was merely scourged and hanged or crucified by way of ' a later mitigation of his sufferings.' [2] Or perhaps he was hanged first, and burned afterwards, as in our good old-fashioned punishment for treason, whereby many Jesuits were cut down alive, and many Jacobites, their bowels being burned before their living eyes.[3] But to burn a man only half hanged and still capable of feeling pain would not mitigate his sufferings.

My own theory pleases me better. When tired of being sacrificed yearly, the Babylonian king provided a substitute in a son, or other member of the royal family, with what sad and ruinous results to the dynasty I have already shown. Let us suppose that the princely substitutes were also really sacrificed by burning. But here the merit of my theory comes in, and, I hope, shines forth. Wearied of sacrificing princes of his house, the king substitutes Elamite prisoners of war. There is no objection to whipping and hanging *them*, except the frivolous objection that they at once cease to be sacrifices, and we can overcome that difficulty by supposing that they were hanged first, and burned afterwards, or ' wirryit at ane

---

[1] *G. B.* iii. 171 ; Movers, *Die Phoenizier*, i. 496.

[2] *G. B.* iii. 171. [3] *G. B.* iii. 171.

stake' (like George Wishart in St. Andrews), and then burned. This makes it needless to regard whipping and hanging as a 'mitigation.'

The next step is, when Elamite wars cease, and Elamite captives are not procurable, to substitute a condemned criminal, who, he also, like the Elamite prisoners, is called Humman, and represents both the king of Babylon, and Humman, an Elamite god of vegetation, who, like Tammuz, has his resurrection. We thus get :

1. Babylonian king. Incarnates the god of vegetation. Is therefore sacrificed annually to keep the god provided with a succession of fresh and sturdy subjects to be incarnated in. The king is burned.

2. His sons or nephews are treated in the same way, for the same reasons, annually. The king escapes.

3. An Elamite war-prisoner becomes the king's substitute. He also represents the Elamite god of vegetation. In mockery of the Elamites and their god he is scourged and hanged. Observe the Aztec analogy, though to be sure the Aztec captive, representing an Aztec god, is merely sacrificed. But *he* represents a friendly god.

4. The substitute is next a condemned criminal. He also is whipped and hanged. Like the Elamite war-captive he represents the king of Babylon, and dies for him. He also dies as the Elamite god of vegetable life, and, as such, has a resurrection, in the shape of Mordecai, who represents the Babylonian supreme god, Marduk (not Tammuz or another), and is not hanged till next year, when he becomes Haman or Humman, represents the king of Babylon, represents the Elamite god of vegetation, and is whipped and hanged, after enjoying (as king) the caresses of the royal harem, and as Humman the embraces of a sacred harlot, Vashti, who personates Ishtar. After being hanged (and perhaps burned) he has a pseudo-

resurrection in the Marduk of that year, the Humman of the next. And so on, both at the Sacæa and at Purim.

This hypothesis appears to be in many ways an advance on any one of Mr. Frazer's hypotheses. It allows us to keep up the Jewish Haman as personating Humman; which seems necessary, for how otherwise is Haman to be explained? We are, moreover, enabled to understand how a victim who represented a vanquished Elamite god, also, and at the same time, represented a victorious Babylonian king. Humman being, by my hypothesis, an Elamite kind of Tammuz, all our anxieties about the appearance of Marduk and Humman, where Tammuz had previously done duty, disappear. Purim, which had been a Tammuz feast (if we accept Jensen's solution) and also a feast where a man died for the king, and then a feast of triumph for the victory of the Babylonian gods, and 'a wholly *secular* merrymaking,' though, if Purim is a Jewish Tammuz feast, it had been, according to Ezekiel (who perhaps knew best), a religious rite of a false religion, now becomes all these things at once, though some may doubt how Purim could be, simultaneously, both religious and secular. But I would not abandon my theory merely because it involves a contradiction in terms. Add to all this that we can now have a Tammuz death and resurrection in June–July, and another in March– April, and all is translucent. At the summer festival we burn a dummy; [1] at the vernal feast we hang a man. [2]

Admirably as my hypothesis colligates the facts, it is not the hypothesis of Mr. Frazer. Though he thinks that 'we can hardly deny the plausibility of' Nöldeke's theory that the Sacæa is a triumph for the victory of the Baby- lonian over the Elamite gods, and that Purim is an adaptation of the Sacæa, [3] Mr. Frazer does not accept

[1] *G. B.* ii. 123, 124.   [2] *G. B.* iii. 152.   [3] *G. B.* iii. 159.

that idea.   Nöldeke is plausible, but not sound ; and this is ruinous to my hypothesis of the Elamite war-prisoner, slain as Humman, merely in a stage of evolution between the sacrificed prince and the hanged criminal.   We have seen how admirably my humble suggestion worked out all round, but it must be abandoned if Nöldeke is wrong.

Mr. Frazer thinks that the Sacæa and Purim did *not* (as in Nöldeke's scheme) mean *originally* a triumph of Babylonian over Elamite gods.   No Elamite prisoner was hanged (as I had sagely conjectured) at any stage of the evolution of the Sacæa.   What occurred was this : At the Sacæa there were originally two divine pairs, let us say Vashti and Haman to represent the dying, Esther and Mordecai to represent the renascent, forces of vegetation.   There was nothing Elamite in the business originally.   But ' it would be natural enough that in time an unfavourable comparison should be drawn between the two pairs, and that people, forgetting their real mean- ing and religious identity, should see in their apparent opposition a victory of the gods of Babylon over the gods of their eternal foes the Elamites.   Hence, while the happy pair retained their Babylonian names of Marduk and Ishtar, the unhappy pair, who were originally nothing but Marduk and Ishtar in a different aspect, were re- named after the hated Elamite deities Humman and Vashti.' [1]

Thus the plausibility of Nöldeke's theory, that Purim was adapted from rejoicings for a victory of the Baby- lonian gods over those of Elam,[2] proves to be no more than merely plausible.   We are thus driven back to Jensen's solution : that the fast and the rejoicings of Purim are a festival of Tammuz, or of a god or hero of his type, and

---

[1] *G. B.* iii. 180, 181.   [2] *G. B.* iii. 159.

they cannot, then, have been borrowed in Babylon, for the Jews had the Tammuz ritual before the exile. And yet [1] Purim *was* probably borrowed at Babylon. It must, apparently, be meant that only the hanging of a mock-king was really borrowed. The victim may thus represent both the king of Babylon and also the god of vegetation whom we are to suppose to be incarnated in the king (?) [2] But why should the Jews borrow that, and why did the prophets and legislators hold their peace, and how do we know that the majesty of Babylon incarnated a god of vegetation ?

As I sometimes understand Mr. Frazer's whole theory, it is this.[3]   The victim of the Sacæa represents the king, who represents Marduk, Humman, Tammuz, or some other deity. He gets his royal robes from the king; his whipping and hanging from the commuted burning alive of the king; his divinity from the king *plus* the god; his resurrection from the king *plus* Tammuz or Eabani, granting that Eabani *had* a resurrection, which I cannot find in Dr. Jastrow's account. But to do a resurrection plausibly we need another man to take the part of the re-arisen victim, king, and god. Now the victim for the year is really, or is called, Marduk, in one shape; his representative in the resurrection is Marduk in another shape; each man being provided with a consort, representing Ishtar, though I have yet to learn that she was the wife, or mistress, either of Marduk or Eabani. But the populace, not understanding the two Marduks and two Ishtars, preferred to call the Marduk who died Humman, after an Elamite god, and his sacred lady of pleasure Vashti, after a possible, but dubious, Elamite

---

[1] *G. B.* iii. 155.   [2] *G. B.* iii. 185.

[3] I assume that Jensen's theory of Zakmuk is accepted, for it gets in a resurrection, through Eabani. This is essential, as we hear nothing elsewhere of a Tammuz resurrection in March at Babylon.

goddess. The Marduk who did not die was still called Marduk till next year, and his consort till next year was called Ishtar.

All this occurred at the Sacæa, which are Zakmuk (though Jensen does not appear to see it), and at Purim (which Jastrow and Nöldeke do not identify with Zakmuk), and in March, not, as chronology has it, in July. By pushing the proceedings forward only a month, from Purim to Passover, we can connect them with the Crucifixion, and account for ' the halo of divinity.' The theory seems too ramified.

It may very naturally be thought that I am introducing these complexities and these difficulties by dint of wilfully or unconsciously misrepresenting Mr. Frazer's argument. But the argument, I sincerely think, is really a very tangled one. It seems plain that originally the victim was only conceived of by Mr. Frazer as dying to save the life of the king, who otherwise would have been slain as a god, on Mr. Frazer's hypothesis of religious regicide, as he could not be trusted ' to remain in full bodily and mental vigour for more than a year.' [1] The king was ' slain in his character as a god,' who could not be trusted for more than a year. Nothing was said to indicate that the mock king incarnated any special known god; say Tammuz. That conjecture appeared later,[2] and the date of the sacrifice was in June–July. Nothing was said, even now, about the victim's sacred harlot. The victim was content with the royal harem. As late as iii. 152 ' the central feature of the Sacæa seems to have been the saving of the king's life,' by the slaying of the victim, and, to that main end of the rite, no sacred harlot was necessary. But the date had now been moved from midsummer to early spring, and into the neighbourhood of the feast of Purim. The

[1] *G. B.* ii. 24, 26. [2] *G. B.* ii. 253–254.

religious character of the Sacæa as a period of wailing and rejoicing in sympathy with a god (Tammuz) now seemed to be overlooked, for Mr. Frazer says that the Sacæa 'was a wild Bacchanalian revel . . .' and that Purim was the same : men and women disguising themselves, drinking, and behaving wantonly.[1]

But Purim was connected, through the Book of Esther, with Haman, Mordecai, Vashti, and Esther ; and now arose the idea of making Haman, the victim, have a double who represented him in his resurrection. The Elamite god Humman and the Babylonian god Mordecai crept in through the Book of Esther, and through the very perilous effort to identify the Sacæa with Zakmuk, and both with Purim. The Book of Esther also introduced two female characters, and parts had to be found for *them* in the Sacæa, though our only authority mentions, in connection with the Sacæa, no female characters whatever, except the ladies of the royal harem. By analogy and conjecture, as to Semiramis and her lovers, parts were next found for the female characters of the Book of Esther as sacred harlots, representing the goddess of love. The consequent amours are supposed to stimulate the crops, and, in this part of the theory, the conjecture that the victim really dies to save the life of the king does appear to be rather dropped out of sight, though this idea is the real starting-point of the whole speculation. There is a come and go between the victim as king, with the royal harem, and the victim as Tammuz, with the sacred harlot. Conjectures about the victim as the Elamite Humman, or as the Babylonian Marduk, or as Marduk representing Eabani, or representing Gilgamesh, flit like the weaver's shuttle through the strangely woven warp and woof of the argument. Throughout we ask in

[1] *G. B.* iii. 155, 156.

vain for any proof that the King of Babylon was ever, at any time, in any text, regarded or spoken of as an incarnation of Tammuz, or of Marduk, or of Humman, or of Gilgamesh, or of Eabani—which the speculation requires.

Meanwhile the known, or at least the alleged, facts are the mock royalty, whipping, and death of the man who yearly lorded it as king for five days in the Persian palace, at the Sacæa, a period of licence, when every house had its slave-king. The extraordinary complexities in a matter really very simple are caused by identifying the Sacæa with Purim and Zakmuk, in the teeth of chronology ; and by introducing into the Sacæa, without any historical evidence, the characters of a Hebrew historical romance about the origin of Purim. The tendency also to find gods of vegetation everywhere adds its bewildering enchantment, till the spirit of system discovers gods of vegetation in the criminals who, on very slender evidence, are said to have been yearly whipped and hanged. Nay, even the hypothetical male issue of the criminal, by a hypothetical harlot, becomes a hypothetical 'infant god,' is brought up as a criminal, and ends as a mock-king and a divine victim.

Mr. Frazer's whole argument, of course, clashes with the higher criticism of Wellhausen, who avers that the Jews could keep no feasts in the exile, and there learned ' the lesson of religious isolation.' On the other hand, the Jews, by Mr. Frazer's theory, did keep a feast, and a very abominable feast, and, far from learning the lesson of religious isolation, borrowed the most execrable heathen cruelties, accompanied by ritual debaucheries. So Wellhausen must greatly err in his opinions, which are much revered by the clergy of this island.

[1] Wellhausen, *History of Israel*, pp. 492-493.

IX

WHY WAS THE MOCK-KING OF THE SACÆA WHIPPED AND HANGED?

THOUGH I have tried to argue against Mr. Frazer's theory of the cause of the ' sacrifice' of the mock Sacæan king, I am not prepared to offer a dogmatic counter-theory. The Sacæan case is unique, is isolated; we are acquainted with no other similar examples, and thus a rite which has an isolated existence may have had a singular cause. The cause may be hidden behind the scenes of history. Though I have not a firm hypothesis as to that cause, I shall end this chapter by throwing out a conjecture, for what it may be worth.

Meanwhile it may be asked why I call the adventure of the Sacæan mock-king ' isolated and unique.' Have we not other examples of temporary kings, holding office for three or four days, in a period of festivity and unreason? Certainly we have such kings, but all of them 'scape whipping and hanging. And none of them was a slave or a criminal. These are not mere verbal, and probably not mere accidental, variations from the solitary Sacæan type. But we have the legend of St. Dasius? Yes, but, accepting the truth of that legend, it rather adds to than diminishes the difficulty of getting a clue to the origin of the Sacæan mock-king and his doom. Let us tabulate the facts :

A. SACÆA	B. SATURNALIA
1. A condemned criminal.	1. A freeman selected by lot.
2. King of a thirty days' revel.	2. King of a five days' revel.
3. Is stripped and scourged.	3. Is not stripped or scourged.
4. Is hanged.	4. Is sacrificed at the altar of Saturn ; or sacrifices himself.
5. Is guessed to represent (a) a Tammuz god, or (b) the king of Babylon ; or both.	5. Represents Saturn.
6. Has a pseudo-resurrection.	6. Has no known pseudo-resurrection.
7. Lies with (a) the royal concubines, (b) with a sacred harlot.	7. Does not lie with royal concubines or with a sacred harlot.
8. In a period of topsy-turvy licence to slaves and free.	8. In a period of topsy-turvy licence to slaves and free.
9. Which is supposed to commemorate a victory over the Sacæ.	9. Which is supposed to commemorate the Golden Age of Saturn.

Under A, number 5—the item that the Sacæan mock-king represents the king of Babylon, or Tammuz, or both —number 6, the mock-king's pseudo-resurrection, and number 7 (b), his amour with the sacred harlot, are all conjectures of Mr. Frazer's. The real points of resemblance between the Sacæan and the Mœsian victim are (1) their mockery of royalty, (2) their death, occurring in very different circumstances, (3) during a period of licence, including the pretence of lordship by slaves in each household at Babylon ; by free men at Rome.

The points of difference are numerous and essential, and the dates and durations of the Babylonian and Roman festivals vary widely.

Thus, I think, the Sacæan and Mœsian cases do not explain the meaning of what is a religious rite in Mœsia : a secular custom (as I believe) in Babylon. Again, the differences make it hard to conjecture, with MM. Cumont and Parmentier, that the Mœsian rite was introduced by Oriental soldiers of Rome, accustomed to the Babylonian

Sacæa.   But to suppose a native Roman survival or recrudescence is also difficult, because Greek and Roman poets, historians, antiquaries, and essayists, all writing on the Saturnalia, know of no such survival.   Again, if originally Italian mock-kings were sacrificed yearly in many places, did they die as proxies for real local Italian kings, who would otherwise have been sacrificed?   This, as we have seen, is impossible: men would never have accepted the crown on such conditions.   Or did they die, like the Mexican victims, as man-gods slain for a real god Saturn ?   But the Mexican victim was a captive : free men would hardly draw lots for death.

There is no trace in Roman folk-custom of any mock slaying of the actual Roman Saturnalian kings of the brawls in each household.   The Saturnalia were so remote in Lucian's day from cruelty, that Dickens might have written, as Christmas papers, Lucian's essays and letters on the subject.   Universal kindness—the Scrooges feasting the Trotty Vecks of the period—universal giving of presents, and family games of forfeits and of chance (played for nuts) were the features of the Saturnalia. Wine flowed like water; but as to amorous licence at the Saturnalia, we only hear the complaint of the rich that the poor guests make too free with the ladies of the house.

The connection of the Saturnalia with Saturn, recognised by the Romans as ' that old savage ' the Greek Cronos, may, or may not, have been original.   The Saturnalia were not ' saturnine.'   Was the theory of a golden age under Saturn not a reflection from the festive period, ' the best day in the year,' says Catullus, which had become associated with the name of Saturn ?

Our evidence for sacrifice or hanging of a mock-king is so meagre and shadowy (in one case the dubious

Dasius legend; in the other what Athenæus cites from
Berosus, coupled with what Dio puts into the mouth of
Diogenes, and with what Strabo tells about the Sacæa)
that the ground will not bear the weight of Mr. Frazer's
high-piled, eighteen-storied castle of hypotheses. I do
not, even so, absolutely impugn the truth of the two tales
of the deaths of mock-kings; the undesigned coincidence
of testimony I am willing to take for presumption of truth,
though of four ancient witnesses who speak of the Sacæa,
only one, Dio, alludes to the crowning, robing, stripping,
scourging, and hanging of the mock-king of the festival.[1]

I. PERIODS OF LICENCE

How are we to explain the obscure facts? Let us
begin with a feature common to the Mœsian event of
303 A.D. and to the Sacæa. Both occur in a period of
chartered licence, when slaves play the masters, and all is
topsy-turvy. Mr. Frazer has collected many examples
of festivals of licence, when laws lose their force.[2] The
Roman slaves at the Saturnalia were not even reproved
'for conduct which at any other season might have been
punished with stripes, imprisonment, or death.'[3]

Now pass the conjecture that in just one known place,
Babylon, the stripes and death for the conduct usually
punished with these penalties *were* inflicted, after the
period of licence, on just one person, and you get Dio's
case of the mock-king of the Babylonian Sacæa.

Meanwhile observe that there was a Zoganes, or
slave-lord, ruling in every Babylonian household, including that of the king. Each Zoganes was royally attired,

See Appendix B, 'Martyrdom of Dasius.'

[2] *G. B.* iii. 76, 78, 84, 85, 86, 138, 119, note 1; ii. 326; iii. 139; iii. 141,
143; iii. 145; iii. 147.

[3] *G. B.* iii. 139; Horace, *Sat.* ii. 7, 4; M crobius, i. 7, 26; Justin, xliii.
i. 4; Plutarch, *Sulla*, 18; Lucian, *Sat.* 5, 7.

and bore sway in the dwelling where, except in the five
days of licence, he served. But for all that was done in
these five days only one man was punished, and he was
the king's Zoganes. Athenæus does not mention this ;
Hesychius is silent; Strabo does not even speak of the
lordship of slaves. Our only evidence for the slaying of
the king's Zoganes is Dio Chrysostom, putting the
anecdote into a feigned discourse of Diogenes. The
slaying occurs only in one place, as the Persians had only
one king.

Meanwhile let us study in various regions the periods
of licence. It seems as if human nature needed an
annual 'burst.' Mr. Frazer suggests, as a magical
motive, that the farmers thought by swilling and guzzling
just before they proceeded to sow the fields that they
thereby imparted additional vigour to the seed.[1] In fact,
whether men fasted or feasted, were chaste or amorous,
in all cases they acted for the benefit of the crops. Be it
so, but why should non-agricultural savages have periods
of licence ? I venture to suggest that the agricultural
motive in religion and ritual is at present rather over-
worked. It is becoming as common an explanation of
custom and belief as the recognition of the sun and the
dawn everywhere used to be in mythology. To show
that a period of licence with express and purposeful
breach of the most sacred laws may exist without an
agricultural motive, I shall prove later that it occurs
among a non-agricultural set of savages, and, consequently, when found among agricultural peoples, may
descend from some non-agricultural motive. Mr. Frazer
himself elsewhere assigns a motive, not necessarily agricultural, for these chartered explosions of unlaw.

1. On the Gold Coast the period of licence precedes

[1] *G. B.* iii. 145.

the annual ceremony of 'banishing the devil.' The season of the year is not given.

2. The feast of licence of the Hos of North-East India is called by Dalton 'a saturnale.' It is held in January, 'when the granaries are full of grain, and the people, to use their own expression, are full of devilry.' With prayers for a good new year the devil is beaten out of the bounds.

3. At the similar Mundari festival 'the servants are feasted by their masters.' So far nothing is noted about swilling for the good of the crops; *that* is not 'an excuse for the glass.'

4. In the Hindoo Koosh a little licence exists at the end of harvest: devils are driven out, and then seed is sown.

5. In Tonquin from January 25 to February 25 was a season of dormant law: 'only treason and murder were taken account of, and the malefactors detained till the great seal should come into operation again.' Then offerings were made to evil spirits, for 'it is usual and customary among them to feast the condemned before their execution.' The devils were then expelled.[1]

6. In Cambodia, after the expulsion of devils (*diabolo-fugium*), gambling is universal.

7. In Nepaul, in October, feasting and drinking occur, and presents are made by masters to slaves. There may be, perhaps, expulsion of devils; for the army fire salutes.[2]

In these cases of licence Mr. Frazer thinks that men rejoice either before the expulsion of devils, because that ceremony will carry off their sins, or after the expulsion, when their minds are at ease.[3] Thus men enjoy these bursts either, by the first hypothesis, to improve the

[1] *G. B.* iii. 84.   [2] *G. B.* iii. 119, note 1.   [3] *G. B.* iii. 119.

prospects of agriculture; or, on the second theory, because a ceremony will cleanse the sins of the 'burst;' or because a ceremony has freed their minds from fear of devils. When the harvest is just in, then, in fact, men have plenty of food, and, as we saw, are 'full of devilry.' So they play it off. In at least four out of our seven cases fulness of bread and drink appears to me to account for the 'burst.'

This also explains (8) the Zulu licence at the rejoicing for the first fruits, 'a saturnalia, people are not supposed to be responsible for what they say or do.' [1]

9. The same facts mark the Pondo feast of first fruits.[2]

10. In Ashanti the harvest feast is in September. 'During its continuance the grossest licence prevails; theft, intrigue, and assault go unpunished, and both sexes abandon themselves to their passions.' [3] By an extraordinary coincidence, which Mr. Frazer does not quote, 'on the *fifth* day' of the Ashanti harvest festival 'a criminal is sacrificed,' says Sir A. B. Ellis, 'sent as a messenger to the deceased kings.' Is the criminal attired as a mock-king?

I would venture to suggest, as a conclusion, that people indulge in these lawless excesses not so much to improve the prospects of farming as because they are 'full of devilry,' and that often they are full of devilry because they have ended their labours and are full of meat and drink. *Sine Bacche et Cerere friget Venus.* They therefore permit themselves a regular debauch; ranks are reversed, slaves lord it over their masters, laws are in abeyance; in Tonquin reviving law only takes notice of treason and murder. In Rome, at the Saturnalia, and at Purim among the Jews, however, a kind of

---

[1] *G. B.* ii. 326.   [2] *G. B.* ii. 327.

[3] *G. B.* ii. 460; Ellis, *Tshi-speaking Peoples*, p. 229.

Dickensite Christianity prevailed at the period of licence; also in Persia, at the period called Purdaghân, which Hyde compares to the Sacæa and Purim: as does Lagarde, in writing on Purim.[1]

The reader will have observed that at not one of these many periods of licence, in widely severed regions and grades of civilisation, is a mock-king put to death. Indeed, nobody is put to death, except in Ashanti, and nobody is scourged. Thus, as I remarked before, the case of the mock-king at the Babylonian Sacæa is isolated, as far as our knowledge goes.

II. THE DIVINE SCAPEGOAT

In many cases, however, at expulsion of the devils, the part of devil is played by a man who is driven away, often he is beaten away. Now I have already said that, by Mr. Frazer's theory (as I understand it), the mock-king at the Sacæa was 'sacrificed' in a double *rôle*; namely both as the king's proxy (the king being a god) and also as Tammuz, not to speak of Marduk and Humman. To this, of course, I replied (1) that no case seemed to be given of killing a king yearly to benefit a god; (2) that I could find no case of a king being killed by proxy; (3) that when kings really were killed, it was not annually nor by the infamous death of a malefactor (hanging); (4) that there was no proof of a man being killed as Tammuz; (5) that Tammuz is nowhere said to have been hanged, or crucified, or scourged; (6) that in no case known to me is sacrifice performed by hanging, still less (if possible) by hanging after a whipping. These arguments convince me that Mr. Frazer's theory (if it *is* his theory) is unconvincing.

But I am not quite sure that Mr. Frazer really holds his Sacæan victim to have played two parts, at two

[1] Hyde, *Hist. Rel. Pers.* pp. 260–267.

distinct times of year. Now, however, in connection
with human scapegoats, our author does certainly make
a victim 'double a part.' First, it was usual to kill a
beast-god or man-god 'to save his divine life from being
weakened by the inroads of age.' Next, there were
human scapegoats, driven away with all evil on their
heads. But, suggests Mr. Frazer, ' if it occurred to people
to combine these two customs, the result would be the
employment of the dying god' (god-man, king, or his
proxy) 'as a scapegoat. He was killed, not originally to
take away sin, but to save the divine life from the degene-
racy of old age ; but, since he had to be killed at any rate,
people may have thought that they might as well seize
the opportunity to lay upon him the burden of their
sufferings and sin in order that he might bear it away
with him to the unknown world beyond the grave.' [1]

Even so, when a Dublin mob was about to throw a
man over from the gallery of the theatre, some economist
cried, ' Don't waste him : kill a fiddler with him ' !

As proof that people might reason in this thrifty way
we learn that, on March 15, a scapegoat man, called ' Old
Mars,' was beaten at Rome and expelled. Mars, of
course, was a god of vegetation, and here the man-god,
' Old Mars,' is both god and scapegoat. But he is not
sacrificed, nor even hanged.[2]

In Athens during plague, drought, or famine two
human scapegoats were done to death, and Mr. Frazer
infers, but doubtfully, were stoned to death. This
also occurred yearly at the Thargelia ; the stoning is a
conjecture. In Greek cities of Asia Minor, in times of
calamity, an ugly or deformed man was made to eat
dried figs, a barley loaf, and cheese. Then he was beaten
seven times in a special manner, with squills and myrtle

[1] *G. B.* iii. 120, 121.   [2] *G .B.* iii. 122, 123.

boughs, was burned, and the ashes were thrown into the sea. The beating at once expelled evil influences and was good for the crops. So in this ugly poor devil ' we must recognise a representative of the creating and fertilising god of vegetation.' I really must try to save him from this general doom ! These stupid cruelties, if they had the usual agricultural motive, worked *magically*, not *religiously*, worked by sympathetic magic, not by divine interference. This creature, though supposed to be a god of vegetation, was confessedly in appearance no Adonis ! [1]

In rejecting the idea that this hideous wretch did duty as a god, Adonis, so fair that he won and so cold that he rejected the love of the golden Aphrodite, I may justify myself by Mr. Frazer's example. I argue that the deformed victim was, if anything, used in *magic*, not in *religion*—not as embodying a god. In the same way Mr. Frazer himself says of the rites of the dying god of vegetation, all over Western Asia, that the ritual was ' fundamentally a religious, or rather a magical, ceremony.' [2] So was the beating and death of the ugly deformed man (as to whom no evidence hints that he did duty for a god) a merely magical ceremony.

Now let us see where we are. Mr. Frazer's point was to prove that a man, whom he regarded as a proxy of a god-king, was put to death, at a period of chartered licence, to save the divine life. But people also had human scapegoats. So they perhaps argued (this is my own suggestion) : ' As the proxy of the man-god (himself *ex officio* a man-god) has to be killed at any rate, and as a scapegoat has to be thumped, why not thump the man-god who has to die at any rate ? Let him double the part, nay, as we are economising, let him treble the part, let

[1] *G. B.* iii. 125-128.   [2] *G. B.* iii. p. 179

him be beaten as a scapegoat, be hanged as a proxy for the divine life of the king, and also be hanged as Tammuz.'

But to prove that all this was deliberately thought out, where have we a case of a scapegoat god-man who is put to death? We have none, unless we let Mr. Frazer persuade us that his ugly deformed person, 'a degraded and useless being,' '*must* be recognised as a representative of the creative and fertilising god of vegetation, whose reproductive powers are stimulated that these might be transmitted in full activity to his successor, the new god or new embodiment of the old god, who was *doubtless* supposed immediately to take the place of the one slain.' [1] I must decline to obey Mr. Frazer's 'must,' and to recognise an Adonis in the ugly deformed person. Next, I demur to the idea that 'doubtless' the dying deformed one handed over his powers to a new god. Thirdly, if all this is meant to show that the Sacæan criminal was not only (1) a proxy, saving the royal divine life, and enjoying the royal harem; and (2) was a representative of Tammuz, enjoying a sacred harlot; but (3) was, moreover, a human scapegoat, scourged as such, and to stimulate his reproductive powers, and to expel evil influences, then I really cannot accept the portentous hypothesis. No attested examples of human scapegoats at Babylon are offered, but that is a trifle.

If Mr. Frazer really means to add the duties of a scapegoat, and the consequent beating,[2] to the duties of proxy king and Tammuz man in his chapter on the Saturnalia, he does not say so. It does not appear, then, that he wishes to explain the scourging of the mock-king

---

[1] The italics are mine.

[2] When explaining the flogging of the Sacæan victim, Mr. Frazer does not say that the purpose was 'to stimulate his reproductive powers.' He speaks of a 'mitigation' of burning.

at the Sacæa by his theory of a human scapegoat, and
it does not appear that he ever explains the stripping of
the royal robes from the unlucky man. Yet if the man
really died as a mock-king, there must have been some
reason for stripping him of his royal raiment. We never
hear that the representative of King Saturnus was either
stripped or whipped before being sacrificed. Nor do I remark that, in Anahuac, the human victim who personated
a god was stripped of the god's robes and ornaments.
Why then was the Sacæan victim, and he alone (as far
as we know), reduced from his royalty by being stripped
before execution, and also brought down to the estate of
a slave by being scourged ?

III. MORE PERIODS OF LICENCE

I am going with more than diffidence to offer a guess
at the reasons, asking it to be remembered that I do so
merely because the case is isolated, and cannot at present
be illustrated by parallel ceremonies. But first, returning
to the periods of licence, I must show that they are not
peculiar to agricultural races, nor, therefore, necessarily
instituted to aid the farmer. This in itself is a great
comfort, for one wearies of being told that the crops are
so eternally the cause of custom and rite. Among the
Arunta of Central Australia, in many ways a backward
race and not agricultural, 'considerable licence is allowed
on certain occasions, when a large number of men and
women are gathered together to perform certain corroborees ' (or sacred dances). So say Messrs. Spencer and
Gillen.

The laws of marriage are then turned upside down.
A man is ordered to have relations with the woman who
is his ' Mura—that is, one to whom he may not, under

ordinary circumstances, even speak, or go near, much less have anything like marital relations with.' Every man is expected to send his wife to these dances, for the express purpose of violating, in this period of licence, the most sacred laws of the tribe.[1] These backward persons, the Arunta, have no native strong drink, and cannot get intoxicated, but what they can they do in the way of licence, like more civilised races, and necessarily not for agricultural reasons, as they have no agriculture. They break their most sacred law, just as the Jews, at Purim, deliberately broke the law of Moses.[2] Conceivably, then, even stripping, scourging, and hanging a mock-king at the Sæca may also have been done for some reason not agricultural.

What view did the Persians themselves take of their festival ? I do not think that Mr. Frazer insists enough on this point. The Persians regard the Sacæa as commemorative of a great massacre of the Sacæ near the Euxine. In both forms of the Persian legend, in Strabo, their ancestors fell on the Sacæ when that tribe was hopelessly intoxicated : ' drunk and frantic, drowsy and asleep, or dancing and maddened with wine.' The Sacæ were massacred, and the Sacæa, a feast of licence, was dedicated to the Persian goddess Anaitis ; obviously in memory of the intoxicated revels of the Sacæ,[3] or so tradition averred.

The Persians thus, by dint of a popular etymology (Sacæa from Sacæ), accounted to themselves for the origin

---

[1] Spencer and Gillen regard these authorised and enforced breaches of sacred laws as testifying to the existence in the past of a time when no such laws existed, when promiscuity was universal, or at least as pointing in the direction of wider marital relations ' than exist at present' (op. cit. 111). In the same way the Romans thought that the Saturnalia pointed back to a golden age when there was no law.

[2] G. B. iii. 156.

[3] Strabo, 511.

of a period of chartered licence, in which, says Strabo, 'both men and women, dressed in the Scythian habit, drink and sport wantonly by night and day.' As in many other cases, collected by Athenæus, the lawless revel had its kings of unreason : slaves acting as masters and kings. Just one of these kings, the Zoganes in the royal household, was afterwards stripped, scourged, and hanged. What could the reason be? We have seen that in Tonquin all crimes committed in the period of licence are overlooked, except treason and murder.[1] We have been told that in the Roman Saturnalia a slave might do, unreproved, what at any other time would be punished 'with stripes, imprisonment, or death.'[2] We have read that, at the Pondo period of licence, nobody was later made responsible for his actions, though at Tonquin murder and treason were excepted.[3] The same irresponsibility pervades the Zulu period of licence.[4]

To reinforce this fact, that the most sacred laws are purposefully broken at some periods of licence, I cite the Nanga orgies in old Fiji. 'The Nanga is frequently spoken of as the Mbaki, or harvest ; ' people being 'full of devilry and food ' at harvest, which, perhaps, they need not be in March-April. All distinctions of property were suspended at the Nanga. Men and women, in fantastic dresses, publicly 'practised unmentionable abominations.' Even the relationship of brother and sister ' seemed to be no bar to the general licence.' But after the Nanga, as before the Nanga, brothers and sisters might not even speak to each other. This precisely answers to the Australian incest with the Mura. Brothers and sisters at the Nanga were 'intentionally coupled.' The ceremonies included initiatory mysteries, like the Bora of the Australian blacks.

[1] *G. B.* iii. 84.
[2] *G. B.* iii. 139.
[3] *G. B.* ii. p. 327.
[4] *G. B.* ii. p. 326.

As at the Arunta corroborees, the great point was to break the most sacred laws: those of incest.[1] This peculiar 'burst' then is in Australia pre-agricultural, though, as in Fiji, it survives among an agricultural people.

IV. THE SACÆA AS A PERIOD OF LICENCE

Well, the Sacæa was such a period of licence. Each household was then ruled by a slave, the Zoganes, as Athenæus quotes Berosus. The royal household was not an exception. Now to rule the royal household, in the royal robes, and above all to take liberties with the royal harem (compare Fijian and Australian licence), is treason; one of the two crimes excepted from the Saturnalian amnesty in Tonquin. To overlook treason would be, for a Persian monarch, to set a dangerous precedent. Therefore the royal Zoganes, or slave-king of the five days' revel, unlike the Zoganes of private houses, would deserve death, technically speaking. At this point let me adopt Mr. Frazer's theory of a substitute. A criminal already condemned to death is employed instead of a harmless slave, as Zoganes of the royal household, and is then hanged.

In dozens of cases of summer gambols, in European folklore, 'the Whitsuntide representatives of the tree spirit' are put to a mock death.[2] These are in one or two instances called 'kings.' The regular May Kings and May Queens seem to escape: the Grass King merely 'hands his crown to the mayor.'[3] These mock slayings of folklore actors may (I think), like handing the crown to the mayor, merely mean that the actor's reign is over. This is not Mr. Frazer's opinion: the summer monarchs when killed

---

[1] Fison, *J. A. I.* xiv. p. 28.   [2] *G. B.* ii. 60–66.
[3] *G. B.* i. 218.

in sport are killed, he thinks, as their precursors were really slain, for the god of vegetation. O vegetation, what crimes are wrought in thy name !

In any case the royal Zoganes, or criminal substitute for the slave-king of the royal household in Babylon, deserved a hanging, to discourage the precedent of treason set by him in the period of licence. Only in the king's house was the reign of the Zoganes high treason.

Now, before hanging him, it was actually necessary to demonstrate by symbolic action that he was no real king, but a common slave or criminal. He was reduced to his true level by being stripped of his royal robes, and by being whipped, a specially servile punishment. He was then hanged.

But to treat a real slave thus merely because, as in every other household, he played the Zoganes or slave as master, would be a shame. The man's only fault was the accident, thrust on him by custom, of playing lord in the royal household of a jealous monarch. So a criminal already condemned took the part, and, as the slave would have been, he was finally reduced to his level by being stripped of his royal robes and scourged, before suffering death ; technically for treason, really for the crime on which he was originally condemned.

This mere guess at the origin of a unique custom has certain advantages. It explains (and I fail to see that Mr. Frazer explains) why the Sacæan mock-king (unlike the Saturn victim) was stripped of his royal robes and whipped. These sufferings proclaimed the man no king, but a slave. Again, his hanging was just what, as condemned on a capital charge, a low-born malefactor might expect. With the best will in the world, no Babylonian could follow Mr. Frazer and take a hanged felon for a god or a divine sacrifice. Why only one man was thus treated, though there was a Zoganes or slave-lord in every house, is explained by the fact that there was only one royal house, only one household in which the slave-lord's conduct was treason.

With paternal fondness I contemplate my own little guess. But, alas! we are not told that the other slave-lords at the Sacæa actually invaded the ladies of the house. So why should the slave-lord of the royal household be allowed to do so? How is my conjecture to weather this point of danger? Well, we are never told (as far as I am aware) that a subject in the East enfeoffed himself of private demesne by invading the harem of the man to whose estate he was a pretender. But in the case of royal demesne to invade the harem was the first step of a young pretender, like Absalom, ' for the purpose of making known and strengthening his claim to the throne,' says Movers.[1]

Remembering the tenacity of traditional usage, sanctioning deadly sexual crimes in some periods of licence, remembering that, in them, the ' primitive ' Arunta delibe-rately break, as did the Jews at Purim, and the Fijians, the most sacred and stringent of their taboos, shall we not allow Sacæan custom to encroach, for the purpose of making the royalty of the king's Zoganes indisputable, on the king's harem? For in that way was Oriental royalty proclaimed and asserted. Sir Alfred Lyall says : ' We believe that a few unfortunate concubines would have been of no account at all for the due performance of a popular Babylonian masquerade, which might just as well mimic earthly kingship as symbolise divine mysteries.'

And now we see a simple and conceivable reason why

---

[1] *G. B.* iii. 160, note 1, citing Movers, *Die Phœnizier*, i. 490, *seq.*; 2 Samuel xvi. 21 ; cf. xii. 8 ; Herodotus, iii. 68 ; Josephus, *Contra Apion.* i. 15.

the mock-king of the Sacæa invaded the king's harem, ruled all royally, was crowned, robed in the king's robes, and then, to restore his servile status and wipe away his royalty, was stripped of the royal robes, whipped as a slave was whipped, and hanged as a condemned criminal deserved to be.

My guess, unlike Mr. Frazer's hypothesis, colligates all the facts. It explains the stripping, which Mr. Frazer does not, I think, explain. It explains the scourging and hanging, which Mr. Frazer is obliged to account for as a mitigation of burning. It does not require us to believe (what is incredible) that of old the Persian kings were sacrificed annually. It accounts for the occurrence of the execution at a season of secular licence just as in Ashanti. It involves us in no double, and, to my thinking, contradictory theory, that the sufferer is both king's proxy and also a representative of Tammuz, or Marduk, or Humman, or Gilgamesh, or Eabani.

But my guess is only a guess, and is offered chiefly to prove that guessing is easy. We cannot be certain about any explanation of a custom so remote, so unparalleled, and reported on evidence so late and so dubious as that of Dio Chrysostom.

Some student may point out that, though I boast of my theory as colligating all the facts, I have left out the sacred harlot. But she was only the child of an hypothesis of Mr. Frazer's. A scientific hypothesis is not required to colligate more than the known facts in each case. And I am by no means certain that the facts given by our only authority, Dio, were facts of history.

X

CALVARY

It is, fortunately, not needful to dwell long on the disproval of Mr. Frazer's theory that his facts 'seem to shed fresh light on some of the causes which contributed to the remarkably rapid diffusion of Christianity in Asia Minor. . . . The new faith had elements in it which appealed powerfully to the Asiatic mind. . . . We have seen that the conception of the dying and risen god was no new one in these regions. . . . A man whom the fond imagination of his worshippers invested with the attributes of a god gave his life for the life of the world. . . . A chain of causes which, because we cannot follow them, might in the loose language of daily life be called an accident, determined that the part of the dying god in this annual play should be thrust on Jesus of Nazareth. . . .' His death as the Haman of the annual mystery play of the dying god 'impressed upon what had been hitherto mainly an ethical mission the character of a divine revelation culminating in the passion and death of the incarnate Son of a heavenly Father. In this form the story of the life and death of Jesus exerted an influence which it could never have had if the great teacher had died the death of a vulgar malefactor. It shed round the Cross on Calvary a halo of divinity,' &c.[1]

But all this halo could only be shed if the victim was

---

[1] *G. B.* iii. 195–197.

recognised by the world as dying in the character of a god, and as rising again in the person of Barabbas, the Mordecai of the year. We know on the best historical evidence that there was no such recognition. ' To the Greeks foolishness, and to the Jews a stumbling block,' was the Cross, as St. Paul assures us. Moreover, we know that ribaldry, not reverence, marked the multitude at the Crucifixion. By Mr. Frazer's theory Barabbas represented the re-arisen god, ' The Son of the Father.' Was Barabbas revered ? No ; ' some pretended to salute his mock majesty, and others belaboured the donkey on which he rode.' [1] Therefore, by Mr. Frazer's own explicit statement, the divine facts about Barabbas were not recognised. Yet he was the counterpart of the sacred Victim.

Mr. Frazer's theory demands, I think, the general recognition of the godhead of the yearly victim, who gave Christ's mission 'the influence which it could never have had if the great teacher had died the death of a vulgar malefactor.' [2]

Yet Mr. Frazer himself assures us that the idea of the divinity of the victim may have been forgotten ; that his ' sacrifice ' might seem ' the execution of a criminal.' I cite the passage : ' The divine character of the animal or man is forgotten, and he comes to be regarded merely as an ordinary victim. This is especially the case when it is a divine man who is killed. For when a nation becomes civilised, if it does not drop human sacrifices altogether, it at least selects as victims only such wretches as would be put to death at any rate. Thus, as in the Sacæan festival at Babylon, the killing of a god may come to be confounded with the execution of a criminal.' [3] Yet within eighty pages Mr. Frazer attributes the ' halo of

---

[1] *G. B.* ii . 192.   [2] *G. B.* iii. 197.   [3] *G. B.* iii. 120.

divinity ' to the happy accident which enabled the victim to die as a *recognised* representative of a dying god.[1]

Mr. Frazer puts forth his hypothesis ' with great diffidence.' [2] He thinks that he may ' have perhaps been led by the interest and importance of the subject somewhat deeper than the evidence warrants.' [3]

That is certain. We have shown that the evidence, in our opinion, warrants none of the hypotheses ; no, not one.

It is not proved that magic is older than religion.

It is disproved that general belief (as distinguished from local legend) in any age regards gods as mortal.

There is no evidence, or none is given, to show that a man has ever been sacrificed for the benefit of a god whom he incarnates.

There is no evidence that a real king was ever yearly sacrificed to benefit a god at Babylon, or in every city-state of early Italy, or anywhere. The idea is incredible.

The evidence for any sacrifice of mock-kings is, historically, of the weakest conceivable kind.

The deaths of the Sacæan mock-kings were infamous executions of criminals ; they were not sacrifices, if they ever occurred at all.

The date of the festival at which, if at all, they perished cannot be made to fit in with Purim or Easter.

There is no evidence that the Jews borrowed the custom of killing a yearly human victim, or practised the habit.

If they did, it was a month after Purim.[4]

If they did, by Mr. Frazer's own statement the killing

---

[1] The passage in which Mr. Frazer thus appears to demolish his own theory represents his opinion before his theory was evolved. It appeared in his first edition, but he retains it in his remodelled work.

[2] *G. B.* iii. 193.   [3] *G. B.* iii. 195.

[4] See the contradictory attempts to get out of this difficulty in iii. 189.

might be thought that of a vulgar malefactor,[1] and could not cast on all or on any one of the victims a halo of divinity.

Finally, our own history, in the case of the Earl of Atholl (who pretended to the crown at the murder of James I. of Scotland) and in the case of Sir William Wallace (who was accused of saying that he would be crowned in Westminster Hall), proves that pretenders to royalty have been mocked by being indued with symbols of royalty. Wallace was crowned at his trial with laurel; Atholl was tortured to death with a red-hot iron crown. The Victim of Calvary was accused of aiming at a kingdom, and, like Wallace and Atholl, was crowned—with thorns. The preliminary scourging is illustrated by the tyranny of Verres in Sicily.

May we not conclude that Mr. Frazer's ' light bridges ' of hypothesis have ' broken down ' ?[2]

' The importance and interest of the subject' have induced me to examine the hypotheses. But it was needless.

One point has been clear from the beginning. Even if the Sacæan victims were *originally* supposed to be gods, they could not bequeath a halo of divinity to Christ, unless, as late as the reign of Tiberius, their own godhead was still commonly recognised. Now it certainly was *not* recognised. When Mr. Frazer published the first edition of his ' Golden Bough,' he doubted that the Sacæan victim could, as civilisation advanced, be identified with a god. But, before publishing his second edition, Mr. Frazer evolved his theory of the origin or partial origin of the belief in the divinity of Christ, as inherited from the criminal slaves at the Sacæa. In his second edition, therefore, the godhead of the Sacæan victims is usually regarded as commonly recognised; though Mr. Frazer had doubted the possibility of this in his first, and preserves

---

[1] *G. B.* iii. 120.　　　　[2] *G. B.* i. xv, xvi.

the doubt in his second edition. It is needless to say more.

Mr. Frazer, in vol. iii. 120, had already shaken his own theory as given in vol. iii. 195–198.[1] I might have contented myself with comparing these two passages, but in the interest of the nascent science of religion it seemed desirable to point out what I am constrained to think the errors of method that now prevail. In the following essay criticism is applied to an hypothesis with which modern orthodoxy has no concern.

[1] See also Appendix C, pp. 303–304.

XI

THE GHASTLY PRIEST

THE spirit of system, of finding master keys for all the locks of old religion and mythology, has confessedly been apt to misguide students. ' Macrobius was the father,' says Mr. Frazer, ' of that large family of mythologists who resolve all or most gods into the sun. According to him Mercury was the sun, Mars was the sun, Janus was the sun, Saturn was the sun, so was Jupiter, also Nemesis, likewise Pan, and so on through a great part of the Pantheon. It was natural, therefore, that he should identify Osiris with the sun. . . .'[1]

Mythology has been of late emancipated from the universal dominion of the sun, but only to fall under that of gods of vegetation, whether of vegetable life at large, or of the corn spirit and the oak spirit in particular. What Mr. Frazer says about Macrobius, Macrobius would retort on Mr. Frazer, thus :

' According to him Mars was a god of vegetation, Saturn was a god of vegetation (of sowing), so was Zeus, also Hera, and so on through a great part of the Pantheon. It was natural, therefore, that he should identify Osiris with a god of vegetation—and Mr. Frazer does so.'

Far be it from me to say that Mr. Frazer is wrong, when his gods are gods of vegetation, or even that Macrobius is wrong, when his gods are gods of the sun.

[1] *G. B.* ii. 147.

It appears to me that when a god had obtained a firm hold of public favour, the public might accept him as a god of this, that, and the other aspect or phenomenon of nature.

Still, the new school of mythology does work the vegetable element in mythology hard ; nearly as hard as the solar element used to be worked. Aphrodite, as the female mate of Adonis, gets mixed up with plant life.[1] So does Attis with Cybele, so does Balder,[2] so does Death,[3] so does Dionysus[4] with undoubted propriety ; so does Eabani, so does Gilgamesh, so does Haman, so does Hera,[5] so does Iasion with Demeter,[6] so does Isis,[7] so does Jack-in-the-Green, so does Kupalo,[8] so do Linus and Lityerses,[9] so does Mamurius Veturius,[10] so does Merodach or Marduk (if he represents Eabani or Gilgamesh), so does Mars,[11] so does Osiris,[12] so, I think, does Semiramis,[13] so does Tammuz, so does Virbius,[14] so does Zeus, probably ;[15] so does a great multitude of cattle, cats, horses, bulls, goats, cocks, with plenty of other beasts.

The solar mythologists did not spare heroes like Achilles ; they, too, were the sun. But the vegetable school, the Covent Garden school of mythologists, mixes up real human beings with vegetation. Jesus Christ derives his divinity, or some of it, as we have seen, from a long array of criminals who were hanged partly as kings, partly as gods of vegetation. I do not feel absolutely assured that Judas Iscariot, at his annual burnings in effigy, escapes the universal doom any more than the ugly deformed person who was whipped and killed in old Attica. But an unexpected man to be a representative

---

[1] *G. B.* iii. 166.
[2] *G. B.* iii. 346.
[3] *G. B.* ii. 95.
[4] *G. B.* ii. 160.
[5] *G. B.* i. 227.
[6] *G. B.* ii. 217.
[7] *G. B.* ii. 145.
[8] *G. B.* ii. 129.
[9] *G. B.* ii. 253 ; ii. 250.
[10] *G. B.* ii. 123.
[11] *G. B.* iii. 122.
[12] *G. B.* iii. 127.
[13] *G. B.* iii. 163.
[14] *G. B.* iii. 456.
[15] *G. B.* iii. 456, 457.

of a god of vegetation is the priest of the grove of Diana near Aricia. He is known to all from the familar verse of Macaulay—

> These trees in whose dark shadow
> The ghastly priest doth reign,
> The priest who slew the slayer,
> And shall himself be slain.

Why, Mr. Frazer asks, in effect, had the priest of the grove of Diana, near Aricia, to slay his predecessor, subject, in turn, to death at the hands of a new competitor for the office? First, let us ask what we know about this ghastly priest. Let us begin with the evidence of Virgil, in the Sixth Book of the ' Æneid ' (line 136 and so onwards). Virgil says nothing about the ghastly priest, or, in this place, about Diana, or the grove near Aricia. Virgil, indeed, tells us much about a bough of a tree, a golden branch, but, as to the singular priest, nothing. But some four hundred years after Virgil's date (say 370 A.D.) a commentator on Virgil, Servius, tries to illustrate the passage cited from the ' Æneid.' He obviously knows nothing about Virgil's mystic golden bough, but he tells us that, in his own time, ' public opinion ' (*publica opinio*) placed the habitat of Virgil's bough in the grove haunted by the ghastly priest, near Aricia. It is, in fact, not known whether Virgil invented his bough, with its extraordinary attributes, or took it from his rich store of antiquarian learning. It may have been a folklore belief, like *Le Rameau d'Or* of Madame d'Aulnoy's fairy tale. Virgil's bough, as we shall see, has one folklore attribute in common with a mystic sword in the Arthurian cycle of romances, and in the Volsunga Saga. I think that Mr. Frazer has failed to comment on this point. If I might hazard a guess as to Virgil's branch, it is that, of old, suppliants approached gods or kings with boughs in their hands. He who would approach Proserpine carried, in Virgil, a bough of pure gold, which only the favoured and predestined suppliant could obtain, as shall be shown.

In the four centuries between Virgil and Servius the meaning and source of Virgil's branch of gold were forgotten. But people, and Servius himself, knew of another bough, near Aricia, and located (conjecturally ?) Virgil's branch of gold in that district. Servius, then, in his commentary on the 'Æneid,' after the manner of annotators in all ages, talks much about the boughs of a certain tree in a certain grove, concerning which Virgil makes no remark. Virgil, as we shall see, was writing about a golden branch of very peculiar character. Knowing, like the public opinion of his age, something about quite other branches, and nothing about Virgil's branch, Servius tells us that, in the grove of Diana at Aricia, there grew a tree from which it was unlawful (*non licebat*) to break a bough. If any fugitive slave, however, could break a branch from this tree, he might fight the priest, taking his office if successful. In the opinion of Servius the temple was founded by Orestes, to the barbaric Diana of the Chersonese, whence he had fled after a homicide. *That* Diana received human sacrifices of all strangers who landed on her coasts. The rite of human sacrifice was, in Italy, commuted, Servius thinks, for the duel between the priest and the fugitive slave, Orestes having himself been a fugitive. The process is, first a Greek wanderer on a barbarous coast is in danger of being offered, as all outlanders were offered, to the local goddess. This rite was a form of *xenelasia*, an anti-immigrant statute. Compare China, the Transvaal, the agitation against pauper immigrants. Having escaped being sacrificed, and having killed the king in an unfriendly land, Orestes flies to Italy and appeases the cruel Diana by erecting her fane at Aricia.

But, instead of sacrificing immigrants, he, or his successors, establish a duel between the priest and any other fugitive slave. Why? For the priest of the cruel Diana was not accustomed to be sacrificed, nor had he been a fugitive slave. Servius then, not observing this, goes off into an allegorising interpretation of *Virgil's* branch, as worthless as all such interpretations always are.

The story about Orestes appears to myself to be a late ' ætiological myth,' a story invented to explain the slaying of the slayer—which it does not do ; in short, it is an hypothesis. The priesthood is open not to men flying the blood feud like Orestes, but only to runaway slaves. The custom introduced by Orestes was the sacrifice of outlanders, not of priests. The story has a *doublette* in Pausanias.[1] According to Pausanias, Hippolytus was raised from the dead, and, in hatred of his father, and being a fugitive, he went and reigned at the Arician grove of the goddess.

For these reasons, apparently, Statius calls the Arician grove ' profugis regibus aptum,' a sanctuary of exiled princes, Orestes and Hippolytus.[2] From Suetonius we learn that the ghastly priest was styled *Rex Nemorensis*, King of the Wood, and that the envious Caligula, thinking the priest had held office long enough, set another athlete to kill him.[3] The title of 'king,' borne by a priest, suggests, of course, the sacrificial king at Rome. Also Mr. Frazer adduces African kings of fire and water, credited with miraculous powers over the elements. They kill nobody and nobody kills them. Then we have Jack-in-the-Green = May-Tree = the Spirit of Vegetation = the May *King* and the *Queen* of the May. ' These titles,' as Mannhardt observes, ' imply that the spirit incorporate in vegetation is a ruler, whose creative power extends far

---

[1] Pausanias, ii. xxvii. 4.   [2] *Sylvæ*, iii. i. 55.   [3] *Caligula*, 35.

and wide.' Possibly so. Now, the King of the Wood, the ghastly priest, lived in the grove of Diana, who (among other things) has the attributes of a tree-spirit. ' May not, then, the King of the Wood, in the Arician grove, have been, like the King of the May . . . an incarnation of the tree-spirit, or spirit of vegetation ? ' Given a female tree-spirit, we should rather expect a *Queen* of the Wood ; and we assuredly do not expect a priest of Diana to represent the supreme Aryan god, nay to incarnate him. But this Mr. Frazer thinks probable.[1] Again, ' since the King of the Wood could only be assailed by him who had plucked the golden bough, his life was safe from assault as long as the bough, or the tree on which it grew, remained uninjured.' [2]

Here we remark the nimbleness of Mr. Frazer's method. In vol. i. 4 he had said : ' Tradition averred that the fatal branch ' (in the grove near Aricia) ' was that golden bough which, at the Sibyl's bidding, Æneas plucked before he assayed the perilous journey to the world of the dead.' But I have tried to show that, according to Servius, this identification of two absolutely distinct boughs, neither similar nor similarly situated, was the conjecture of ' public opinion ' in an age divided from Virgil's date by four hundred years.

In the space between vol. i. 4 and i. 231 the averment of tradition, as Mr. Frazer calls it, the inference of the curious, as I suppose, to the effect that Virgil's golden branch and the Arician branch were identical, has become matter of fact for Mr. Frazer. ' Since the King of the Wood could only be assailed by him who had plucked the Golden Bough,' he says ; with what follows.[3]

But who has told us anything about the breaking, by a fugitive slave, near Aricia, of a *golden* bough ? Nobody,

---

[1] *G. B.* iii. 457.   [2] *G. B.* i. 231.   [3] *G. B.* i. 231.

as far as I am aware, has mentioned the circumstance.
After an interval of four hundred years, the golden bough
of Virgil is only brought by Servius into connection with
the wood at Aricia, because Servius, and the public opinion
of his age, knew about a branch there, and did not know
anything about Virgil's branch of gold.

That branch is a safe passport to Hades.   It is
sacred, not to a tree-spirit named Diana, but to Infernal
Juno, or Proserpine.   It cannot be broken by a fugitive
slave, or anybody else ; no, nor can it be cut with edge of
iron.   None but he whom the Fates call can break it.
It yields at a touch of the predestined man, and another
golden branch grows instantly in its place.

> *Ipse volens facilisque sequetur,*
> *Si te fata vocant.*
> *Primo avulso non deficit alter*
> *Aureus.*

Virgil's bough thus answers to the magical sword set
in a stone in the Arthurian legends, in a tree trunk in the
Volsunga Saga, as Mr. H. S. C. Everard reminds me.   All
the knights may tug vainly at the sword, but you can
draw it lightly, *si te fata vocant*, if you are the predestined
king, if you are Arthur or Sigmund.   When Æneas bears
this bough, Charon recognises the old familiar passport.
Other living men, in the strength of this talisman, have
already entered the land of the dead.

> *Ille admirans venerabile donum*
> *Fatalis virgæ, longo nunc tempore visum.*

I have collected all these extraordinary attributes of
Virgil's bough (in origin, a suppliant's bough, perhaps),
because, as far as I notice, Mr. Frazer lays no stress on
the many peculiarities which differentiate Virgil's bough
from any casual branch of the tree at Aricia, and connect
it with the mystic sword.   The ' general reader ' (who

seldom knows Latin) needs, I think, to be told precisely what Virgil's bough was.   Nothing can be more unlike a branch, any accessible branch, of the Arician tree, than is Virgil's golden bough.   It does not grow at Aricia.   It is golden.   It is not connected with a tree-spirit, but is dear to Proserpine.   (I easily see, of course, that Proserpine may be identified with a tree spirit.)[1]   Virgil's branch is not to be plucked by fugitive slaves.   It is not a challenge, but a talismanic passport to Hades, recognised by Charon, who has not seen a specimen for ever so long.   It is instantly succeeded, if plucked, by another branch of gold, which the Arician twig is not.   So I really do not understand how Mr. Frazer can identify Virgil's golden bough with an ordinary branch of a tree at Aricia, which anybody could break, though only runaway slaves, strongly built, had an interest in so doing.

Still less do I think that Virgil meant to identify his branch of gold with mistletoe.   He does the reverse : in a poetic simile he compares his bough to mistletoe.   A poet does not compare a thing to itself![2]   Mr. Frazer cites the Welsh for mistletoe—*pren puraur*, tree *d'or pur*. In places, also, mistletoe is used for divining rods, which may be employed by gold-hunters.   What wood is *not* thus used?[3]   Like other magical plants, mistletoe is

---

[1] Who, or what, can escape being a tree-spirit, if Zeus is one ?   Mr. Frazer thinks that the savage must regard all trees used in fire-making as sources of hidden fire.   ' May not this,' he asks, ' have been the origin of the name " the Bright or Shining One " (Zeus, Jove [Dyaus]), by which the ancient Greeks and Italians designated their supreme God ?   It is, at least, highly significant that, amongst both Greeks and Italians, the oak should have been the tree of the supreme God. . . . '—iii. 457.   Zeus, like Num, and countless others, was also a sky god.   The sky is bright and shining, an oak is the reverse.   We do not think that a savage would call an oak or a match-box ' bright,' even if they do hold seeds of fire.

[2] *G. B.* iii. 449 ; *Æn.* vi. 203, *et seq.*

[3] See Professor Barrett's two works on ' the so-called Divining Rod,' in *Proceedings of the Society for Psychical Research.*

gathered at the solstices, when fern-seed is fabled to flame. Must not the golden bough, like the golden fern-seed, be an emanation of the sun's fire ? The older solar mythologists would have had not a doubt of it.[1]

I must admit, then, that I cannot, at present, accept the identification of the branch of gold in Virgil with any branch you please on a certain tree at Aricia. Nor am I aware of any historical evidence that the grove there was an oak grove, or the tree an oak tree, or that the branch to be plucked was a mistletoe bough, or that any branch, for the purpose of the runaway slave, was not as good as another.

That Virgil's branch of gold was mistletoe, that the tree at Aricia was an oak, that the bough to be plucked by the person ambitious of being a ghastly priest was mistletoe, seems (if I follow Mr. Frazer accurately) to be rather needful to the success of the solution of his problem which he finally propounds. He takes, on his road, the Eddaic myth of Balder, which I do not regard as a very early myth ; but on that point there is great searching of hearts among Scandinavian specialists. ' No one now,' writes a Scandinavian scholar to me, ' puts any of the Edda poems earlier than 900 A.D., and most of them, if not all, are probably later than that. We do not even know whether they were composed by Christians or pagans, as the Icelanders never lost their interest in the old mythology. It has never been sufficiently noticed that these poems are not *religious* in any sense ; all that their poets cared for was the story. That it will ever be possible to say where the stories came from, I doubt very much : probably they represent the fusion of several quite different veins of legends, heathen and Christian. The Saga writers knew practically nothing about the old heathen

[1] *G. B.* iii. 454.

worship, and Balder may never have been worshipped at all, or, if he was, it is rather hopeless to conjecture in what capacity.'

Such are the opinions of Mr. W. A. Craigie, whose writings on the Celto-Scandinavian relations of the Northern mythological literature are familiar to students.   We return to Mr. Frazer's handling of the Balder story.

Balder, says the Edda, dreamed of death. A goddess made everything in nature swear not to hurt him, except a mistletoe plant, which she thought too young to understand the nature of an oath ! Loki learned this, plucked the plant, and, when the gods were hurling things at Balder, asked the blind Hödur to throw the mistletoe. It pierced and slew Balder, and his funeral was of a kind which may, or may not, have been used before the period of inhumation in 'howes' or barrows. Balder's dead body was burned on board his ship, 'the hugest of all ships.' [1] I had an impression that this was a not uncommon Viking form of incremation, but Mr. Craigie thinks that it had quite gone out before the historic period. In the legendary period he remembers but one case, in Ynglinga Saga.[2] King Haki, being mortally wounded, had his ship piled with the bodies and weapons of the slain ; a funeral pyre was erected on board and lit, and the body of Haki was borne forth to sea in the flaming vessel. 'The thing was famous long after.' The story may be borrowed from the Balder story or the Balder story from that of King Haki.

In any case Balder was not sacrificed, but cremated, and the 'huge ship,' of course, is a late Viking idea, an idea the reverse of primitive. Mr. Frazer, however, goes on, apparently assuming that in the original form of the myth Balder was sacrificed, to a theory about certain religious or ritual fires, which survive in folklore. These fires are lit

---

[1] *G. B.* iii. 236–237.   [2] c. 27.

by peasants at various seasons, but are best known at midsummer, while a pretence of burning a man is made, and this at a season when mistletoe is gathered as a magical healing herb, not as a weapon of death. He seems to think that Balder was the spirit of the oak, that human victims, representing the oak and Balder, were, of old, periodically sacrificed, and that people deemed that the oak could not be injured by axes before the mistletoe (in which, they thought, lay its life) was plucked off. Unluckily, I see no evidence that people ever did entertain this opinion—namely, that the oak was invulnerable till the mistletoe was plucked.[1]

Mr. Frazer says : ' The mistletoe was viewed as the seat of the life of the oak, and, so long as it was uninjured, nothing could kill or even wound the oak.' He shows how this idea *might* arise. ' The oak, so people might think, was invulnerable,' so long as the mistletoe remained intact.[2] But *did* the people think so ? Pliny says a great deal about the Druidical gathering of mistletoe, which, on oaks, ' is very rarely to be met with.' The Druids, I presume, never observed that oaks in general, in fact by an overwhelming majority, lived very well without having any seat of life (mistletoe) at all. Not noticing this obvious fact, they reckoned, it would appear, that an oak

[1] Mr. Frazer notices that Pliny derived ' Druid ' from Greek *drūs*, oak. ' He did not know that the Celtic word for oak was the same, *daur*, and that therefore Druid, in the sense of priest of the oak, was genuine Celtic, not borrowed from the Greek.' With other authorities Mr. Frazer cites J. Rhys's *Celtic Heathendom*, p. 221 *et seq.* Principal Rhys informs me that he is inclined to think that ' Druid ' is of the same origin as the Celtic word for oak. Mr. Stokes seems to think otherwise, and to interpret *dru* to be the equivalent to ' true,' and to make the word Druid mean ' soothsayer,' to which Principal Rhys sees phonetic objections. He himself sees the difficulty, in both theories, that they make the word ' Druid ' Aryan, whereas the whole Druidical business may be non-Aryan and ' aboriginal,' Pictish, or whatever we like to call it.

[2] *G. B.* iii. 350.

with mistletoe on it could not be cut till the mistletoe was removed. Perhaps they never tried. Pliny does not say that when the Druid had climbed the tree and removed the mistletoe, he next cut down the tree.[1] It does seem desirable to prove that people thought the life of an oak was in the mistletoe (which they might gather without hurting the oak), before we begin to build another theory on our theory that they did hold this opinion.[2]

This new theory Mr. Frazer goes forth to erect on the basis of the first theory. The theory, in brief, comes to this : that as Balder was the spirit of the oak, and was sacrificed (of which I see no proof), so human beings, representing Balder and the oak, were sacrificed, to reinvigorate vegetation. The mistletoe which slew Balder was the soul-box of both Balder and of the oak, and of the human victims who represented, yearly, the oak and Balder.

About all this much might be said. The killing of ' divine kings,' Balder and others,[3] seems to me, as I have already said, in the majority of cases, to be a mere rude form of superannuation. We do not kill a commander-in-chief, or an old professor ; we pension them off. But it is not so easy to pension off a king. I think that most of the cases cited mean superannuation, or dissatisfaction with the ruler, not a magical ceremony to improve vegetation. Regicide is, or was, common. Says Birrel (1560–1605) : ' There has beine in this Kingdome of Scotland, ane hundereth and five Kings, of quhilk there was slaine

---

[1] *G. B.* iii. 327.

[2] The story of mistletoe as the ' life-token ' of the Hays of Errol (iii. 449) seems to rest on a scrap of recent verse, cut from a newspaper of unknown name and date. I suspect that it is from the pen (*circ.* 1822) of ' John Sobieski Stolberg Stuart,' *alias* John Hay Allan, author of other apocryphal rhymes on the Hays of Errol, and of their genealogy.

[3] *G. B.* iii. 1–59.

fifty-sex,' often succeeded by their slayers, like the ghastly priest. I am not convinced that the ghastly priest represented vegetation, and endured the duel ordeal as a commutation of yearly sacrifice, though there is a kind of parallel in the case of the king of Calicut. But that modern mummers are put to death, in a mock ceremony (as Mr. Frazer holds, to quicken vegetation), is proved by much folklore evidence.[1]

If we admit (which I think far from inevitable) that the ghastly priest was once a kind of May King, periodically slain, and was analogous to Balder, and represented the life of an oak, we are next invited to suppose that the tree at Aricia was also an oak, that the only branch on it to be plucked by the would-be successor was mistletoe, and that the mistletoe was the soul-box of the tree and of the ghastly priest, who could more easily be killed when his life-box (the mistletoe) was damaged.[2]

There is hardly a link in this chain of reasoning which to me seems strong. I do not see that Balder, in the Edda, was sacrificed. I do not see that the mistletoe was his soul-box. I conceive that the use of so feeble a weapon to kill him is analogous to the slaying of an invulnerable hero, in North American myth, by the weapon of a bulrush : an example of the popular liking for weakness that overcomes strength. I find no evidence that the mistletoe was ever thought to be the soul-box of the oak ; none to prove that the tree at Aricia was an oak ; nothing to show that the branch to be plucked was the branch of gold in Virgil, and nothing to indicate that Virgil's branch was the mistletoe. To reach Mr. Frazer's solution—that the ghastly priest was an incarnate spirit of vegetation, slain, after the plucking of mistletoe, in order that he might be succeeded by a stronger soul, more apt to increase

[1] *G. B.* ii. 59–67.   [2] *G. B.* iii. 450.

the life of vegetation—we have to cross at least six 'light bridges' of hypothesis, 'built to connect isolated facts.' [1] To me these hypotheses seem more like the apparently solid spots in a peat-bog, on which whoso alights is let into the morass. I feel like Mr. Frazer's 'cautious inquirer,' who is 'brought up sharp on the edge of some yawning chasm.' [2]

I ought to propose an hypothesis myself. In doing so I shall confine myself (the limitation is not unscientific) to the known facts of the problem. In the grove of Diana (a goddess of many various attributes) was a priest of whom we know nothing but that he was (1) a fugitive slave, (2) called King of the Grove, (3) might be slain and succeeded by any other fugitive slave, (4) who broke a bough of the tree which the priest's only known duty was to protect. These are all the ascertained facts.

Why had the priest to be a runaway slave? Mr. Frazer says : 'He had to be a runaway slave in memory of the flight of Orestes, the traditional founder of the worship. . . . .' [3] But the *Greek* story of Orestes, and its *doublette* as to Hippolytus, are only ætiological myths, fanciful 'reasons why,' attached to a *Latin* usage. Neither Orestes nor Hippolytus was a slave, like the ghastly priest. The story about Orestes, a fugitive, arises out of the custom of Aricia, and does not explain that custom. Mr. Frazer, I presume, admits this, but thinks that the ghastly priest might perhaps, at one time, save himself by being a runaway. But why a slave? If I might guess, I would venture to suggest that the grove near Aricia may have been an asylum for fugitives, as they say that Rome originally was. There are such sanctuaries in Central Australia.

Here, fortunately, Mr. Frazer himself supplies me with the very instances which my conjecture craves. He

[1] *G. B.* i. xv.   [2] *G. B.* i. xx.   [3] *G. B.* ii. 67.

cites Mr. Turner's 'Samoa' for trees which were sanctuaries for fugitives. These useful examples are given, not
in 'The Golden Bough,' but in an essay on 'The Origin
of Totemism.' [1]

' In Upolu, one of the Samoan islands, a certain god,
Vave, had his abode in an old tree, which served as an
asylum for murderers and other offenders who had incurred
the penalty of death.'

I gather from Mr. Turner's 'Nineteen Years in Polynesia ' (p. 285) that the death penalty was that of the
blood feud. In his ' Samoa,' Mr. Turner writes concerning
trees which were sanctuaries :

' If that tree was reached by the criminal, he was safe,
and the avenger of blood could pursue no farther, but wait
investigation and trial. It is said that the king of a
division of Upolu, called Atua, once lived at that spot.
After he died the house fell into decay, but the tree was
fixed on as representing the departed king, and out of
respect for his memory it was made the substitute of a
living and royal protector. It was called *o le asi pulu
tangata*, ' the asi tree, the refuge of men.' This reminds
me of what I once heard from a native of another island.
He said that at one time they had been ten years without
a king, and so anxious were they to have some protecting
substitute that they fixed upon a large O'a tree (*Bischoffia
Javanica*), and made it the representative of a king, and
an asylum for the thief or the homicide when pursued by
the injured in hot haste for vengeance.[2]

There seem to have been three sanctuary trees : one
inhabited by a god, Vave ; one respected in memory of a
king ; and one doing duty as a kind of figure-head, or
representative of a king.

If my guess that the tree in the Arician grove was once a

[1] *Fortnightly Review*, April 1899, p. 652.
[2] Turner, *Samoa*, p. 64, *seq.*

sanctuary, or asylum for fugitives, including fugitive slaves, is plausible, I cannot, of course, conjecture as to the reason of its protective sanctity. It may have been one of the three Samoan reasons (which none of us could have guessed correctly), or any other motive may have taken effect. A fugitive slave, of course, was not awaiting trial and chance of acquittal. By custom he would be restored to his master's tender mercies, or live on under the tree.

But an unlimited asylum of fugitive slaves was an inconvenient neighbour to Aricia. Hence (it is physically conceivable, but I lay no stress on it) the asylum was at last limited to one fugitive slave at a time. It was not like the forest in the Indian fable, populated by ' millions of hermits,' who cannot have been very solitary anchorites. Any fugitive slave who took sanctuary had to kill and dispossess the prior occupant. There was only sanctuary for one at a time. More would have been most inconvenient. In any case the one solitary duty of the ghastly priest (as far as we know) was to act as *garde champêtre* to one certain tree. Why this one tree, we do not and cannot know. I am averse to Sir Alfred Lyall's plan of suggesting singular solutions arising out of some possible historical accident in the veiled past, when the problem to be solved is a practice of wide diffusion. The causes, in such cases of wide diffusion, cannot be regarded as mere freaks or recurring accidents. But this affair of the tree and its inviolate branches is isolated, unless we regard the tree as a taboo or sanctuary tree, which it might be for many reasons, as in Samoa, perhaps because it was the residence of a tree-spirit. At all events, the priest's only known duty was to guard the tree.

Then, why had his would-be successor to break a bough before fighting ? Obviously as a challenge, and also as a warning. The priest in office was to ' have a fair show ; '

some ' law ' was to be given him.   When he found a branch
broken, any branch, he was in the position of the pirate
captain on whom ' the black spot ' was passed.[1]   He was in
the situation of the king of the Eyeos, to whom a present of
parrots' eggs meant that it was ' time for him to go.' [2]   If
the bough was mistletoe, and if the fugitive slave, like the
Druids in Pliny,[3] had to climb for it, then the ghastly
priest ' had him at an avail.'   It was any odds on the
priest, who could ' tree ' his man or cut him down as he
descended.   However, our authorities tell us about no
bough in particular, still less about mistletoe.   Let me add
that, if the bough was mistletoe, the sacred tree would need
to be changed every time (of which we hear nothing), for
it is not a case of

Uno avulso non deficit alter

with mistletoe.

The bough was broken, then, as a taunt, a challenge,
and a warning.   ' You can't keep your old tree, make
room for a better man ! '   That is the spirit of the business.   The fugitive, utilised as a priest of the grove, was
slain when the better man appeared, not that a new soul
might keep the vegetation lively, but merely because the
best man attainable was needed to guard the taboo tree.

The sacred and priestly character of a runaway fighting
slave does not, to me, seem pronounced.[4]   We know not
that he ever sacrificed.   Ladies who wished to be mothers
visited the shrine, indeed,[5] as this Diana was a goddess
like Lucina, presiding over birth.   I do not deny that
the priest might have worked miracles for them (like the
Indian forest sages who do the miracle for childless rajahs).
But his one known duty, guarding the tree, was inconsistent with much attention to this branch of his sacred

---

[1] See *Treasure Island*.   [2] *G. B.* ii. 13.
[3] *G. B.* iii. 327.   [4] Compare i. 232.   [5] *G. B.* i. 5

calling. ' He prowled about with sword drawn, always on
the look out.' [1]   That is all !

We have not, in this theory, to invent a single fact, or
introduce a single belief where we do not know that it
existed.   Sanctuaries or asyla did exist, we have given
examples of sanctuary trees, and the tree was a sanctuary for just one runaway slave at a time :   he could
not run to burg, as in our old and more merciful law.
If he wanted the billet of ghastly priest he had to fight
for it :

> Lads, you'll need to fight
> Before you drive ta peasties.

Before fighting he had to get through the priest's guard
and break a branch of the tree which the priest protected,
the act being a warning as well as a challenge.   This
hypothesis introduces no unknown and unproved facts, and
colligates all the facts which are known.   The title of
' King of the Grove' may mean no more than the title of
' Cock of the North ; ' or it may be a priestly title, not,
even so, *necessarily* implying that the runaway slave
embodied the ruling spirit of the vegetable department.

I have been favoured with objections to my guess.
First, if I am right, where is the sanction for the custom
at which I conjecture ?   Well, where is the sanction of
the Samoan customs ?   They reposed (1) on the residence
of a god in a tree, (2) on respect for a king who had lived
near a tree, (3) on a legal fiction.   The sanctuaries of the
Arunta *Ertnatulunga* derive their sanction from hoards of
churinga, sacred objects of which, till recently, we knew
nothing.[2]   Obviously I cannot say which of many conceivable and inconceivable primeval reasons gave a sanction
to the tree-asylum of Aricia.   Once instituted, custom did

---

[6] Strabo, v. 3, 12.   [2] Spencer and Gillen, pp. 134–135.

the rest. The tree was a sanctuary for one fugitive slave, and, next, for another who could kill him.

Secondly, my guess is thought to disregard Mr. Frazer's many other analogies from folklore. Which analogies? Where else do we find a priestly fugitive slave, who held his sacred office by the *coir na glaive*, the Right of Sword? I am acquainted with no other example. As I have shown already, the kings who are killed (admitting the Arician fugitive to be a *rex*) are killed for a considerable variety of reasons, and are never shown to be killed that a sturdier vehicle may be provided for a vegetable deity; while the kings said to incarnate a deity are never said to be killed for religious reasons. If the reverse were the case, then the Arician fugitive, the ghastly priest, might take the benefit of the analogies. I hope that my bald prosaic theory, abjectly Philistine as it is, has the characteristics of a scientific hypothesis. But, like my guess as to the real reason for the death of the Sacæan victim, this attempt to explain the office of the ghastly priest is but a conjecture. The affair is so singular that it may have an isolated cause in some forgotten occurrence. I remember no other classical instance of a priest whose duty was to be always watching a single sacred tree, a thing requiring a vigilance of attention not compatible with much other priestly work: a post so unenviable that only a fugitive slave would be likely to care for the duties and perquisites. Naturally he would not know that he was ' an incarnation of the supreme Aryan god, whose life was in the mistletoe or golden bough.' And, as he did not know, he would not be ' proud of the title.'

XII

SOUTH AFRICAN RELIGION

THE provisional hypothesis by which I try to explain the early stages of religion may be stated in the words of a critic, Mr. Hartland. 'Apparently it is claimed that the belief in a supreme being came, in some way only to be guessed at, first in order of evolution, and was subsequently obscured and overlaid by belief in ghosts and in a pantheon of lesser divinities.'[1]   I was led to these conclusions, first, by observing the reports of belief in a relatively supreme being and maker among tribes who do not worship ancestral spirits (Australians and Andamanese), and, secondly, by remarking the otiose unworshipped supreme being, often credited with the charge of future rewards and punishments, among polytheistic and ancestor-worshipping people too numerous for detailed mention.   The supreme being among these races, in some instances a mere shadow of a children's tale, I conjectured to be a vague survival of such a thing as the Andamanese Puluga, or the Australian Baiame.

Granting the validity of the evidence, the hypothesis appears to colligate the facts.   There is a creative being (not a spirit, merely a being) before ghosts are worshipped. Where ghosts are worshipped, and the spiritual deities of polytheism have been developed, and are adored, there is

---

[1] *Folk Lore*, March 1901, p. 21.   Presidential address.

still the unworshipped maker, in various degrees of repose and neglect. That the belief in him 'came in some way, only to be guessed at,' is true enough. But if I am to have an hypothesis like my neighbours, I have suggested that early man, looking for an origin of things, easily adopted the idea of a maker, usually an unborn man, who was before death, and still exists. Round this being crystallised affection, fear, and sense of duty; he sanctions morality and early man's remarkable resistance to the cosmic tendency : his notion of unselfishness. That man should so early conceive a maker and father seems to me very probable ; to my critics it is a difficulty. But one of Dr. Callaway's native informants remarks: 'When we asked " By what was the sun made ? " they said " By Umvelinqangi." For we used to ask when we were little, thinking that the old men knew all things.' [1] What a savage child naturally asks about, his yet more savage ancestors may have pondered. No speculation seems more inevitable.

As soon as man was a reasoning being he must have wondered about origins; he has usually two answers : creation, complete or partial, and evolution. Like Topsy 'he 'specs things growed,' when he does not guess that things were made by somebody. As far as totemism is religious, it accepts the answer of evolution, men were evolved out of lower types, beasts and plants, their totems. But these are not always treated with *religious* reverence, as sometimes are such creative beings and fathers as Baiame. In many cases, as I have kept on saying, the savage creative being has a deputy, often a demiurge, who exercises authority. Where this is the case, and where ancestor-worship is the working religion, the deputy easily comes to be envisaged as the first man, unborn of human parents, maker of things, or of many things, and culture hero. Mr.

---

[1] Callaway, *Religion of the Amazulu*, p. 10 1868.

Tylor says : ' In the mythology of Kamchatka the relation between the Creator and the first man is one not of identity, but of parentage.' It is clear that, in proportion to the exclusive prevalence of ancestor-worship as a working religion, the idea of the Creator might be worn away, and the first man might be identified with him. It would not follow that the idea of creation was totally lost. The first man might be credited with the feat of creation. Mr. Tylor observes that 'by these consistent manes-worshippers, the Zulus, the first man, Unkulunkulu, is identified with the Creator.' [1]

Mr. Tylor's statement, of course, involves the opinion that the idea of creation is present to the Zulu mind. Un-kulunkulu made things, as Baiame, and Puluga, and other beings did. Like them he is no spirit, but a magnified non-natural man. Unlike them, he is subject to the competition of ancestral ghosts, the more recent the better, in receipt of prayer and sacrifice. Having no special house which claims him as ancestor, and being very remote, he is now believed by many Zulus to be dead. His name is a fable, like that of Atahocan, a thing to amuse or put off children with ; they are told to call on Unkulunkulu when their parents want to send them out of the way.

All this is exactly what my theory would lead me to anticipate, if the Zulus had once possessed the idea of an unworshipped creative being, and had lost it under the competition of worshipped, near akin, and serviceable ghosts. Their ancestral character would be reflected on him. It is just as if the Australian Kurnai were to take to ancestor-worship, glorify Tundun, the son and deputy of Mungan-ngaur ; neglect Mungan-ngaur, look on Tundun as the creator, and finally neglect *him* in favour

---

[1] *Primitive Culture*, ii. pp. 312, 313, 1873.

of ancestral spirits less remote, and more closely akin to themselves. This process is very readily conceivable, and, from our point of view, it would look like degeneration in religion, under stress of a new religious motive, the *do ut des* of sacrifice to ancestral ghosts. That Unkulunkulu should come to be thought dead is the less surprising, as a Zulu in bad luck will be so blasphemous as to declare that the ancestral spirits of his worship are themselves dead. ' When we sacrifice to them, and pray that a certain disease may cease, and it does not cease, then we begin to quarrel with them, and to deny their existence. And the man who has sacrificed exclaims : " There are no Amadhlozi ; although others say there are, but for my part I say that the Amadhlozi of our house died for ever." ' [1] . . .

Thus I can easily suppose that the Zulus once had an idea of a creative being ; that they reduced him, on the lines described, to a first man ; that they neglected him in favour of serviceable ghosts ; and that they now think him extinct ; like the ghosts themselves when they cease to be serviceable.

Mr. Hartland's theory is the reverse of mine. He says : ' In fact, so far as can be gathered, the very idea of creation was foreign to their minds.' . . . 'The earth was in existence first, before Unkulunkulu as yet existed.' [2] But heaven, and the sun, and all things were not in existence before Unkulunkulu : he made them, according to other native witnesses, and Dr. Callaway, in his first page, says that the Zulus regard Unkulunkulu as the Creator.

The evidence, as Mr. Hartland urges with truth, is ' contradictory.' But its contradictions contradict his statement that ' the very idea of creation was foreign to

[1] Callaway, p. 29. [2] Callaway, p. 41 ; *Folk Lore, ut supra,* p. 23.

their minds.' Many witnesses attest the existence in the Zulu mind of the idea of creation.

' It was said at first, before the arrival of missionaries, if we asked, "By what were the stones made?" "They were made by Umvelinqangi." ' ' The ancients used to say, before the arrival of the missionaries, that all things were made by Umvelinqangi; but they were not acquainted with his name.' ' The natives,' says Dr. Callaway, ' cannot tell you his *name*, except it be Umvelinqangi.' [1] ' The sun and moon we referred to Unkulunkulu, together with all the things in this world, and yonder heaven we referred to Unkulunkulu. . . . We said all was made by Unkulunkulu.' [2] ' At first we saw that they were made by Unkulunkulu, but . . . we worshipped those whom we had seen with our eyes ' (the ghosts of their fathers), ' so then we began to ask all things of the Amadhlozi.' This convenient Zulu, Umpengula Mbanda, states my very hypothesis.[3] But he seems to have been a Christian convert, and probably constructed his theory after he heard of the Christian God. ' We seek out the Amadhlozi that we may not be always thinking about Unkulunkulu.' So spiritualists are more interested in ghosts than in the Christian God. ' In process of time we have come to worship the Amadhlozi only, because we knew not what to say about Unkulunkulu,' just as the spiritualist ' knows what to say ' about his aunt, who speaks to him through the celebrated Mrs. Piper.[4]

Dr. Callaway consulted a very old Zulu, Ukoto, whose aunt was the mother of King Chaka (Utshaka). Mr. Rider Haggard dates Chaka about 1813–1828. With him began seventy years of Zulu conquest and revolution, in which old ideas might be obliterated. Ukoto answered Dr.

---

[1] Callaway, p. 10, note 25.   [2] *Ibid.* p. 21.
[3] *Ibid.* p. 17.   [4] *Ibid.* pp. 26, 27.

Callaway's inquiries thus : ' When we were children it was said the Lord is in heaven. . . . We heard it said that the Creator of the world (Umdabuko) is the Lord which is above. When I was growing up, it used to be said the Creator of the world is above.' [1]

So far we must either reject most respectable evidence, going back to the earliest years of last century, before the Zulu period of revolution, or dismiss Mr. Hartland's opinion that the very idea of creation is foreign to the Zulu mind. A very old woman, whose childhood was prior to Chaka's initiation of the revolutionary period of conquest (1813), being interrogated by the Zulu, Umpengula, said that ' when we asked of the origin of corn, the old people said " it came from the Creator who created all things. But we do not know him." The old people said ' the Creator of all things is in heaven.' [2] The old woman then abounded in contradictions. She said that Unkulunkulu was the Creator in heaven, but only the day before she had denied this. Dr. Callaway thought not that her mind was wandering, but that ' there appears in this account to be rather the intermixture of several faiths, which might have met and contended or amalgamated at the time to which she alludes '—the early days of Chaka—' 1. Primitive faith in a heavenly Lord or Creator. 2. The ancestor-worshipping faith, which confounds the Creator with the first man. 3. The Christian faith, again directing the attention of the natives to a God who is not anthropomorphic.' She might also, in a part of her tale, allude to the fabled ascension of the father of King Chaka prior to 1813.

From my point of view, Dr. Callaway's theory seems

---

[1] *Umdabuko* is derived from *ukadabuka*, to be broken off, a word implying the pre-existence of something from which the division took place. Callaway, i. note 3, 50, note 95. It is usually a vaguely metaphysical term.

[2] Callaway, pp. 52, 53.

possible. The memories and ideas of people who were 'ancient,' when Chaka and this old woman were young, before the Zulus entered on a 'wolf age, a war age,' went far back into the Zulu past, when their belief may have been nearer to that kind of savage deism which Waitz regards as unborrowed and indigenous to Africa.[1]   Another very old man, Ubebe, who had fought against Chaka, said : ' As to the source of being ' (*Umdabuko*), ' I know only that which is in heaven.   The ancient men said *Umdakuko* is above . . . for the Lord gives them life.'   *Umdabuko*, source of ife, may be ' local or personal, the place in which man was created, or the person who created him.' . . . Here the Umdabuko is called ' the lord which gives them life.'[2]   Here, too, the evidence is of Zulu antiquity, the words of the ancients of Chaka's time.   The use of the same name for a person and a place is familiar to us in ' Zeus ' and ' Hades,' and we use ' Heaven ' ourselves for God, as in ' the will of Heaven.'   The old man uses Umdabuko as a personal name ; elsewhere it is equivalent to Uthlanga, the impersonal metaphysical source of being, *not* identical with *Umhlanga*, ' a bed of reeds,' from which mankind arose in Zulu myth.   ' Um*h*langa is the place where they broke off, or out came, from U*h*langa.'[3]

Old Ubebe said to Umpengula : ' Do you not understand that we said Unkulunkulu made all things that we see or touch.'   And Unkulunkulu, he added, was a man, and now a dead man ; then he considered, and added : ' It is evident that all things were not made by a man who is dead ; they were made by one who now is.'   He began with the creator vouched for by the other old people ; he relapsed into the confusion of him with the first man, and either reverted to

[1] Waitz, *Anthropologie*, i. 167.   [2] *Ibid.* p. 59, and note 12.
[3] *Ibid.* 61, and note 17, 9, and note 22.

the original idea, or to a natural reflection of his own. Dr. Callaway found Ubebe declaring that tradition averred the maker to have been a man, but that the missionaries averred the Creator to be ' the heavenly Lord.' ' The old men said that Unkulunkulu was an ancestor and nothing more, an ancient man who begat men, and gave origin to all things.' [1] In fact the primal being of lower savages, Andamanese and Australians, *is* a man, without human limitations, and creative. My hypothesis, like Dr. Callaway's, is that Ubebe and the rest wandered between three faiths : a faith analogous to that of the Andamanese and Australians ; that faith modified by ancestor-worship carried to a great pitch—the creator being identified with the first man, and the doctrine of the missionaries. It is no wonder that these ancients are confused, but perhaps my hypothesis, which is Dr. Callaway's, so far, helps to explain their contradictions. ' They talk of Providence, but I reckon there is One above he,' said the British agriculturist, quite as confused as Ubebe.

Dr. Callaway interrogated another very old man, Ulangeni. He denied that Utikxo, his name for God, was a Hottentot word, introduced by missionaries, misled by what Dr. Callaway thinks their erroneous idea that the Hottentot Utikxo represented a lofty and refined theistic belief. Ulangeni utterly rejected with extreme contempt the idea that his tribe borrowed Utikxo from a people broken and contaminated by the Dutch.[2] ' We have learnt nothing of them.' In Ulangeni's opinion, Utikxo created Unkulunkulu, but, being invisible, was disregarded in favour of his visible deputy, as Mungan-ngaur might come to be disregarded in favour of Tundun. ' And so they said Unkulunkulu was God.' I am grateful to Ulangeni for again anticipating my humble theory. He gave

---

[1] Callaway, 63, and note 23.   [2] *Ibid*. p. 65.

a humorous account of the arrival of the first missionary, Unyegana (Gardiner ?), of his 'jabbering,' of his promise to give news of Utikxo, and of the controversies of Zulu theologians. A native convert won the day and composed a hymn : all this is recorded by Umpengula. With all respect for Ulangeni, he appears to have been in the wrong about Utikxo. Kolb (1729) gives Gounja Ticquoa (Utikxo) as the Hottentot word for a supreme deity ; but, if Dr. Callaway is right, Kolb was in error.

'Nothing is more easy than to inquire of heathen savages the nature of their creed, and during the conversation to impart to them great truths and ideas which they never heard before, and presently to have these come back to one as articles of their own original faith. . . .'[1]

But Kolb's Hottentots, as Dr. Callaway notes, say that Ticquoa 'is a good *man.*' They did not get that from Kolb, or any missionary : as I have said it is the regular preanimistic savage theory, as in Australia and the Andaman Isles. Later investigations down to Hahn tell us of Tsui Goab, 'wounded knee,' a Hottentot being who is only an idealised medicine-man. Shaw says that 'the *older* Kaffirs used to speak of Umdali, the Creator ; ' but Moffat found no trace of anything higher than Morimo, another mythical first ancestor, who came out of the earth. Livingstone asserts just the reverse. 'There is no necessity for beginning to tell even the most degraded of these people of the existence of God, or of a future state, the facts being universally admitted.'[2] As to the Bechuana Morimo, Mr. Hartland gives the etymology of his name : it is said to be derived from *gorimo*, above, with the singular prefix *mo*. It would thus mean 'Him who is above.' But why, then, did Morimo come out of

---

[1] Waitz, *Anthropologie*, pp. 105, 106.　　[2] *Missionary Travels*, p. 158.

a hole in the earth? Was he once 'He who is above,' and was he confused with the first man? The plural, *Barimo*, seems to mean the spirits of the dead. Molsino, *teste* Cassilis, is used for an ancestral ghost. Mr. Hartland is 'inclined to regard Morimo not as a once supreme deity fading away, but as a god in process of becoming.'[1] I feel that I have no grounds whereon to base even a conjecture.

A curious piece of evidence by Dr. Callaway is given in a note not in his book. One Zulu account is that Unkulunkulu was created by Utikxo. Now Unkulunkulu was visible, Utikxo was invisible, and so was more prominent and popular.[2] Thus regarded, Unkulunkulu is the demiurge and deputy of Utikxo, as sometimes are Daramulun, Tundun, Hobamok, Okee, Bobowissi, the deputies of Baiame, Mungan-ngaur, Kiehtan, Ahone, Nyankupon, and so on. The idea is usual in savage theologies. Now Dr. Callaway cites the evidence of another Zulu: 'We had this word before the missionaries came; we had God (Utikxo) long ago; for a man when dying would utter his last words, saying, "I am going home; I am going up on high." For there is a word in a song which says:

> Guide me, O Hawk!
> That I may go heavenward,
> To seek the one-hearted man,
> Away from double-hearted men,
> Who deal in blessing and cursing.

We see, then, that those people used to speak of a matter of the present time, which we clearly understand by the word which the missionaries teach us. . . . So we say there is no God' (no new God) 'who has just come to us.' Dr. Callaway explains: 'That God of whom the

---

[1] *Folk Lore*, March 1901, pp. 26, 27.
[2] Callaway, *Rel. of Amazulu*, p. 67.

missionaries speak is not a new God, but the same God of whom we spoke by the terms Ukqamata and Utikxo.' [1]

Dr. Callaway could not produce this testimony, or translate it, owing to the archaisms and allusions demanding familiarity with ancient Zulu songs, till he got the aid of a Kxosa Kaffir.

I am apt to regard the archaic character of the piece as fairly good proof of genuine antiquity. If the testimony is accepted, it settles the question in my sense. The Zulu religion, in its higher elements, was a waning religion. Utikxo was, 'with his one foot in the grave,' like John Knox; he was not, as by Mr. Hartland's theory, a god in the making. Old hymns are our best authorities, and the hymn proves a belief in a future far nobler than the transfiguration of Zulu souls into serpents. A deity is also attested by the witness. But from the use of the word Utikxo by this witness, he may be speaking of ideas borrowed by Hottentots from the Dutch, and by Kaffirs from Hottentots.

Another odd example occurs elsewhere. Mr. Frazer quotes the King of Sofala, or of Quiteva, or 'The Quiteva.' [2] This king ranks with the deity; in fact, 'the Caffres acknowledge no other gods than their monarch,' says Dos Santos. But Mr. Frazer omits the circumstance that the same author adds : 'They acknowledge a God who both in this world and the world to come they fancy measures retribution for the good and evil done in this. . . . Though convinced of the existence of a deity they neither adore nor pray to him.' [3] Here we have a belief in a future life and a god (Molunga) analogous to that revealed

---

[1] *Folk Lore Journal*, South Africa, ii. iv. 1880, p. 59, *et seq.*

[2] *Golden Bough*, i. 155 ; ii. 10. Dos Santos, in Pinkerton, xvi. 682–687, *et seq.*

[3] Dos Santos, in Pinkerton, xvi. 687. He confuses Quiteva, the country, and the king, the Quiteva. Cf. supra, p. 97 note 3.

in the archaic Zulu hymn.   But Dos Santos only recognised as god a god who receives prayer and adoration ;
hence he says that the Kaffirs have no gods, and also that
they ' acknowledge a god '—unworshipped.   The name
of that god, Molunga, is the same, I presume, as Mulungu,
who now, ' in the world beyond the grave, is represented as
assigning to spirits their proper places.' [1]

To myself, then, Zulu religion, now almost exclusively
ancestor-worship, does seem to contain a broken and
almost obliterated element of belief in a high unworshipped god, presiding over a future life.   Obviously
archaic hymns are better evidence, with their native
interpretation, than the contradictory statements of
individual Zulus, who speak dubiously of what the
fathers used to say.   The analogy between the Utikxo
and Mulungu belief also counts as corroboration, while the
unworshipped supreme being, with a deputy or deputies
(Utikxo—Unkulunkulu), is a pervading feature of savage
religion.   If philology could throw any certain light on
the meanings of names like Mulungu, and so forth, more
sure ground might be reached.   Again, when the name of
a relatively supreme being may be regarded as a plural,
like *Elohim*, the inference may be that many ancestral
spirits are being blended, or have been blended, into one
being.   The case of the Mura Mura of the Australian
Dieri has met us already, in the essay on ' Magic and
Religion.'   Is it a case of ' They ' or ' He ? '   ' Mulungu=
God,' a native told Mr. Clement Scott ; ' you can't put
the plural, as God is One.'   ' Spirits are spirits of people
who have died ' (*Mzima*), ' not gods.'   On the other hand,

[1] Macdonald, *Africana*, i. 66, 67. For etymological guesses, and the
application of *Mulungu* (as of *Barimo*) to ancestral spirits, and the statement that ' all things in the world were made by Mulungu,' who was prior
to death, see *Africana*, and Mr. Clement Scott's *Dictionary of the Mang'anja
Language in British Central Africa*, and *Making of Religion*, pp. 232–238.

Mr. Macdonald learned that 'people who have died become Mulungu.' Yet he is also regarded as a separate and supreme being, who assigns their places to the spirits of the dead. His very name is variously interpreted as 'sky' or 'ancestor.'

We may argue that Mulungu is primal, and that the spirits of the dead, *Mzima*, are only 'the people of Mulungu,' who was, in the myth, prior to death. Or we may argue that many Mzima have been combined in a later conception of Mulungu as a single being. Such beings do occur, it is certain, where spirits of the dead are held of no account in religion. I fear that, in the condition of the evidence, students will take sides in accordance with their bias : at least both parties will think that their opponents do so. I have observed that many writers appear only to be aware of the existence of the religious bias, which denotes lack of humour.

As to Utikxo, Mr. Beiderbecke, like Dr. Callaway, thinks that Kaffirs, living near Hottentots, borrowed their name for god, Tixo (Utikxo), and dropped Unkulunkulu. Among the Ovaherero, in a region 'which had not yet been under the influence of civilisation and Christianity' (1873), Mr. Beiderbecke found that a god called Karunga was believed in. 'Look at our oxen and sheep : is it not Karunga who has made us so rich,' as Jehovah made the Israelites ? Mukuru was used by believers in Kuringa as the name for the missionaries' God. Mukuru 'is in Otyihereró *the* name for god.' The derivation is unknown, but Omurunga, the sacred fan-palm tree, must be derived from Omuru, not Omuru from Omurunga. The Otyihereró word for spirit differs from both : it is *Otyimbosi*. As a god, Karunga seems to have no sacrifices : these are made to ancestral spirits. Karunga does not appear to be offended by sin, but this seems merely to be inferred from his receiving no atonement, as the spirits do. When people are dying they say 'Karunga has bid them come.' Traces of him as a creator are very dubious, but rain, thunder, and so on come from him, as proverbial sayings prove, and he is prayed to in time of danger—the prayers may be post-Christian. The Omuambo creation tale, or one of the tales, makes Kalunga, like Morimo, come out of the earth, and create men and women. He is no ghost. 'They also had ghosts,' the witness said, 'but Kalunga was quite a distinct and unique being.' [1]

My bias in favour of my own theory is unconcealed, but I conceive that South African belief in a god, 'a unique being,' indicates itself in Mr. Beiderbecke's evidence.

There are different words for this being and for ghosts and spirits; though in other cases philology finds cognate African words for both.

Dr. Callaway concludes : ' It appears that in the native mind there is scarcely any idea of deity, if any at all, wrapped up in their sayings about a heavenly chief. When it is applied to God it is simply the result of teaching. Among themselves he is not regarded as the Creator, nor as the preserver of men ; but as a power, it may be nothing more than an earthly chief, still celebrated by name—a relic of the king worship of the Egyptians ; another form of ancestor-worship'—only he is *not* worshipped ! [2] Dr. Callaway, a most impartial inquirer, has given several cases of very old Zulus, who in childhood heard from their elders about a creator, a creative lord. But this excellent collector had just a trifle of most justifiable bias. He was arguing to prove that Unkulunkulu, Uthlanga, Utikxo, and the rest were

---

[1] Beiderbecke, *F. L. Journal*, South Africa, iv. v. 88–97.
[2] Callaway, p. 124.

not safe equivalents to be used by missionaries for God. And they were not safe equivalents. Umpengula argued that point to perfection. Unkulunkulu, he said, was a name to deceive children with ; you must not come to us with a new great god, and call him by the name of a being whom every adult Zulu despises.[1]   But that the name was despised, say in 1860, by 'convinced manes-worshippers,' by no means proves the non-existence of a higher belief in the past.   Mr. Ridley deemed Baiame a fit name for the Christian God : probably it was imprudent to employ it in teaching natives.

Urged by his justifiable objection to the use of native names to indicate the Christian God, Dr. Callaway, in the conclusion just quoted, forgot, or had abandoned, his opinion that the evidence of old Zulus represented a blend-ing of beliefs, beginning with 'a primitive faith in a heavenly Lord or Creator.'[2]   I entirely go with his con-clusion that the natives at large, of his generation, did not regard ' the heavenly chief as the Creator or preserver of men,' and that ' they had scarcely any notion of deity at all.'   But, on the evidence collected from very old people by Dr. Callaway, I feel disposed to think it probable enough that, under stress of military life, conquest, and ancestor-worship, the Zulus may have forgotten and almost obliterated the higher belief which the old men had heard of in their infancy.   If so, the Zulus fall into the general line of my argument.   Their faint traditions (as in the case of Atahocan) have dwindled to children's tales.   They are not the ' theoplasm ' of a god who was in course of becoming.   But, of course, it may be argued that these faint rudiments came in, with Utikxo, through the Hottentots, who picked them up in conversa-tion with the Dutch.   This process, however, does not

---

[1] Callaway, pp. 74-76.   [2] Callaway, p. 55, note 4.

apply to the belief in superior beings, carefully concealed from the native women, the children, and the Europeans, by the Australians. Nor does it apply to the American Kiehtan, Ahone, Andouagni, Atahocan, and many others. Such are the hesitating conclusions which I venture to draw from what we are told about religion among the peoples of South Africa. In favour of my theory is the fact that the oldest evidence, that of persons born before the genius of Chaka revolutionised Zulu life, agrees with what I expect to find, a creative tradition.

The success of either of the competing theories—that which sees elements of a high religion among low savages, and that which denies the existence of these elements—does not appear to me to affect our ideas about ' the truth of religion.' Each theory regards religion as a thing evolved by mankind in accordance with their essential nature. The only question is as to the sequence of stages of evolution. Suppose that the beginning of religion was (as in my hypothesis) regard for a maker and father, who was credited with sanctioning morality, and, in some cases, with rewarding or punishing the good or bad in a future life. These ideas occur in modern religion. But the circumstance that they also occurred in primitive religion would not prove modern religion to be ' true.' It would only prove that the men who evolved primitive religion were really human : very like their descendants. Why not ? They did not produce the higher ideas pure : or at least, as we find them, they are always contaminated, often overlaid, by myths of every degree of absurdity and viciousness. But it is to be observed that the faith of primitive man, as far as it is represented by the evidence which I offer as to very backward man, had not some of the worst elements of the creeds of more advanced races. Sacrifices there were none. But when agriculture arose, it brought with it hecatombs of human sacrifices, especially if we agree with Mr. Frazer's theory stated in ' The Golden Bough.' So far it cannot be doubted that, as man advanced in social progress, he became more deeply stained with religious cruelty. In similar fashion the religion of peace and goodwill came to be accompanied, thanks to the nature of mankind, by religious cruelties as barbarous as those of the Aztecs. *Tantæ molis erat* : so hard has it been to elevate the race in any one direction without introducing new depressions in other directions.

XIII

'CUP AND RING:' AN OLD PROBLEM SOLVED

HISTORY and antiquity supply our curious minds with many pleasant profitless exercises. Even in these days of education there are still many persons who have heard of the Man in the Iron Mask, and would like to know who he was. Nobody, of course, reads the 'Letters of Junius,' but many would be glad to be certain as to who wrote them.

My riddle is infinitely more remote, but it has this merit : that I think I can unriddle it. If ever you roamed on that moor of the Cheviot Hills which is near Chatton Park (I think on Lord Tankerville's ground), you may have noticed, engraved on the boulders, central cup-like depressions, surrounded by incised concentric circles. Who hollowed out these devices, why, and in what age ?

I remember putting these questions when I first saw the 'scalps' of whinstone, just swelling out of the turf among the heather, on a beautiful day of September. It was a lonely spot, where victual never grew ; about us were the blue heights of the Cheviots, below us the *fabulosus amnis* of Till, that drowns three men to one drowned by Tweed. My friend told me that some said the stones were places of Druid human sacrifice, and others, men of common sense, held that the herd-boys carved the circles out of sheer idleness.

But these answers will not pass. There were no

herd-boys nor Druids in Central Australia, nor on the
Rio Negro in Brazil, among the Waimara Indians, nor
in Fiji, nor in Georgia of old, nor in Zululand, where
these decorative markings occur with others of primeval
character.   In our own country they are found, not only
on scalps of rock, but on the stones of ' Druid circles,' from
Inverness-shire to Lancashire, Cumberland, and the Isle of
Man.   They also occur on great stones arranged in avenues ;
on cromlechs (one huge horizontal stone supported on
others which are erect) ;   on the stones of chambered
tumuli (artificial mounds) in Yorkshire ; on stone ' kists '
or coffins, in Scotland, Ireland, and in Dorset ; on prehistoric obelisks, or solitary ' standing stones,' in Argyll ;
on walls in underground Picts' houses in the Orkneys and
Forfarshire ; in prehistoric Scottish forts ; near old camps ;
as well as on isolated rocks, scalps, and stones.   Analogous
double spirals occur at New Grange, in Ireland, at the
entrance of the great gallery leading to the domed
chamber ; in Scandinavia ; in Asia Minor ; in China and
Zululand ; in Australia, India, America, North and South,
and in Fiji.[1]

Now, who made these marks, when, and why ?   Sir
James Simpson says : ' They are archæological enigmas,
which we have no present power of solving.'   He cites
some guesses.   The markings are ' archaic maps or plans
of old circular camps and cities.'   They are sundials—but
they occur in dark chambers of sepulchres, or underground
houses !   They stand for sun, or moon, or for Lingam
worship.   They are Roman, or they are Phœnician—a
theory on which much learning has been wasted.

To all these guesses Sir James Simpson opposed the

---

[1] For India see *Archæological Notes on Ancient Sculpturings on Rocks in
Kumaon, India*, by Mr. J. H. Rivett-Carnac, Calcutta, 1883.   The form of
the Jew's harp is common to India and Scotland.

solution that the markings are merely decorative. 'From the very earliest historic periods in the architecture of Egypt, Assyria, Greece, &c., down to our own day, circles, single or double, and spirals have formed, under various modifications, perhaps the most common types of lapidary decoration.' It appears in Polynesian tattooing, this love of spirals and volutes. But, added Sir James, 'that they were emblems or symbols, connected in some way with the religious thoughts and doctrines of those that carved them, appears to me to be rendered probable, at least, by the position and circumstances in which we occasionally find them placed,' as on the lids of stone coffins and mortuary urns. Their date must be 'very remote.' They preceded writing and tradition. They are found in company with polished neolithic stone weapons, as in Brittany, without any remains of the metals, save in one case, of gold. The markings are certainly, in Australia, earlier than the use of metals. Sir James found by experiment that the markings could be made even on Aberdeen granite with a flint celt and a wooden mallet. He reckoned them earlier than the arrival of the Celtic race, and asked for evidence of their existence in Africa, America, or Polynesia. He did not know the Fijian example in Williams's work on the Fijians, nor the American and Australian examples.

Sir James did not live to hear much about these mysterious marks in remote and savage lands. But, in 1875, Professor Daniel Wilson discovered, or rather reported his discovery of, cups and rings on a granite boulder in Georgia. The designs are quite of the familiar orthodox sort, and rocks covered with deep cup-marks occur in Ohio.[1] Now there are romantic antiquaries, all for Druids and Phœnicians ; and there are sardonic

[1] *Proceedings S.A.S.*, June 1875. 'Ohio Rock Markings.'

antiquaries, who like to rub the gilt off the gingerbread. Dr. Wilson was of the latter class, and explained the cups as holes made by early men in grinding stone pestles. The concentric rings may have been drawn round the cups 'for amusement.' This is damping, but early man did not use stone kists and the inner walls of sepulchres as grindstones ; yet on these the marks occur. Nor would he climb an almost inaccessible rock to find his grindstone ; yet the summit of such a rock has the decorations, in the parish of Tannadyce (Forfarshire). We may, therefore, discard Dr. Wilson's theory as a general solution of the problem. Sir James Simpson left it with the answer that the marks are decorative, *plus* religious symbolism.[1]   His guess, as I think I can prove, or, at least, cause to seem probable, was correct. The cups and circles, with other marks, were originally decorative, with a symbolical and religious meaning in certain cases. How I have reached this conclusion I go on to show.

When you want to understand an old meaningless custom or belief, found in the middle of civilisation, you try to discover the belief or custom in some region where it possesses intelligible life. Then you may reckon that, where you now find it without meaning, it once meant what it now does where it is full of vitality, or meant something analogous.

The place where the concentric circles and other markings have a living and potent signification I discovered by pure accident. I had been reading the proofs of Messrs. Spencer and Gillen's valuable book on the ' Native Tribes of Central Australia ' (Macmillan). There I had noted plenty of facts about the native churinga, or ' sacred things,' flat oval pieces of wood or stone, covered with concentric circles, cups, and other decorations, which

---

[1] *Ancient Sculpturings of Cups, Circles, &c.* Edinburgh, 1871.

are read, or deciphered, as records of the myths and legendary history of the native race. These churinga are of various sizes, down to a foot or less in length. I did not think of them in connection with our cups, circles, and so forth on our boulders and standing stones. But a friend chanced to come into my study, who began to tell me about the singular old site, Dumbuck, discovered by Mr. W. A. Donnelly (July 1898), under high-tide mark in the Clyde estuary, near Dumbarton. 'The odd thing,' said my friend, 'is that they have found small portable stones, amulets marked in the same way as the cup and ring marked rocks,' and he began to sketch a diagram. 'Why, that's a churinga,' said I, 'a Central Australian churinga,' enlightened by Messrs. Spencer and Gillen. My friend, after being informed as to churinga, told me that other examples had been dug up, also by Mr. Donnelly, in an ancient fort near the other site, at a place called Dunbuie. Here, then, I had things very like churinga, and of the same markings as our boulders, kists, and so on, in two Scottish sites, where I understand neither pottery nor metal has yet been detected. Next, I found that the marks which the Australians engrave on their small churinga, they also *paint* on boulders, rock-walls, and other fixtures in the landscape, on sacred ground, tabooed to women.

The startling analogy between Australian and old Scottish markings *saute aux yeux*.

On the cover of Sir James Simpson's book, stamped in gold, is a central set of six concentric circles, surrounding a cup. From the inmost circle a groove goes to the circumference of the outer circle (the circles often occur without this radial groove), and there the line gives a wriggle, suggesting that the circle was evolved out of a spiral. Above and below this figure are a similar one with three and another with four concentric circles; at each side are two-circled and one-circled specimens with the wriggled line, and two cups and circles with no wriggle. Now compare fig. 131, p. 631, of Messrs Spencer and Gillen. Here we have the churinga ilkinia, or sacred rock-drawing, in red and white, of the honey ant totem in the Warramunga tribe. Here are, first, seven concentric circles, through the centre of which goes a straight line of the same breadth (only found among the Warramunga), while to each extremity are added two concentric circles of small dimensions, ending in a cross. Around, as on Sir James's cover, are smaller sets of less numerous concentric circles, exactly like Sir James's, except for the radial groove which ends in a wriggle. Again (fig. 124, p. 615), we have two sets of concentric circles with white dots answering to cups, and, where the third set of circles should be, is a volute, as at New Grange, in Ireland, and in many other examples in our islands.

Now, in Central Australia the decorative motives, or analogous motives, of the permanent rock-paintings are repeated on the small portable churinga, which are deciphered by the blacks in a religious, or rather in a mythical, sense. It is, therefore, arguable that the small portable Scottish cup and circle marked stones, only recently discovered, bore the same relation to the engravings on permanent stones, scalps, and boulders as do the Australian churinga to the Australian sacred rock-paintings. They may have been portable sacred things.

I have been unable to visit Dumbuck, now in course of excavation, and have only seen some casts and pen-and-ink sketches sent to me by Mr. Donnelly. But I have examined the similar objects from Dunbuie, in the museum at Edinburgh. The antiquaries looked dubiously on them, because they had seen no such matters before (they might have done so in Ireland), because a shell, with a very modern scratched face, was among the finds, and because a few of the markings on one or two stones look recent and fresh. But I argue that a Dumbarton humorist wishing to hoax us Monkbarnses would hardly 'salt' an old site with objects unknown to Scottish antiquaries, yet afterwards discovered in Central Australia. How could the idea occur to him? A forger would forge things known, such as flint weapons; he would not forge novelties, which, later, are found to tally with savage sacred things in actual use.

Many of the Dunbuie finds are engraved in Mr. Millar's paper on Dunbuie.[1] But he has not engraved the most unmistakable churinga, a small oval slab of stone, with an ornament of little cups following its outline (much as in an Irish instance), and provided, like stone churinga in Australia, with a hole for suspension.

He does engrave certain hitherto unheard-of articles—spear-heads of slate, two supplied with suspension holes. One (p. 294) has a pattern of the simplest, like a child's drawing of a larch, which recurs in Australia.[2] That these slate spear-heads, pierced for suspension, were used in war I doubt, though some Australians do use spearheads 'of a flinty slate;' and where flint is so scarce, as in Scotland, hard slate may be used—for example, in North America.[3] I rather regard the slate weapons as amulets, or churinga, analogous to the very old and rare boomerang-shaped churinga of the Arunta (lizard totem)

[1] *Proceedings S.A.S.* vol. xxx. 1896, pp. 291–316.

[2] Spencer and Gillen, p. 632, Nos. 14–23. 'Ilkinia and Plum Tree Totem.'

[3] The evidence for Australian slate spear-heads is not strong. Capt. King acquired a bundle of bark in a raid on natives. It contained 'several spear-heads, most ingeniously and curiously made of stone . . . the stone was covered with red pigment, and appeared to be *of a flinty slate.*'—See *The Picture of Australia*, p. 243. London, 1829.

of Central Australia. Mr. Millar observes: ' They have all been saturated with oil or fat, as water does not adhere to them, but runs off as from a greasy surface.' Now the Australian churinga are very frequently rubbed with red ochre, and made greasy with ' hand grease '—a singular coincidence. Footmarks are among the sacred Australian rock-paintings with a legendary sense. They also occur, engraved on rock in Brittany, Ireland, on ' The Fairy Stone' (ilkinia) in Glenesk, and on ' The Witches' Stone ' at Monzie, associated with cups and concentric circles.[1] These close analogies point all in one direction.

Meaningless in Europe, what meaning have these designs in Australia? Though certainty is impossible, I take it that they were first purely decorative, before the mythical and symbolical meaning was read into them by the savages. They occur on the mystic ' bull-roarers ' of Central Queensland, but I do not learn that in Queensland the circles and so on are interpreted or deciphered as among the Arunta.[2] Still, they occur here in a religious connection—the bull-roarer being swung at the mysteries—and they are carved on trees at mysteries held far south in New South Wales.[3] But even in Central Australia the markings sometimes occur as purely decorative, on one rock or other object, while on others they are sacred, and are interpreted as records of legends,[4] according to Spencer and Gillen. There are ' ordinary rock-paintings,' and ' certain other drawings, in many cases not distinguishable from some of the first series, so far as their form

---

[1] Simpson, pp. 182–184.

[2] Roth, *Natives of N. W. Queensland*, p. 129, pl. xvii.

[3] *Journal Anthrop. Institute*, May 1895, p. 410, pl. 21, fig. 7.

[4] Some wooden churinga are engraved, as ' Australian Magic Sticks,' in Ratzel's popular *History of Mankind*, i. 379. They exactly answer to the churinga of the Arunta.

is concerned, but belonging to a class all of which are spoken of as churinga ilkinia, and are regarded as sacred because they are associated with totems. Each local totemic group has certain of these specially belonging to the group, and in very many cases preserved on rock-surfaces in spots which are strictly *tabu* to the women, children, and uninitiated men.’ One of the commonest ‘represents a snake coming out of a hole in a rock,’ which the wriggle out of the cup in our circle-marked stones would stand for fairly well. Some designs are only ‘play-work;’ others exactly similar, on another spot, have a definite meaning. The meaning is read, where the spot is sacred ground. The concentric circles are ‘believed, on good ground, to have been derived from an original spiral.’ ‘It is much more easy to imagine a series of concentric circles originating out of a spiral than to imagine a spiral originating out of a series of concentric circles.’ In this country the spiral seems to be later than the circle.

These devices not only occur on fixed rocks and portable churinga, they are also painted on the bodies of boys when initiated in the mysteries: ‘concentric circles with radiating lines preponderate.’

In Mr. Haddon’s ‘Decorative Art of British New Guinea’ he describes designs of concentric circles and spirals which are clearly derivatives of drawings of the human face.[1] Thus our concentric circles and spirals *may*, in the last resort, have been derived from drawings of the human face, though *diablement changés en route*.

What, then, however we interpret the origin, decorative or symbolic, of the sacred designs, is their significance as understood by the Arunta of Central Australia at the present time?

[1] Royal Irish Academy, *Cunningham Memoirs*, No. x. 1894.

The Arunta are totemistic—that is, they believe in close relations which bind up the groups of their society with certain plants and animals. But they differ vastly from other totemistic races all over the world, and even in Australia. So much do they differ that it may be doubted whether their totems can properly be called totems at all. Elsewhere a man of a given totem—say the emu—cannot marry a woman of that stock; it is incest. The children inherit their totem, either from the mother, or, less frequently, the father. Any local group in a given region contains persons of various totems. People may not kill, eat, or make any use of the plants and animals which, in each case, are their totems.

Among the Arunta all is otherwise. A child's totem may be that of his father, of his mother, or different from that of either parent. A man may marry a woman of his own totem, which elsewhere is incest, and capitally punished. Thus, father is a grub; mother is a grub; one child may be a grub, another an emu. Moreover, here totems are *local*; almost every one in a given place will be, for example, a lizard or a plum tree. Usually people do eat their own totems, though sparingly, at magical rites, intended to multiply the animal or plant with which it is associated, in the interests of the general food supply. The Grubs work a rite to cause plenty of grubs, and they give the other groups a lead by eating sparingly of the first fruits of the grubs. This bears, in my opinion, no strong analogy to the so-called 'totem-sacrament.' To work the magic, the men of the grub or other totem must eat a little of it. This probably confirms their relation to the grub, but involves no *religious* element. They do not adore the grub. If any one likes to call this a 'totem-sacrament,' he is rather easily satisfied. Nor does it agree with the notion that a man's totem is the receptacle of his 'life' or 'soul;' if so, why should he encourage his neighbour to kill and eat it? Nay, he even helps them to destroy it.

Whether Arunta totemism is the most archaic kind, from which all other totemism has varied, or whether it is a private 'sport' from the main stock, does not concern us here, and is matter of conjecture. The Arunta, and other Central Australian tribes, look back to a mythic past, when ancestors, closely connected with this or that plant or animal, perhaps transformations of such animal or plant, roamed the country in groups, each of the same totem name, each feeding freely on its own totem.

This was 'the Alcheringa time,' and existing rites are explained by ' ætiological myths,' stating how such or such a mummery, still practised, was originally practised in the Alcheringa. Nothing of the sort, of course, need have been the case, and such myths cannot tell us what the manners and customs of that dim age really were. Demeter was a woman of the Greek Alcheringa, and the Eleusinian rites were explained by the Greeks as originating in her Alcheringa adventures. But these obviously were invented purely to account for the rites themselves, not *vice versa*.

Now, among the Arunta the blacks of to-day are regarded as reincarnations of the Alcheringa fabulous ancestors. Each of these carried about (both men and women) churinga, the portable decorated stones. When an Alcheringite died, a rock or tree rose to mark the place, but his or her spirit ' remained in the churinga.' Plenty of churinga were dropped at different sites, and round these now hover the spirits associated with them. In one place is a crowd of wild cat ghosts; at another, a mob of frog or lizard or emu ghosts. These want to be reincarnated. Consequently, a woman who desires to have a baby goes to one of them (in Argyll she would slide down a cup-marked rock !), a woman who does *not* want to have a baby keeps away. A child's totem is derived, not from father or mother, but from the totem of the ghosts at the place where the woman thinks she conceived it. When the baby is born her relations hunt the spot, and find for it the churinga left by the spirit which is reincarnated in it.

Thus, first there is the fabulous Alcheringite, himself a transformation of an emu, lizard, water, fire, or what not. Then there is his spirit haunting, after his death, a spot where churinga of his totem were deposited. That spirit enters into and is born again from a passing woman, and the spirit's churinga is found and is henceforth the child's churinga—an oval plate of stone, with cup and ring or other decorations.[1] All these churinga are kept at sacred central stores, caves, or crevices. Each member of the tribe is represented by her or his ' churinga nanja ' in these repositories. Women may not go near these sacred stores, nor may they see a churinga.[2] If they do, their eyes are burned out with a fire stick. A man's churinga is *not*, to him, like the egg in which was the life of the giant in the fairy tale. If it comes to grief, he does not die, but expects bad luck, as we do if we break a mirror. Not till he has been through the mysteries and the most cruel mutilations, and just before he has been painted with the pattern on the sacred rock of his totem, can a man see the store-houses of the churinga. Now, in the witchetty grub totem this sacred painting tallies with the lines incised, under concentric circles, on the covering

---

[1] For cups, see Spencer and Gillen, p. 129 ; for concentric circles, see p. 131.

[2] The tribal stores of churinga are *not* the same as the places where churinga were dropped in the Alcheringa.

of a stone kist at Tillicoutry.[1] There are circles above
the lines in the Australian example, or rather circular
dabs of paint, called ' the decorated eyes,' painted on the
rocks ; the corresponding patterns are incised on the
portable churinga. In Scotland the patterns are incised
both on fixed rocks and portable stones ; the latter at
Dumbuck and Dunbuie.

I observe many patterns common to both regions.
There are the concentric circles, the spiral, the marks like
horseshoes, the tree pattern, the witchetty grub pattern,
the volute, the long sinuous snake-like pattern, and a
number of these recur in Brazil, on the banks of the
Rio Negro.[2] Now, though we have those patterns on *rocks*
in Ohio, Brazil, Australia, in this country, in France, in
Asia Minor, I only know the patterns *on portable small
stones* in Australia, at Dunbuie, on the Dumbuck site,
and, I think, in a cairn near Lough Crew, in County
Meath.   The curious, for this last case, may consult
' Proceedings of Scottish Society of Antiquaries,' 1893,
p. 299, where in figs. 6 and 7 he will see what in Australia
would be called two stone churinga, with any number of
Scoto-Australian patterns on large stones. On one the
pattern is like that of a stone from Dunbuie.

In Australia members of each totem decipher the
marks, purely conventional, as representative of the totem,
and of adventures in the Alcheringa time. For example,
a mark like two croquet hoops, or horseshoes, is ' an old
woman gathering frogs.' The concentric circles are frogs ;
the dots round them are tracks of women ; dull, often dirty,
stories are told about the adventures of the Alcheringites

---

[1] *Proceedings S.A.S.* vol. xxix. p. 193. Spencer and Gillen, fig. 132,
No. 6.
[2] *S.A.S.* 1884–5, vol. vii. pp. 388–394. Compare, for County Meath,
the same work, 1892–93, pp. 297–338.

commemorated by the patterns. At the sacred pattern-painted rocks, magic ceremonies, extremely puerile, are performed to ensure a supply of the edible totem which the pattern represents. Some event occurred there in the Alcheringa ; the rite repeats what, in myth, was then done, and the stomachs of the men are rubbed with the churinga ' for luck.' Such are the uses of the churinga. Did they once exist wherever the similarly decorated fixed rocks exist ? Did the makers of the decorations in Scotland decipher the churinga as the Central Australians do now ? Were the dwellers by Clyde (much more advanced in culture than the Australians) totemists, looking on their small decorated stones as associated with the spirits of Alcheringa ances-tors ? Do women in Argyll slide down a cup-marked rock, in hope of offspring, because totemistic ghosts once hovered round it, eager to be reincarnated ? The fact of the sliding is attested by a chief of Clan Diarmid.

Nobody can answer ! I have shown these decorated rocks and small stones to have a living significance, a.vital legendary symbolism, in Central Australia. I cannot prove that they had the same significance in County Meath or Dumbartonshire. The Australians may have begun with mere decoration, and later added a symbolism suited to their amazing theory of life. In our country the decorations may have quite a different symbolical sense, but probably they had some sense. Otherwise, why engrave them, not only on rocks, but on small stones pierced for suspension ? Perhaps men believed in an Alcheringa time on the Clyde ; perhaps they multiplied salmon and deer by magical mummeries at the engraved rocks ; perhaps these were sacred places, tabooed to women. Or quite a different set of fables and customs may have crystallised in Scotland round marked rocks and inscribed small stones. I cannot prove that, as in Australia,

Clydesdale boys of old, when initiated in the mysteries, were painted with the pattern on their sacred totem rock and stone or wood churinga. But, if not these rites, other rites were, I conceive, connected with the decorative patterns found in so many still savage countries.

One piece of evidence rather points in this direction. The Australian stone churinga are shaped like the wooden churinga, and these are shaped like the *tundun*, or 'bull-roarer.' Now the bull-roarer (which occurs in Australia where stone churinga do not) is a sacred oval piece of wood, not to be seen by women, which is whirled at the mysteries, and makes a windy, roaring noise. The same object is used, for the same purpose, at the mysteries in America, Africa, and, of old, in Greece.[1] The roaring noise is taken to be the voice of Tundun, son of Mungan-ngaur, 'Our Father' in the heavens, among the Kurnai, and of gods or culture heroes of other names in other tribes. Now, in Celtic Scotland (as also in England) this instrument, the tundun, occurs as a mere toy, in Gaelic named *strannam*. Does it descend from a sacred object of savage mysteries, and are the Australian stone churinga—in shape like the tundun, and like the tundun tabooed to women—mere lapidary modifications of the wooden tundun? However this may be, the *strannam* looks like a link in the long chain which binds us to the prehistoric past.

While correcting the proof-sheets of this article I read, in the *Glasgow Herald* (January 7, 1899), an article on Dumbuck and Dunbuie, by Dr. Munro, the eminent authority on crannogs, or pile-dwellings, and, generally on prehistoric Scotland. Dr. Munro, as I understand him, does not regard Dumbuck as an older than mediæval site, nor as a

---

[1] See the author's *Custom and Myth : The Bull Roarer.* Prof. Haddon has discovered many other instances; see also *The Golden Bough*, iii. 423 *et seq.*

true crannog. The incised stones he looks on either as of most singular character (if genuine) or as forgeries of to-day, the opinion which he seems to prefer. He was then unacquainted with similar objects in any part of the world. I have here provided references to similar objects from Central Australia, and I suggest examination of the *apparently* similar Irish objects, figured in ' Proceedings of Scottish Society of Antiquaries,' 1893, p. 299, figs. 6 and 7. Not having seen these stones I can only offer the hint suggested by the illustrations in ' Proceedings.' Why a forger should forge such unknown objects, and place them at Dunbuie, in 1895, before the Central Australian stones had been described, I cannot guess. Nor can I enough deplore the stupidity of the same hypothetical forger in not ' salting ' Dunbuie and Dumbuck with neolithic implements, whether antique or made by some Flint Jack of to-day. Both his sins of omission and of commission *donnent furieusement à penser.* Dr. Munro, however, as I gather from his article on Dumbuck in ' The Reliquary' (April 1901), still declines to recognise the Dumbuck decorated portable stones as of genuine antiquity.

XIV

FIRST-FRUITS AND TABOOS

TABOO is one of the few savage words which have struck root in England. Introduced from New Zealand (*tapu*) and other Polynesian islands, it is used in English to denote a prohibition. This, that, or the other thing, or person, or book is 'tabooed.' Many of the Ten Commandments are, in this sense, taboos. But, in anthropological language, 'taboo' generally denotes something more than a prohibition. It commonly means a prohibition for which, to the civilised mind, there is no very obvious meaning. In this way the prohibitive Commandments are not precisely taboos; it is pretty obvious why we ought not to steal or kill, though the *raison d'être* of the Seventh Commandment is obscure to some advanced intelligences. But the reasons why a Sinclair must not cross the Ord on a certain 'lawful day,' or why on another 'lawful day' the fishermen of St. Andrews might not go a-fishing, resemble many savage taboos in the lack of a manifest reason why. Secondly, the infraction of the savage taboo generally, unlike that of the decalogue, carries its own punishment. Forbidden food is poison, tabooed land is dangerous to tread upon, to handle tabooed property may mean death; nobody knows what awful cosmic catastrophe might occur if a tabooed woman saw the sun; many words and names are taboo, and no luck will come of using them—for instance, you must not name 'salmon,' 'pigs,' or the minister when out fishing in some parts of Scotland.

In many cases the reason of this or that taboo is easily discovered. A day is unlucky because all the fishers, as at St. Andrews, were lost on that day in a past century through a storm; or the Sinclairs on another day were cut off in an expedition. Most of us have our lucky or unlucky days, clothes, and other vanities. Again, things are taboo for some reason in that kind of faith which holds that things connected in the association of ideas are mystically connected in fact. You must not mention salmon, lest they hear you and escape; or tin in Malay tin mining, lest the tin should literally ' make itself scarce.' You may not name the fairies, a jealous folk. Therefore you say ' the people of peace,' and so on. But many other taboos have good practical reasons. If women, among ourselves, were tabooed from salmon-fishing, eating oysters, or entering smoking-rooms (all of which things are greatly to be desired), the reason would be the convenience of the men, who wish a sanctuary or asylum in the smoking-room, and want to keep oysters and fishing to themselves. It is pretty plain why the sight of the royal treasury is tabooed to a West African king: to speak colloquially, if admitted to see the hoards he ' would blue the lot.' A taboo often protects by a supernatural sanction the property and persons of the privileged classes. If the umbrella of a bishop or a baronet were taboo, it would not be taken away from the club by accident.

This simple explanation covers the case of many taboos.

Brother and sister may scarcely ever see each other, still less speak to or name each other, where the law against brother and sister marriage or amour is the one most definite law of the community. ' It is not, therefore,

surprising,' says Mr. Jevons, ' that the earlier students of
the custom' (of taboo) 'regarded it as an artificial invention,
a piece of statecraft, cunningly devised in the interests of
the nobility and the priests.   This view is, however, now
generally abandoned,' because taboo ' is most at home
in communities which have no state organisation, and
flourishes where there are no priests or no priesthood.
Above all the belief is not artificial and imposed, but
spontaneous and natural.' [1]

I hesitate about this theory.   Taboo can hardly
flourish more than it does in Polynesia and West Africa,
where there are kings and priests.   Moreover, though
there are human societies without kings or priests (as in
Australia), there are no societies in which artificial
rules are not propagated, instituted, and enforced by the
adult males meeting in councils.   The Arunta of Central
Australia are, of course, far from ' primitive.'   They have
institutions, ceremonies, weapons, rules, and a complete
system of philosophy, which must have needed unknown
ages to develop.   They have local head-men, or Alatunjas,
whose office passes always in the male line : from father to
son, if the son be of age to succeed, or, if he is not, to the
brother, on whose death it reverts to the son.   An Alatunja
dying without a son nominates a brother or nephew to
succeed him.   Messrs. Spencer and Gillen know no
equivalent to this law among other Australian tribes, and
it indicates, among the so-called ' primitive ' Arunta, a
marked advance beyond other tribes in social evolution.
The Alatunja is hereditary Convener of Council, and if an
able man has considerable power.   He is guardian of the
Sacra of the group, determines the date of the cessation
of close-time for certain sorts of game, the date of the
magical ceremonies for fostering the game or edible

[1] *Introduction to the History of Religion*, p. 82.

plants, and directs the ceremonies. In the councils called by the Alatunja it appears that changes in stereo-typed custom may be introduced. Men learned in the customs and skilled in magic 'settle everything.' Definite proof of fundamental innovations thus introduced Messrs. Spencer and Gillen do not possess; but tradition indicates alterations of custom, and it is quite possible that a strong Alatunja, well backed, might bring in even a radical reform.[1] There are also recognised grades of skill among the medicine-men and the dealers with spirits, who must have their own share of social influence.

In brief, though without priests or kings these backward tribes have councils, and conveners, and directors whose office is hereditary in the male line. These persons, through unknown ages, have moulded customs and taboos, which are just as much sanctioned by traditoin and authority just as little 'spontaneous and universal,' as if kings and priests had invented them for purposes of statecraft. Mr. Jevons next argues that taboo 'cannot have been derived from experience. It is prior to and even contradictory of experience. In fine, it is an inherent tendency of the human mind.' In the same way Gibbon's ancestor, Blue Gown herald, when among North American Indians, declared that heraldry is an inherent tendency of the human mind, an innate idea.

An opinion is not necessarily erroneous because it is obsolete, nor a view wrong because 'it is generally abandoned.' I am here supporting the 'generally abandoned' hypothesis that many taboos, at least, are artificial and imposed, against Mr. Jevons's idea that the taboo, like armorial bearings, results from 'an inherent tendency of the human mind ' 'prior to and even contra-

[1] Spencer and Gillen, pp. 10-16.

dictory of experience.' [1]   That ' a new-born baby is dangerous,' or that ' the water in which a holy person has washed
is dangerous,' my private experience does not tell me ; in
fact, I never made either experiment : never tubbed in
the water previously used by a bishop.   But I am
prepared to admit that neither babies nor bishops are
proved by our experience to be dangerous.   That is not the
question.   The savage argued, not from unbiassed and
impartial scientific experiment, but from *fancied* experience.   Thus Mr. Jevons mentions a Maori who died after
finding out that he had eaten, unawares, the remains of the
luncheon of a holy person, a chief.   There was experience
produced by suggestion.   The suggestion was suggested
in the interests of holy chiefs ; they were ' tabooed an inch
thick,' as Mr. Manning writes.   As to the baby, the Dyaks,
as in our own fairy belief, hold that ' new-born children
are the especial prey of evil spirits,' just as corpses were in
Scotland, where, if the door was left ajar, the corpse sat
up, and mopped and mowed.   If the watchers left it, and
dined in the ' but,' an awful *vacarme* arose in the ' ben.'
The minister entered, stilled the tumult, asked for the
tongs, and came back holding in the tongs *a bloody glove* !
This he dropped into the fire.

This kind of thing is contradictory to the experience
of Mr. Jevons, but not to the *fancied* experience of Dyaks,
Scots, and other races.   Opinion therefore makes taboos in
accordance with experience, or what is believed to be
experience, and the belief is fortified by suggestion,
which produces death or disease when the taboo is broken.
On the analogy of infectious diseases, the mischief of the
tabooed thing is held to be contagious.

Thus I cannot hold with Mr. Jevons that the human
mind is provided with an *a priori* categorical imperative

[1] Jevons, p. 85.

' that there are some things which must not be done,' ' a feeling ' ' independent of sense experience.' [1]   If the choice of what things are ' not to be done ' seems to us ' irrational,' that is merely because our reason is more enlightened than that of the savage.   He prohibited just such things as his philosophy, and what he believed to be his experience, showed him to be dangerous for obscure reasons.   Any fool could see that it was dangerous to eat poison berries or frolic with a bear.   But it took reflection to discover that a baby or a corpse was dangerous by reason of evil spirits, *Iruntarinia*, whom the *Alkna Buma*, or clairvoyant, could see, and describe, though Mr. Jevons and I could not discern them.[2]   These Iruntarinia notoriously carry off women, and probably, like the fairies, have their best chance in the hour of child-birth : at all events, the fairies have.[3]   The belief is socially useful : it prevents young Arunta women from wandering off alone, and philandering out of bounds.

Thus these taboos are sanctioned by the tribal counsellors as the results of experience, not their own perhaps, but that of the *Alkna Buma*, or clairvoyant, or ' sensitive,' or ' medium,' or habitually hallucinated person.   Other taboos, as to women, are imposed for very good reasons, though not for the reasons alleged, and broken taboos are not (in actual ordinary experience) attended by the penalties which, however, suggestion may produce.

Taboo, then, is not imposed irrationally, nor in deference to ' an inherent tendency of the human mind ' (that Mrs. Harris of philosophy), but for a very good reason, as savage reasoning goes, and in accordance with what is believed to be experience, and, by dint of suggestion, really does become experience.

---

[1] Jevons, pp. 85–87.   [2] Spencer and Gillen, pp. 15, 515.   [3] *Ibid.* p. 517.

It was ' irrational' in Dr. Johnson to touch certain posts, and avoid certain stones, and enter a door twice, if he first entered it with the wrong foot. All my life I have had similar private taboos, though nobody knows better that they are nonsense. But some solitary experience in childhood probably suggested a relation of cause and effect, where there was only a fortuitous sequence of antecedent and consequent, and so Dr. Johnson and I (though not so conspicuously as the Doctor) imposed taboos on ourselves in deference to (fancied) experience. Early man has acted in the same way on a large scale, obeying no categorical *a priori* imperative, but merely acting on his philosophy and experience which is real to him, though not to civilised men. They usually do not understand it, but educated persons with a survival of savagery in their mental constitutions find the affair intelligible.

But the reason in actual practical experience for some taboos must be plain to the most civilised minds, except those of Radical voters for the Border Boroughs. Man, in the hunter stage, *must* have game laws and a close-time for edible animals and plants. The Border Radical will not permit a close-time for trout, perferring to destroy them, and with them their offspring, when gravid and unfit for human food, or before they recover condition.

The ' primitive ' Arunta are not so irrational, and have a close-time, protected by taboo, or, at least, by ceremonies of a nature more or less magical. In these ceremonies of a people not pastoral or agricultural, we seem to see the germs of the offerings of first-fruits to gods or spirits, though the Australian produce is offered neither to spirits nor to gods. These tribes recognise a great spirit, indeed, Twanyirika, but that he plays any other part in religion or society than presiding over the tribal mysteries we have at present no evidence to prove. Similar figures, associated with the mysteries, are, in other parts of Australia, provided with an ample mythology, and are subject to a being more august and remote. But either the Arunta are advanced thinkers who have passed beyond such ideas, or they have not yet attained to them, or our witnesses are uninformed on the subject.[1] In any case, the first-fruits of the game, grubs, and plants of the Arunta are not offered to Twanyirika, or to the minor sprites, *Iruntarinia.*

The ceremonies, partly intended to make the creatures used for food prolific, and partly, I think, to indicate that the close-time is over and that the creatures may be taken and eaten, are called Intichiuma. On the mummeries expected to make animals and plants plentiful we need not dwell. In each case the men who belong to the totem of the beast, grub, or plant perform the ceremonies. There is believed to be a close and essential connection between a man of the kangaroo totem and all kangaroos, between a man of the grub totem and all grubs, so each totem group does the magic to propagate its ally among beasts or plants. How these ideas arose we do not know. But if a local group was originally called kangaroos or grubs (and some name it must have), the association of names would inevitably lead, by association of ideas, to the notion that a mysterious connection existed between the men of a totem name and the plant, animal, or what not which gave the name. These men, therefore, would work the magic for propagating their kindred in the animal and vegetable world. But the existence of this connection would also suggest that, in common decency, a man should not kill and eat his animal or vegetable relations. In most parts of the world he abstains from this

[1] Spencer and Gillen, pp. 222, 246.

uncousinly behaviour : among the Arunta he may eat sparingly of his totem, and must do so at the end of the close-time or beginning of the season.

He thus, as a near relation of the actual kangaroos or grubs, declares the season open, and gives his neighbours of other totems a lead. Now they may begin to eat grubs or kangaroos ; the taboo is off. Thus, in 1745, Gask tabooed the corn of his tenants ; they must not reap it, because they refused ' to rise and follow Charlie.' Prince Charles, hearing of this, cut a few ears with his claymore, thus removing the taboo. In the same way the grub or kangaroo men publicly eat a little of their own totem, after which the tribesmen and other totems may fall to and devour. When the grub or whatever it is becomes plentiful, after the magic doings for its propagation, it is collected and placed before some members of the grub totem. The *Alatunja*, or convener, grinds up some of the grub, he and his fellow totemists eat a little, and hand the mass back to the members of other totems. They eat a little of their own totem, partly, Messrs. Spencer and Gillen say, to strengthen their mystic connection with the creature. This, in a way, is a ' sacramental ' idea, though no religious regard is paid to the plants and animals. But the men also partake, to remove the taboo, and to let the rest of the community gorge themselves legally.[1]

The rite has thus a practical purpose. The grubs or other creatures are not prematurely destroyed, like trout on the Border. In fact, trout themselves are sensible enough not to begin feeding on May fly prematurely.

---

[1] The Arunta eating of the totem, at the magic ceremony, is not religious. Mr. Jevons, however, adduces it as proof of ' the existence of the totem-sacrament,' surviving ' in an etiolated form.' But what proof have we that the totems were once ' totem gods,' or in any way divine, among the Arunta ? Jevons, ' The Science of Religion,' *International Monthly*, p. 489, April 1901.

' Throughout the previous week,' says Sir Herbert Maxwell, 'a few May flies had been seen . . . but not a trout would point his nose at one. . . . This hesitation on the part of the trout to begin their annual banquet is one of the best known and, at the same time, least explicable features of the May fly fortnight.'[1] The Arunta also let the grub come on to its full rise before feeding. When a certain bulb is ripe, the men of its totem rub off and blow away the husks, then the general public may begin feeding. There is nothing sacramental in *this* ceremony, which merely opens the season for tuber eating. The taboo is off. And so in other cases : the kangaroo men are smeared with the fat of the kangaroo, and eat a little of the animal.[2] The non-kangaroo tribesmen may then eat kangaroo. The traditions of the Arunta represent their mythical ancestors as in some cases feeding *solely* on their totems. But this cannot possibly be true. A grub man would die, when grubs were out, of starvation, and so with the rest. ' When fruits is in, cats is out,' and a man of the gooseberry totem, who only ate gooseberries, would perish miserably.

The Arunta eating of the totem has nothing to do with consecrating the first-fruits of grubs or kangaroos to a god or with absorbing the qualities of a spirit. When Swedish peasants bake a cake shaped like a girl, from the last sheaf of the new corn, they perhaps originally ate the cake ' as the body of the corn spirit.'[3] But when the Lithuanian farmer takes the first swig of the new beer— ' the second brew was for the servants '—perhaps he is only declaring his ownership, and opening the beer season.[4] In an unnamed part of Yorkshire the parson cuts the

---

[1] *Memories of the Months*, 1900, pp. 132, 133.
[2] Spencer and Gillen, chapter vi.
[3] *G. B.* ii. 318.   [4] *Ibid.*

first corn ; he is the *Alatunja,* and opens the harvest.   In
the Celebes the priest opens the rice harvest; all eat of it ;
' after this every one is free to get in his rice.'   At St.
Andrews on the Medal Day (which is in harvest time) the
Alatunja (that is the new captain) drives a ball from the
first tee; after this every one is free to drive off in his
turn—but not before.   In some places, as in Indo-China,
the first-fruits are offered to a god ; in Zululand the
king pops a little into the mouth of every man present, who
' may immediately get in his crops.'   If he began harvest
before he would die, or, if detected, would be speared, or
forfeited.   Sometimes the first-fruits are offered to ' the
holy spirit of fire.'   There are all sorts of ways and
ceremonies of opening the season and taking off the taboo.
I really don't think it follows that the first fruits are
dangerous to eat, before the ceremony, *because* ' they are
regarded as instinct with a divine virtue, and consequently
the eating of them is a sacrament or communion.' [1]   It is
dangerous to eat them, as it would be dangerous to steal
a tabooed umbrella.   They are tabooed because it is close-
time.

The other ideas may come to be entertained, an automatic punishment may be thought to follow the breach of
the taboo, though we do not learn that this is the case
among the Arunta.   But the origin of the taboo on the
immature food, I think, is the perfectly practical idea of
a close-time; plants are not to be gathered, nor animals
killed, prematurely.   The more or less supreme being of
the Fuegians is angry—if you shoot flappers.   ' Very bad
to shoot little duck, come rain, come wind, blow, very
much blow.' [2]   The ' great black man, who cannot be
escaped, and who influences the weather according to
men's conduct,' is right about the flappers.   He sanctions

[1] *G. B.* ii. 335.   [2] Fitzroy, *Cruise of the Beagle,* ii. 180.

a necessary game law. The *How* (king), in Tonga, used to wait till the yams were ripe, then he fixed a day for gathering them, and had a religious function. The sort of function depends on the stage at which local religion has arrived; but a close-time—no premature killing or gathering—is the practical idea at the base of all these affairs of first-fruits. Any other superstition, sacrificial or sacramental, may crystallise round the practical primitive prohibition, especially when it was sanctioned by the good old device of automatic punishment, following on infringement of taboo.

If Sir Herbert Maxwell could persuade Mr. Thomas Shaw, M.P., that the proverbially execrable weather on the Border is the direct result of fishing, especially with salmon-roe, out of season; if there was to be no fishing till Mr. Shaw, after tasting of the first trout, declared the season open; if the clergy of all denominations lent their presence to the imposing ceremony, then I believe that Tweed, Ettrick, Teviot, Yarrow, Ail, and Kale would be worth fishing in again.

Taboo, as Mr. Frazer and Mr. Jevons agree, has had its uses in the evolution of morality; but remark that strictly moral offences are nowhere under taboo. You may steal (as long as the object stolen is not tabooed and does not belong to a chief or priest), you may kill, you may interfere with the domestic bliss of your neighbour, you may lie, but the automatic punishment of taboo-breaking nowhere follows. Baiame or Pundjel may punish you; but there is no instant mechanical penalty, as under taboo.

After writing this paper, I found that Mr. Robert Louis Stevenson's experience of *tapu*, in the Pacific, led him to form the same opinions as are here expressed. ' The devil-fish, it seems, were growing scarce upon the reef; it was judged fit to interpose what we should call a close season . . . a tapu had to be declared.' The tapus described ' are for thoroughly sensible ends.' There are tapus which, to us, appear absurd, ' but the tapu is more often the instrument of wise and needful restrictions.' [1]

These taboos are imposed from above, by Government. In other cases, where the taboo expresses an inference from savage superstition (say that a baby or a corpse is dangerous), the taboo is not imposed except by public opinion. That opinion is sanctioned (as in the case of first-fruits) by the action of the Alatunja, or headman : in more advanced societies, by the king. In many cases, taboos are imposed on the king himself by the priestly colleges. But the greatest authority is tradition, resting on fancied experience.

[1] *In the South Seas*, pp. 47-50.

XV

WALKING THROUGH FIRE

PERHAPS the topic of this paper may be ranged under the head of ' Magic,' though in many cases the rite of passing through fire is sanctioned by religion, and the immunity of the performers is explained by the protection of gods. The immunity is really the curious feature. Mr. Frazer describes the Chinese vernal festival of fire in spring, connected as it is with the widespread custom of ' renewing the fire ' at a certain season. The chief performers are labourers, who must fast for three days and observe chastity for a week ; while they are taught in the temple how to discharge the difficult and dangerous duty which is to be laid upon them. ' The fire is made in an enormous brazier of charcoal, sometimes twenty feet wide.' The fire is gratified with salt and rice, thrown on it by a Taoist priest. Further, ' two exorcists, barefooted, and followed by two peasants, traverse the fire again and again till it is somewhat beaten down.' The procession of performers then walks through amidst much excitement. Their immunity is ascribed to the horny consistency of the soles of their feet, and they suffer if the fire touches their ankles.[1] Various Indian examples are given by Mr. Frazer. Captain Mackenzie found the performance remote from the ' sensational,' and thought that only girls with tender

---

[1] *G. B.* iii. 307, 308, citing *Internationales Archiv für Ethnographie* (1896), pp. 193–195.

soles were likely to suffer. A case is also quoted from Strabo, women being the performers, and the instance of the Hirpi of Soracte is well known.[1] Mr. Frazer is interested mainly in the religious, magical, or ritual significance of the rite, which varies in different places. To me, on the other hand, the immunity of the performers appears a subject worthy of physiological inquiry.

The subject occurs everywhere in history, legend, folklore, law, and early religion, and yet nobody has thought it worth while to collect the ancient reports and to compare them with well-authenticated modern examples. In Mr. Tylor's celebrated work, 'Primitive Culture,' only one or two casual allusions are made to the theme. 'They built the high places of Baal, in the valley of the son of Hinnom, to cause their sons and daughters to pass through to Moloch,' that is to pass through the fire, 'whether in ritual or symbolical sacrifice.'[2] As a supposed rite of purification the ceremony is again touched upon lightly.[3] Again: 'The ancient ceremony of passing through a fire, or leaping over burning brands, has been kept up vigorously in the British Isles,'[4] namely, at the midsummer ceremonies, when it is, or was, the custom to jump over, or run through, light fires. Nobody would guess that a rite of passing deliberately. and unscathed, through ovens or furnaces yet exists in Japan, Bulgaria, the Society Islands, Fiji, Southern India, Trinidad, the Straits Settlements, the Isle of Mauritius, and, no doubt, in other regions.

We must distinguish between such sportive playing with fire as prevailed recently in our isles and the more serious Fire Ceremony of Central Australia, which tests endurance

---

[1] *G. B.* iii. 311, 312; Strabo, xii. 2-7, for Castabala in Cappadocia; Virgil, *Æn.* xi. 784; and Servius's Commentary.

[2] *Primitive Culture*, ii. p. 281.

[3] *Ibid.* ii. p. 429.

[4] *Ibid.* i. p. 85.

on the one hand, and the apparent contravention of a natural law on the other. Again, we must discount the popular reply that the hand can be rapidly plunged into molten metal and withdrawn without injury, for we do not happen to be concerned with such a brief exposure to heat. Once more, the theory of the application of some unknown chemical substance must be rejected, because, as we shall prove, there are certainly cases in which nothing of the kind is done. Moreover, science is acquainted with no substance—alum or diluted sulphuric acid, or the like—which will produce the result of preventing cauterisation.[1] Sir William Crookes, at least, is not familiar with any such resources of science. His evidence as to fire-handling by D. D. Home is familiar, and I understand that Mr. Podmore can only explain it away by an hypothesis of a trick played in a bad light, by means of an asbestos glove or some such transparent trick.[2] Perhaps he adds a little ' hallucination ' on the part of the spectators. But asbestos and hallucination are out of the question in the cases which I am about to quote.

Home was, or feigned to be, in a state of trance when he performed with fire. The seeress of Lourdes, Bernadette, was also in religious contemplation when she permitted the flame of a candle to play through her clasped fingers (which were unscathed) for a timed quarter of an hour.[3] Some Indian devotees, again, aver that they ' meditate ' on some divine being while passing over the glowing embers, and the Nistinares of Bulgaria, who dance in the fire, are described as being in a more or less abnormal mental condition. But even this condition is absent in the well-attested Raiatean and

---

[1] See note at end of chapter.
[2] *Studies in Psychical Research*, pp. 58–59.
[3] Dr. Dozous timed the ' miracle.' Boissarie, *Lourdes*, p. 49.

Fijian examples, in which also no kind of chemical preparation is employed. Finally, where savages are concerned, the hardness of the skins of their feet is dwelt upon, as in the Chinese case already quoted. But, first, the sole of the boot would be scorched in the circumstances, while their feet are not affected ; next, the savages' feet were *not* leathery (so Dr. Hocken avers) ; thirdly, one of the Europeans who walked through the fire at Rarotonga declares that the soles of his own feet are peculiarly tender. Thus every known physical or conjectured psychical condition of immunity fails to meet the case, and we are left wholly without an ascertained, or a good conjectural, ' reason why ' for the phenomena.

I shall begin with the most recent and the best authenticated cases, and work back in time, and in civilisation. Mr. Tregear, the well-known lexicographer of the Maori and the allied Mangarova languages, lately sent me the twenty-ninth number of ' The Journal of the Polynesian Society,' March 1899, Wellington, N.Z. Professors Max Müller and Sayce were Honorary Members of the Society, which studies Polynesian languages, customs, and conditions. Mr. Tregear attests the upright, truth-telling character of the British official, who is the narrator of his own experiment. As the journal is not widely circulated in England, I quote the whole of the brief report.

THE UMU-TI, OR FIRE-WALKING CEREMONY

By Colonel Gudgeon, British Resident, Rarotonga

[In this Journal, vol. ii p. 105, Miss Teuira Henry describes this ceremony as practised in Raiatea, of the Society group. We have lately received from Colonel Gudgeon the following account of his experiences in walking barefooted across the glowing hot stones of a

native oven, made in Rarotonga by a man from Raiatea.
Since the date of the paper quoted, it has come to light
that the Maoris of New Zealand were equally acquainted
with this ceremony, which was performed by their
ancestors. On reading Colonel Gudgeon's account to
some old chiefs of the Urewera tribe, they expressed no
surprise, and said that their ancestors could also perform
the ceremony, though it has long gone out of practice.—
EDITORS.]

I must tell you that I have seen and gone through the
fire ceremony of the *Umu-ti*.

The oven was lit at about dawn on the 20th of January,
and I noticed that the stones were very large, as also were
the logs that had been used in the oven for heating
purposes.

About 2 P.M. we went to the oven and there found
the *tohunga* (a Raiatea man) getting matters ready, and I
told him that, as my feet were naturally tender, the stones
should be levelled down a bit. He assented to this, and
evidently he had intended to do so, for shortly after, the
men with very long poles, that had hooks, began to level
the stones flat in the oven, which was some 12 ft. in
diameter. He then went with his disciple and pointed to
two stones that were not hot, and instructed him the
reason was that they had been taken from a *marae*, or
sacred place.

He then unwound two bundles, which proved to be
branches of a large-leaved *Ti* (or *Dracæna*) plucked, it is
said, from two of these trees standing close together, and
it is said that the initiated can on such occasions see the
shadow of a woman with long hair, called *te varua kino*
(evil spirit), standing between the trees. The right-hand
branch is the first plucked, and it is said that the branches
bend down to be plucked.

So much for the Shamanism, and now for the facts.

The *tohunga* (priest) and his *tauira* (pupil) walked
each to the oven, and then halting, the prophet spoke
a few words, and then each struck the edge of the
oven with the *ti* branches. This was three times repeated,
and then they walked slowly and deliberately over the two
fathoms of hot stones. When this was done, the *tohunga*
came to us, and his disciple handed his *ti* branch to

Mr. Goodwin, at whose place the ceremony came off, and they went through the ceremony. Then the *tohunga* said to Mr. Goodwin, ' I hand my *mana* (power) over to you ; lead your friends across.' Now, there were four Europeans —Dr. W. Craig, Dr. George Craig, Mr. Goodwin, and myself—and I can only say that we stepped out boldly. I got across unscathed, and only one of the party was badly burned ; and he, it is said, was spoken to, but, like Lot's wife, looked behind him—a thing against all rules.

I can hardly give you my sensations, but I can say this : that I knew quite well I was walking on red-hot stones and could feel the heat, yet I was not burned. I felt something resembling slight electric shocks, both at the time and afterwards, but that is all. I do not know that I should recommend every one to try it. A man must have *mana* to do it; if he has not, it will be too late when he is on the hot stone of Tama-ahi-roa.

I cannot say that I should have performed this wizard trick had I not been one of the fathers of the Polynesian Society, and bound to support the superiority of the New Zealander all over Polynesia—indeed all over the world. I would not have missed the performance for anything.

To show you the heat of the stones, quite half an hour afterwards some one remarked to the priest that the stones would not be hot enough to cook the *ti*. His only answer was to throw his green branch on the oven, and in a quarter of a minute it was blazing. As I have eaten a fair share of the *ti* cooked in the oven, I am in a position to say that it was hot enough to cook it well.

I walked with bare feet, and after we had done so, about 200 Maoris followed. No one, so far as I saw, went through with boots on. I did not walk quickly across the oven, but with deliberation, because I feared that I should tread on a sharp point of the stones and fall. My feet also were very tender. I did not mention the fact, but my impression as I crossed the oven was that the skin would all peel off my feet. Yet all I really felt when the task was accomplished was a tingling sensation not unlike slight electric shocks on the soles of my feet, and this continued for seven hours or more. The really funny thing is that, though the stones were hot enough an hour afterwards to burn up green branches of the *ti*, the very tender skin of my feet was not even hardened by the fire.

Many of the Maoris thought they were burned, but they were not—at any rate not severely.

Do not suppose that the man who directed this business was an old *tohunga*. He is a young man, but of the Raiatea family, who are hereditary fire-walkers.

I can only tell you it is *mana—mana tangata* and *mana atua*.

On this report a few remarks may be offered. (1) No preparation of any chemical, herbal, or other sort was applied to the Europeans, at least. (2) 'The handing over the *mana*' (or power) was practised by Home, sometimes successfully (it is alleged), as when Mr. S. C. Hall's scalp and white locks were unharmed by a red-hot coal; sometimes unsuccessfully. A clergyman of my acquaintance still bears the blister caused when he accepted a red-hot coal from the hand of Home, as he informs me by letter. (3) The 'walk' was shorter than seems common : only 12 ft. (4 paces). (4) A friend of Colonel Gudgeon's was badly burned, and the reason assigned was a good folklore reason, since the days of Lot's wife, of Theocritus, and of Virgil : he looked behind. (5) The feeling as if of ' slight electric shocks ' is worthy of notice. (6) Colonel Gudgeon clearly believes that a man without *mana* had better not try, and by *mana*, here, he probably means 'nerve.' As we can hardly suppose, in spite of Home, that *mana*, in a supernormal sense, can be ' handed over ' by one man to another, Colonel Gudgeon's experience seems equally to baffle every theory of ' how it is done.' Perhaps we can all do it. People may make their own experiments. Perhaps Colonel Gudgeon faced fire in a manner so unusual as a result of Dr. Hocken's description of the Fijian rite at Mbenga, an isle twenty miles south of Suva. This account was published in the ' Transactions of the New Zealand Institute,' vol. xxxi. 1898, having been read before the Otago Institute on

May 10, 1898, and is here reprinted in full as follows : —

AN ACCOUNT OF THE FIJI FIRE CEREMONY

By Dr. T. M. Hocken, F.L.S.

Amongst the many incidents witnessed during a recent visit to the tropical island of Fiji, probably none exceeded in wonder and interest that of which I propose to give some account this evening, and to which may be applied the designation of ' fire ceremony.' It is called by the natives ' *vilavilairevo*.' In this remarkable ceremony a number of almost nude Fijians walk quickly and unharmed across and among white-hot stones, which form the pavement of a huge native oven—termed ' *lovo* '—in which shortly afterwards are cooked the succulent sugary roots and pith of the *Cordyline terminalis*, one of the cabbage trees, known to the Maoris as the ' *ti*,' and to the Fijians as the ' *masawe*.' This wonderful power of fire-walking is now not only very rarely exercised, but, at least as regards Fiji, is confined to a small clan or family—the *Na Ivilankata*—resident on Bega (=Mbenga), an island of the group, lying somewhat south of Suva, and twenty miles from that capital.

A small remnant of the priestly order at Raiatea, one of the Society Islands, is yet able to utter the preparatory incantation, and afterwards to walk through the fire.

It exists also in other parts of the world, as in parts of India, the Straits Settlements, West India Islands, and elsewhere. Very interesting accounts of the ceremony as seen at Raiatea and at Mbenga are to be found in the second and third volumes of the ' Journal of the Polynesian Society,' and in Basil Thomson's charming ' South Sea Yarns.' These descriptions filled our small party of three—my wife, Dr. Colquhoun, and myself—with the desire to witness it for ourselves, and, if possible, to give some explanation of what was apparently an inexplicable mystery. Our desires were perfectly realised.

The Hon. Mr. A. M. Duncan, a member of the Legislative Council of Fiji, and agent at Suva of the Union Steamship Company, to whom I carried a letter of introduction from Mr. James Mills, the managing director of that Company, was most courteous and obliging, and promised his best efforts in the matter. His energy and ready response succeeded, with the result that a large party from Suva enjoyed such a day as each one must have marked with a red letter.

It was necessary to give the natives three days in which to make their preparations—constructing the oven and paving it with stones, which then required heating for thirty-six or forty-eight hours at least with fierce fires fed with logs and branches. They had also to gather their stores of food to form the foundation of the huge feast whose preparation was to succeed the mystic ceremony. During these three days we lost no opportunity of collecting from former witnesses of the ceremony whatever information or explanation they could afford, but with no very satisfactory result : the facts were undisputed, but the explanations quite insufficient. Some thought that the chief actors rubbed their bodies with a secret preparation which rendered them fireproof; others that lifelong friction on the hard hot rocks, coral-reefs, and sands had so thickened and indurated the foot-sole that it could defy fire; but all agreed as to the *bona fides* of the exhibition. The incident recounted in the 'Polynesian Journal' was also confirmed—where Lady Thurston threw her handkerchief upon the shoulder of one of the actors, and, though it remained there but a few seconds before being picked off by means of a long stick, it was greatly scorched.[1]

The story or legend attached to this weird gift of firewalking was told us, with some variation, by two or three different people, and it is mainly as follows : A far-distant ancestor of the present inheritors of this power was walking one day when he espied an eel, which he caught, and was about to kill. The eel squeaked out, and said, ' Oh ! Tui Na Galita (=Eng-Galita), do not kill me ; spare me. I am a god, and I will make you so strong in war that none shall withstand you.' ' Oh, but,' replied Na Galita, ' I am already stronger in war than any one else, and I fear no one.' ' Well, then,' said the eel, ' I will make your canoe the fastest to sail on these seas, and none shall come up with it.' ' But,' replied Na Galita, ' as it is, none can pass my canoe.' ' Well, then,' rejoined the eel, ' I

---

[1] I have not seen this account.

will make you a great favourite among women, so that all will fall in love with you.' 'Not so,' said Na Galita, ' I have one wife, of whom I am very fond, and I desire no other.' The poor eel then made other offers, which were also rejected, and his chances of life were fading fast when he made a final effort. ' Oh, Na Galita, if you will spare me, I will so cause it that you and your descendants shall henceforth walk through the *masawe* oven unharmed.' ' Good,' said Na Galita, ' now I will let you go.' This story varies somewhat from that told in the ' Polynesian Journal.' [1]

The eventful morning was blazingly hot and brilliant, and the vivid-blue sky was without a cloud as we steamed down towards Mbenga in the s.s. *Hauroto*. Mr. Vaughan, an eminent inhabitant of Suva, who has charge of the Meteorological Department there, was of our party, and carried the thermometer. This was the most suitable for our purpose procurable ; it was in a strong japanned-tin casing, and registered 400° Fahr. We had also three amateur photographers.

Owing to the numerous coral-reefs and shallows, we finally transhipped into the *Maori*, a steamer of much less draught. Approaching the silent verdure-clad islet, with its narrow beach of white coral sand, we saw a thin blue haze of smoke curling above the lofty cocoanut trees at a little distance in the interior, which sufficiently localised the mysterious spot. We now took the ship's boat, and soon, stepping ashore, made our way through a narrow pathway in the dense bush until we came to an open space cleared from the forest, in the midst of which was the great *lovo*, or oven.

A remarkable and never-to-be-forgotten scene now presented itself. There were hundreds of Fijians, dressed according to the rules of nature and their own art—that is, they were lightly garlanded here and there with their fantastic *likulikus* of grass, ornamented with brilliant scarlet and yellow hibiscus flowers and streamers of the delicate ribbonwood. These hung in airy profusion from their necks and around their waists, showing off to advantage their lovely brown glossy skins. In addition, many wore clean white cotton *sulus*, or pendant loincloths. All were excited, moving hither and thither in

---

[1] See also Mr. Thomson's *South Sea Yarns*.

wild confusion, and making the forest ring again with
their noisy hilarity.   Some climbed the lofty cocoa-palms,
hand over hand, foot over foot, with all the dexterity of
monkeys.   The top reached, and shrouded amongst the
feathery leaves, they poured down a shower of nuts for
the refreshment of their guests.

The celerity with which they opened the nuts was
something astonishing, and afforded an example, too, as
to the mode of using stone implements.   A stout strong
stick, 3 ft. long, and sharpened at both ends, was driven
into the ground, and a few smart strokes upon it soon
tore from the nut its outer thick covering.   The upper
part of the shell was then broken off by means of a long
sharp-edged stone as cleanly and regularly as the lid of an
egg is removed with a knife, and then was disclosed a pint
of delicious milk—a most welcome beverage on that over-
poweringly hot day.

The great oven lay before us, pouring forth its torrents
of heat from huge embers which were still burning fiercely
on the underlying stones.   These were indeed melting
moments for the spectators.   The pitiless noontide sun,
and the no less pitiless oven-heat, both pent up in the
deep well-like forest clearing, reduced us to a state of
solution from which there was no escape.   Despite this
the photographers took up their stations, and others of us
proceeded to make our observations.   The *lovo*, or oven,
was circular, with a diameter of 25 ft. or 30 ft.; its
greatest depth was perhaps 8 ft., its general shape that of
a saucer, with sloping sides and a flattish bottom, the
latter being filled with the white-hot stones.   Near the
margin of the oven, and on its windward side, the thermometer marked 114°.

Suddenly, and as if Pandemonium had been let loose,
the air was filled with savage yells ; a throng of natives
surrounded the oven, and in a most ingenious and effective
way proceeded to drag out the smouldering unburnt logs
and cast them some distance away.   Large loops of
incombustible lianas attached to long poles were dexte-
rously thrown over the burning trunks, much after the
manner of the head-hunters of New Guinea when securing their human prey.   A twist or two round of the loop
securely entangled the logs, which were then dragged out
by the united efforts of scores of natives, who all the

while were shouting out some wild rhythmical song. This accomplished, the stones at the bottom of the oven were disclosed, with here and there flame flickering and forking up through the interstices. The diameter of the area occupied by those stones was about 10 ft., but this was speedily increased to a spread of 15 ft. or more by a second ingenious method. The natives thrust their long poles, which were of the unconsumable wi-tree (*Spondias dulcis*), between the stones at intervals of perhaps 1 ft. A long rope-like liana—*wa*—previously placed underneath the poles, and 1 ft. or 2 ft. from their extremities, was now dragged by scores of lusty savages, with the effect of spreading and levelling the stones. This done, our thermometer was suspended by a simple device over the centre of the stones, and about 5 ft. or 6 ft. above them ; but it had to be withdrawn almost immediately, as the solder began to melt and drop, and the instrument to be destroyed. It, however, registered 282° Fahr., and it is certain that had not this accident occurred, the range of 400° would have been exceeded, and the thermometer burst.

During all these wild scenes we had seen nothing of the main actors—of the descendants of Na Galita. Doubtless to give more impressive effect, they had been hiding in the forest depths until the signal should be given and their own supreme moment arrive. And now they came on, seven or eight in number, amidst the vociferous yells of those around. The margin reached, they steadily descended the oven slope in single file, and walked, as I think, leisurely, but as others of our party think, quickly, across and around the stones, leaving the oven at the point of entrance. The leader, who was longest in the oven, was a second or two under half a minute therein. Almost immediately heaps of the soft and succulent leaves of the hibiscus, which had been gathered for the purpose, were thrown into the oven, which was thus immediately filled with clouds of hissing steam. Upon the leaves and within the steam the natives, who had returned, sat or stood pressing them down in preparation for cooking the various viands which were to afford them a sumptuous feast that evening or on the morrow.

But for us the most interesting part of the drama was over, and it only remained to review observations and

draw conclusions.   Just before the great event of the day,
I gained permission to examine one or two of the fire-
walkers prior to their descent into the oven.   This was
granted without the least hesitation by the principal
native magistrate of the Rewa district, N'Dabea by name,
but generally known as Jonathan.   This native is of great
intelligence and influence, is a member of the Na Galita
Clan, and has himself at various times walked through
the fire.   On this occasion he took no other part in the
ceremony than that of watching or superintending it.
The two men thus sent forward for examination disclosed
no peculiar feature whatever.   As to dress, they were
slightly garlanded round the neck and the waist; the pulse
was unaffected, and the skin, legs, and feet were free from
any apparent application.   I assured myself of this by
touch, smell, and taste, not hesitating to apply my tongue
as a corroborative.   The foot-soles were comparatively
soft and flexible—by no means leathery and insensible.
Thus the two Suvan theories were disposed of.   This
careful examination was repeated immediately after egress
from the oven, and with the same result.   To use the
language of Scripture, 'No smell of fire had passed upon
them.'   No incantations or other religious ceremonial
were observed.   Though these were formerly practised,
they have gradually fallen into disuse since the introduction of Christianity.   I did not succeed in procuring
the old incantation formula; doubtless it was similar to
that of the old Raiatean ceremony, which is given in the
second volume of the 'Polynesian Society's Journal,'
p. 106.

Whilst walking through the fire, Dr. Colquhoun
thought the countenances of the fire-walkers betrayed
some anxiety.   I saw none of this; nor was it apparent
to me at either examination.   The stones, which were
basaltic, must have been white-hot, but due to the
brilliance of the day this was not visible.

Various natives, being interrogated for an explanation,
replied, with a shrug, 'They can do this wonderful thing;
we cannot.   You have seen it; we have seen it.'   Whilst
thus unable to suggest any explanation or theory, I am
absolutely certain as to the truth of the facts and the *bona
fides* of the actors.   A feature is that, wherever this power
is found, it is possessed by but a limited few.   I was assured,

too, that any person holding the hand of one of the fire-walkers could himself pass through the oven unharmed. This the natives positively assert.

My friend Mr. Walter Carew, for thirty years a Resident Commissioner and Stipendiary Magistrate in Fiji, has frequently conversed with Jonathan (referred to above), who, whilst withholding no explanation, can give none. He says, ' I can do it, but I do not know how it is done; ' and, further, that at the time he does not experience any heat or other sensation.

Does any psychical condition explain these facts, as suggested in Lang's 'Modern Mythology'?[1] I certainly did not observe any appearance of trance or other mental condition. In connection with this Mr. Carew thinks that intense faith is the explanation, and that if this were upset, the descendants of Na Galita would be no longer charmed. But it is difficult to see how any mental state can prevent the action of physical law. Hypnotism and anæsthetics may produce insensibility to pain, but do not interfere with the cautery.

Many of the so-called fire miracles are remarkable indeed, but are readily explained, and by no means come within the present category. Such, for instance, as plunging the hand, which is protected by the interposed film of perspiration assuming the globular state of water, into boiling lead. Similarly, many conjuring feats. At the beginning of this century an Italian—Lionetti—performed remarkable experiments : rubbed a bar of red-hot iron over his arms, legs, and hair, and held it between his teeth; he also drank boiling oil. Dr. Sementini, of Naples, carefully examined these experiments, and experimented himself until he surpassed the fireproof qualities of his suggestor. He found that frequent friction with sulphurous acid rendered him insensible to red-hot iron ; a solution of alum did the same. A layer of powdered sugar covered with soap made his tongue insensible to heat. In these and similar instances, however, an explanation, though probably not a very sufficient one, has been given, but in that forming the subject of this paper no solution has been offered. Lang's chapter on the 'Fire Walk' should be consulted; his account of the Bulgarian Nistinares is as wonderful and inexplicable as

[1] I would now withdraw the suggestion in the light of recent evidence.

anything here recited. The whole subject requires thorough scientific examination.

My next case occurs among a civilised race, the Japanese, and is vouched for by Mr. Lafcadio Hearn, an American writer, whose book I have not at hand, and by Colonel Andrew Haggard.[1] Colonel Haggard saw the fire-walk done in Tokio, on April 9, 1899. The fire was 6 yards long by 6 ft wide. The rite was in honour of a mountain god. Ablutions in cold water were made by the performers, and Colonel Haggard was told by one young lady that she had not only done the fire-walk, but had been 'able to sit for a long time, in winter, immersed in ice-cold water, without feeling the cold in the least.' After some waving of wands and sprinkling of salt, people of all ages walked through, not glowing stones in this case, but 'red-hot charcoal.' 'I examined their feet afterwards : they were quite soft, and not a trace of fire upon them.' Colonel Haggard says that the rite is 'a very unusual thing' in Japan : many of the Japanese living in Tokio had never heard of it before. Colonel Haggard was unable to get any clear answer as to why the rite is performed. The priest talked something about a good God who had power over the bad element of fire. It is not clear how, the rite being so unusual, two Japanese ladies told Colonel Haggard that they had 'frequently gone through the fiery ordeal.'

If any one is anxious to know the particulars of the rite as practised in the isle Mauritius, he may communicate with our police officials there, who annually superintend the performance. Coolies from southern India do just what is done by Japanese and Fijians. Our administration, however, does not permit women to pass through the fire.

[1] *The Field*, May 20, 1899, p. 724.

After giving these recent examples in Mauritius, Japan, Rarotonga, and an isle of the Fijian group, I am obliged to fall back on the evidence already set forth in Chapter XII. of my book, 'Modern Mythology' (1897). The Bulgarian practice I take from the 'Recueil de Folklore, de Littérature et de Science,' edited by the Bulgarian Minister of Public Instruction, with the aid of Drs. Schischmanof (whom I know personally) and Mastov. In a private letter, Dr. Schischmanof hints at *extase religieuse*, as in the self-mutilations of Dervishes and Fakirs. *Their* performances are extraordinary enough, but there was no religious ecstasy in the little Japanese boy of six, whom Colonel Haggard saw pass through the fire, none in Colonel Gudgeon, none in the Fijians observed by Dr. Hocken. The fire-walkers in Bulgaria are called *Nistinares,* and the faculty is regarded as *hereditary.* We find the same opinion in Fiji, in ancient Italy, and in the Spain of the last century. In Spain the fire-walkers were employed to help to put out fires. The story is given in the essay on the last Earl Marischal in my 'Companions of Pickle' (p. 24), and is derived from d'Alembert's account of the Earl : 'There is a family or caste in Spain, who, from father to son, have the power of going into the flames without being burned, and who, by dint of charms permitted by the Inquisition, can extinguish fires.' The Duchess of Medina Sidonia thought this a proof of the verity of the Catholic faith, and, wishing to convert the Earl, asked him to view the performance. But he insisted on lighting the fire himself, and to that the Spaniards would not consent, the Earl being a heretic.

To return to the Bulgarian Nistinares, they dance in the fire on May 21, the feast of SS. Helena and Constantine. Great fires of scores of cartloads of dry wood are made. On the embers of these the Nistinares (who turn blue in the face) dance and utter prophecies, afterwards placing their feet in the muddy ground where libations of water have been poured forth. The report says nothing as to the state of their feet. The Nistinare begins to feel the effect of the fire after his face has resumed its wonted colour and expression.

As for India, I may cite Mr. Stokes, in ' The Indian Antiquary ' (ii. 190); Dr. Oppert, in his ' Original Inhabitants of India ' (p. 480); and Mr. Crookes, in ' Introduction to Popular Religion and Folklore in Northern India ' (p. 10). Mr. Stokes uses evidence from an inquest on a boy that fell into the fire and died of his injuries, at Periyângridi. The fire-pit was 27 ft. long by 7½ ft. broad, and a span in depth. Thirteen persons walked through. Mr. Stokes did not witness the performance (which is forbidden by our law), but explains that the fire ' would hardly injure the tough skin of the sole of a labourer's feet.' Yet it killed a boy !

The incredulous say that the fire-walkers smear their feet with oil from the fat of the green frog. Dr. Oppert, admitting that ' the heat is unbearable in the neighbourhood of the ditch,' says that the walkers ' as a rule do not do themselves much harm.' This is vague. Equally vague is the reference to rumours about ' a certain preservative ointment.'

In Trinidad, British West Indies, Mr. Henry R. St. Clair, writing to me, describes (September 14, 1896) the feat as performed by Indian coolie immigrants. He personally witnessed the rite, which was like that described to me by Mr. Stephen Ponder. In both cases the performers were Klings. The case witnessed by Mr. Ponder took place in the Straits Settlements, Province Wellesley. The trench was about 20 yards long by 6 ft. wide and 2 ft.

deep. A pyre of wood, 4 or 5 ft. high, was lighted at noon ; by 4 P.M. it was a bed of red-hot embers. The men, who with long rakes smoothed the ashes, could not stand the heat 'for more than a minute at a time.' A little way from the end of the trench was a hole full of water. Six coolies walked the whole length, and thence into the water. 'Not one of them showed the least sign of injury.' They had been prepared by a 'devil-doctor,' not a Brahmin. On a later occasion Mr. Ponder heard that one of them fell 'and was terribly burnt.'

In these cases, Trinidad (and Mauritius) and the Straits Settlements, the performers are South Indian coolies. In all cases there were multitudes of European spectators, except in Mauritius, where, I learn, Europeans usually take no interest in the doings of the heathen.

Turning to Tonga, we have the account of Miss Teuira Henry.[1] The sister and sister's child of Miss Henry have walked over the red-hot stones, as in the Rarotonga and Fijian cases. The ovens are 30 ft. in diameter. The performance was photographed by Lieutenant Morné, of the French Navy, and the original photograph was sent to the Editor of the 'Polynesian Journal,' with a copy from it by Mr. Barnfield, of Honolulu. The ceremony, preparatory to cooking the *ti* plant, is religious, and the archaic hymn sung is full of obsolete words. Mr. Hastwell, of San Francisco, published a tract, which I have not seen, on the Raiatean rite, witnessed by himself. The stones were 'heated to a red and white heat.' The natives 'walked leisurely across' five times; 'there was not even the smell of fire on their garments' (cited in the 'Polynesian Journal,' vol. ii. No. 3). There is corroborative evidence from Mr. N. J. Tone, from Province Wellesley, Straits Settlements, in the 'Polynesian Journal,'

---

[1] *Polynesian Journal*, vol. ii. No. 2, pp. 105–108.

ii. 3, 193. He did not see the rite, arriving too late, but he saw the fire-pit, and examined the naked feet of the walkers. They were uninjured. Mr. Tone's evidence is an extract from his diary.

As to Fiji there are various accounts. The best is that of Mr. Basil Thomson, son of the late Archbishop of York. Mr. Thomson was an official in Fiji, and is a well-known anthropologist. His sketch in his 'South Sea Yarns' (p. 195, *et seq.*) is too long for quotation. The rite is done yearly, before cooking the *masàwe* (a *dracæna*) in the oven through which the clan Na Ivilankata walk. 'The pit was filled with a white-hot mass, shooting out little tongues of white flame.' 'The bottom of the pit was covered with an even layer of hot stones . . . the tongues of flame played continually among them.' The walkers planted 'their feet squarely and firmly on each stone.' Mr. Thomson closely examined the feet of four or five of the natives when they emerged. 'They were cool and showed no trace of scorching, nor were their anklets of dried tree-fern burnt,' though 'dried tree-fern is as combustible as tinder.' 'The instep is covered with skin no thicker than our own, and we saw the men plant their insteps fairly on the stone.' A large stone was hooked out of the pit before the men entered, and one of the party dropped a pocket-handkerchief upon the stone 'when the first man leapt into the oven and snatched what remained of it up as the last left the stones.' Every fold that touched the stone was charred. Mr. Thomson kindly showed me the handkerchief. He also showed me a rather blurred photograph of the strange scene. It has been rudely reproduced in the 'Folk Lore Journal,' September 1895.

Such is part of the modern evidence; for the ancient, see 'Æneid,' xi. 784 *et seq.*; Servius on the passage;

Pliny, 'Hist. Nat.' vii. 2; Silius Italicus, v. 175. This
evidence refers to the Hirpi of Mount Soracte, a class
exempted from military service by the Roman Government,
because, as Virgil makes Aruns say, 'Strong in faith we
walk through the midst of the fire, and press our footsteps
in the glowing mass.' The Hirpi, or wolves, were perhaps originally a totem group, like the wolf totem of
Tonkaway Red Indians ; they had, like the Tonkaway, a
rite in which they were told to ' behave like wolves.' [1]
The goddess propitiated in their fire-walk was Feronia, a
fire-goddess (Max Müller), or a lightning goddess (Kuhn),
or a corn goddess (Mannhardt). Each of these scholars
bases his opinion on etymology.

I have merely given evidence for the antiquity, wide
diffusion, and actual practice of this extraordinary rite.
Neither physical nor anthropological science has even
glanced at it (except in Dr. Hocken's case), perhaps
because the facts are obviously impossible. I ought to
make an exception for Sir William Crookes, but he,
doubtless, was hallucinated, or gulled by the use of
asbestos, or both. Perhaps Mr. Podmore can apply these
explanations to the spectators whom I have cited. For
my part, I remain without a theory, like all the European
observers whom I have quoted. But, in my humble
opinion, all the usual theories, whether of collective
hallucination (photographic cameras being hallucinated),
of psychical causes, of chemical application, of leathery
skin on the soles of the feet, and so on, are inadequate.
There remains ' suggestion.' Any hypnotist, with his
patient's permission (in writing and witnessed), may try
the experiment.

Since this paper was written I have seen an article,
' Les Dompteurs du Feu,' on the same topic, by Dr. Th.

---

[1] Serv. *Æneid*, vii. 800.

Pascal.[1] The first part of the essay is an extract from the
' Revue Théosophique Française.' No date is given, but
the rite described was viewed at Benares on October 26,
1898. I am unable to understand whether Dr. Pascal is
himself the spectator and narrator of the ' Revue
Théosophique,' or whether he quotes (he uses marks of
quotation) some other writer. The phenomena were of
the usual kind, and the writer, examining the feet of two
of the performers, found the skin of the soles fine and
intact. In four cases, in which the performers had
entered the fire after the procession—with the Master
of the Ceremonies and two excited persons, who
split cocoanuts with swords—had gone, there were
slight cauterisations, healed two days later. The author
of this passage speaks of a Brahmin (apparently ' the
Master of the Ceremonies ') who observed to Mr. Govinda
Das, ' that the control of the fire was not so complete as
usual, because the images of the sanctuary had been
touched by Mahomedans and others in the crowd.'

The second case, not given with marks of quotation,
occurred in the park of Maharajah Tagore on December 7, 1898. ' A Frenchman, the son of Dr. Javal of
Paris, was present.' The narrator, ' *nous*,' was also
present, and went up after the rite to venture his hand
in the furnace. He was warned that the Brahmin had
left ten minutes before, and that ' the fire had recovered
its activity.' The Maharajah, however, caused the ceremony to be repeated, and some minutes after all was
ready. The narrator then traversed the fire, barefoot, at *un
petit trot*, ' a little less than two paces a second.' As 100
yards can be run in ten seconds, this trot was remarkably
slow. He felt in paces one and two a sensation of burning, in the five following paces a sensation of intense heat.

---

[1] *Annales des Sciences Psychiques*, July–August, 1899.

There were three small brown marks on his feet, which formed blisters, but did not interfere with walking, and healed ' in some days.' He now learned that the Brahmin's *premier aide* did the ceremony not quite successfully. He is convinced that, but for the ceremony, he would have been seriously injured.

The third case was at Benares in February 1899. Three Hindoos collided and fell in : neither they nor their clothes were burned.

The author clearly regards the performers of the ceremony as able ' to tame considerably the destructive energy of the fire.' This, of course, is the theory of the savage devotees. The ceremony was only a procession of sacred images carried in a glazed sanctuary, and words, not known to the spectator, were uttered by the Brahmin. Holy water was sprinkled, and a cocoanut was thrown into the oven. As has been said, incantations are pronounced in Fiji and elsewhere.[1]

The following case is recent : it is culled from ' The Daily Mail,' November 9, 1900.

ORDEAL BY FIRE

According to the ' Japan Herald,' on Monday last a party of distinguished Americans (the American Minister and his wife, two naval officers, and others) attended the religious rites of the Ontake Jinsha, a powerful sect of Shintoists.

A heap of burning charcoal was placed in a large furnace. The officiating priest read a service over the fire, after which the foreign visitors, to the number of seven, including ladies, took off their shoes and walked over the fire, their naked feet showing no sign of scorching.

The performance called forth, says the report, the enthusiastic approval of the spectators.

[1] In the *Wide World Magazine* (December 1899), a Japanese lady describes the performance witnessed by Colonel Haggard, already cited.

Yet more recent is the next case, from Honolulu, the reporter being Mr. Gorten, a correspondent of the 'Boston Evening Transcript,' March 20, 1891. We quote the passage :—

We have already witnessed still another strange sight suggestive of necromancy and the incantations of the East. Papa Ita, a Tahitan, has given us exhibitions of the famous fire-walking which is still practised in the South Sea Islands and parts of Japan and India. On the vacant land swept a year ago by the Chinatown fire a great elliptical pit was dug and a large quantity of wood placed therein, on which were piled the lava rocks. All day the fire burned till the stones were of a white heat ; then the white-haired native from Tahiti approached the fiery furnace dressed in a robe of white tapa, with a girdle and head-dress of the sacred ti leaves and a bundle of leaves in his hand for a wand. Striking the ground with the ti-leaf wand, he uttered an incantation in his own language, which was a prayer to his gods to temper the heat and allow him to pass ; then calmly and deliberately, with bare feet, he walked the length of the pit, bearing aloft the ti-leaf wand. Pausing a moment on the other side, he again struck the ground and returned over the same fiery path. This was several times repeated, and he even paused a few seconds when in the middle of the pit to allow his picture to be taken. The stones were undoubtedly hot and were turned by means of long poles just before the walking, to have the hottest side up, and from between the rocks the low flames were continually leaping up. The heat that radiated to the spectators was intense. It was a fact that others followed with shoes on, but no one could be found to accept the standing offer of 500 dollars to any one who would, with bare feet, follow Papa Ita. None but natives of course believe there is anything supernatural, but we cannot explain how he does it. It cannot be called a fake, for he really does what he claims to do, and none, so far, dare imitate him. The natives fall down before him, as a great Kapuna, and many interested in the welfare of the Hawaiians deplore these exhibitions, feeling it is bad for the natives, in that it strengthens their old bonds of superstition, to the undoing of much of the advancement they have made. Just now Papa Ita is touring the other islands of the group, and rumour has it that his manager will take him to the Pan-American Exhibition at Buffalo. In that case people in the States can see and judge of this curious exhibition for themselves.

I end with the only instance (forwarded from a correspondent by Mr. T. S. O'Connor) of the ascertained use of an ointment to diminish the effect of the fire. Dr. Hocken and Colonel Gudgeon, as we saw, found no trace of this device ; nor is it mentioned in the Japanese evidence.

Port of Spain, Trinidad, B.W.I., June 8, 1897.

You referred some time ago to the fire-walkers. I have seen some of these gents performing quite recently, and got an explanation from a coolie customer of ours who watched the business with me. It seems they rub themselves with an oil, made from the root of the tabi-cutch (don't know the Latin name), which has the property of producing profuse sweat, and the two combine, causing an oily covering which warms very slowly and is difficult to dry up by heat. But even then it is essential that the men be good Stoics. I give the explanation for what it is worth, but saw the preparation myself, and had some of the stuff scraped off a man, who was ready for the rite, put it on a piece of tin and held it in the fire, and it certainly neither dried up nor got hot in a hurry.

It is clear that this explanation does not explain several of the cases wherein no anointing is used. We can only agree with Dr. Hocken that the performances deserve the study of physiologists and physicians. The explanation of Iamblichus, 'they walk on fire unharmed,' is that 'the god within them does not let fire harm them.' This implies that an exalted psychical condition of the performers secures their immunity. But in the cases where Europeans bore a part, and even in Dr. Hocken's examination of the natives, there was no sign of other than the normal mental condition. As fresh evidence comes in, it is perhaps not impossible that science will interest herself in the problem.

APPENDIX A

MR. TYLOR'S THEORY OF BORROWING

I FEEL so nervous about differing from Mr. Tylor as to the borrowing of the idea of a superior and creative being from the Jesuits by the Red Indians that I have reconsidered his essay.[1] He is arguing that ' the Great Spirit belongs not to the untutored but to the tutored minds of the savages.' I am not contending for the use of the words ' Great Spirit ' as of native origin, and as employed to designate what I call a superior being. That the natives had an untaught belief in such a being is my opinion, not that they styled him ' Great Spirit.'

Mr. Tylor refers us to ' Relations des Jésuites,' 1611, p. 20, in the Quebec edition of 1858. Here (to translate the passage) I read : ' They believe in a god, so they say, but can only name him by the name of the sun, *Niscaminou*, and know no prayers, nor manner of adoring him.' When hungry they put on sacred robes, turn to the east, and say, ' Our Sun, or our God, give us to eat.' Here, then, are prayer, vestments, and turning to the east. The Jesuits, then, did not introduce these for the first time ; nor did they introduce the conception of the superior being thus implored.

A similar relation of the sun to the being addressed in prayer exists now among the Blackfoot Indians of America. With them the word *Natos* is ' equivalent to holy or divine,' and is also the name of the sun. To Natos prayer and sacrifice are offered, and the cruel rites of the Natos-dance are performed. Tongues of cattle are served out to the virtuous : ' this rite partakes of the nature of a sacrament.' Youths sacrifice a finger, in recognition of prayers answered by Natos. ' Prayer is made to Natos only, and everything in Okán ' (the ceremony) ' is sacred to him alone.'[2]

[1] *J. A. I.* Feb. 1892.
[2] *The Blackfoot Sun-dance*, Rev. J. MacLean, Toronto, 1889.

These are advanced, elaborate, and thoroughly native observances, of which the germ may be found in the religions described in the Jesuit ' Relations' of 1611.

Mr. Tylor says 'especially through missionary influence, since 1500, ideas of . . . retribution after death for deeds done in life have been implanted on native polytheism in various parts of the world.' But his Jesuit authority of 1611, in the passage cited by him, writes : ' They believe in the immortality of the soul, and in recompenses for good men and bad, confusedly, and in a general way, but they seek and care no further as to the manner of such things' (*comment cela doibt estre*). Mr. Tylor's authority does not, I confess, appear to me to support his opinion. The natives believed in future ' retribution.'

His other texts [1] show us savages consulting each his Manitou, ' a powerful being' (*quelque nature puissante*), or *diable*. A Manitou is 'any superior being, good or bad:' the God of the Jesuits is *le bon Manitou*, Satan is *le mauvais Manitou*.

I am not arguing that these phrases are more than the pigeon-French of the savage flock, or that the ideas expressed did not later become implanted in their minds. But Mr. Tylor, in his essay of 1892, omits what he quotes in his ' Primitive Culture,' the Jesuit evidence of 1633 (p. 16) to ' one Atahocan who made everything. Speaking of God in a hut one day, they asked me, " What is God ?" I replied, " The All Powerful One, who made heaven and earth." They then began to say to each other, " Atahocan, Atahocan, he is Atahocan."' ' They have no worship which they are used to pay to him whom they hold for their god.' (This is the religious condition of the Kaffirs described by Dos Santos in Pinkerton, xvi. 687.) Now it is Atahocan who interests me, as pre-missionary: no doubt he was not called *le bon Manitou*—but there he was! In 1634 Father Le Jeune consulted a very hostile sorcerer, who minimised Atahocan. ' They do not know,' said the sorcerer, ' who was the author of the world, perhaps Atahocan : it was uncertain. They only spoke of Atahocan as one speaks of something so remote as to be dubious. In fact the word *Nitatahocan*

---

[1] *Rel. des Jésuites*, 1633, p. 16 ; 1637, p. 49.

means in their language, "I tell a story, an old tale."' [1] The 'sorcerer,' a servant of familiar spirits, had no interest in Atahocan, though the tribesmen recognised in him the God and Creator of Father Le Jeune. There was but a waning tradition of a primal maker; interesting and important just because it was waning, and therefore could not be of fresh European introduction. The beings in receipt of sacrifice were *Khichikouai*, to whom they threw fat on the fire, with prayer. [2] It appears to me that these affable familiar ghosts, practically serviceable, had cast the otiose Atahocan into the background. But he, like Andouagni, Kiehtan, and others, was certainly there before the Jesuits, and these beings are elsewhere cited by Mr. Tylor. The question is one of the existence of belief in such a being, not (for me at least) of the origin, which may well be post-European, of the words 'Kitchi Manitu, or Great Spirit.' If the Mandans believed, as Mr. Tylor does not deny, in 'Omahank Numakchi, the Creator, whose name appears to mean Lord of Earth,' it is quite unimportant that 'there is no Mandan deity whose name answers to that of Great Spirit.' [3]

I mentioned, in the first essay of this book, Mr. Max Müller's version of Bishop Salvado's account of Motagon, a dead creator in Western Australia. Mr. Tylor recognises him as Sir George Grey's Mettagong, 'an insignificant demon identified with the phosphoric fungus.' But did that demon 'die in decrepit old age long ago,' like Bishop Salvado's Motagon? There seems to be no hope of making anything clear out of Motagon. Mr. Oldfield, cited by Mr. Tylor for Australia, I have never quoted: his account cannot be uncontaminated. Yet the natives may have believed in an evil spirit before they adorned him with horns, as Mr. Oldfield states, which no indigenous beast possesses. 'Their doctrine of a *horned* devil' must be modern, though not necessarily their belief in a bad spirit. With Mr. Tylor's theory of Baiame as 'a missionary translation of the word for creator,' as early as 1850, I have already dealt in my second essay, showing that Baiame is a native pre-missionary word, whatever may be its etymology. Mrs. Langloh Parker renders it, not 'maker' (from *baia*, to cut, or fashion), but 'big man.'

---

[1] *Rel. des Jésuites*, 1634, p. 13.   [2] *Ibid.* pp. 32, 33.
[3] *J. A. I.* Feb. 1892, p. 287.

APPENDIX B

THE MARTYRDOM OF DASIUS

It is difficult to ascertain the facts about this affair. There are first two brief narratives. One is printed in the 'Ménologie de Basile.'[1] The other is in Cod. Ambrosianus, D 74, fol. 65r. M. Cumont thinks that both have a single source—namely, an abridgment of the 'Acts of St. Dasius,' published by himself from the Parisinus 1539, a MS. of the eleventh century. The two brief late narratives say that the *Greeks* in Dorostolum held a yearly feast of Cronos. Thirty days before the feast they chose a handsome young soldier, clad him in royal raiment, and allowed him thirty days of revelry, after which he was to sacrifice himself at the altar of Cronos. The lot fell on Dasius, who preferred to die as a martyr of Christ. Diocletian and Maximian, hearing of this, commanded him to be put to the sword. The second MS. names Bassus as the officer at whose tribunal Dasius was arraigned.

The long MS. first published by M. Cumont says that the man on whom the lot fell personated Cronos himself. On the thirtieth day of revelry he died by the sword as a victim to the 'unclean idols.' The author then adds that, in his own time, so-called Christians do devil-worship by dancing about in skins of beasts at the new year—which is not the date of the Saturnalia (December 17–23). Unlike these sinners, who thus give themselves to the devil, Dasius determined to refuse to be a sacrifice to heathen gods. He would never sacrifice himself to Cronos. He proclaimed himself a Christian, was thrown into a dark cell, and was brought before Bassus, 'the Legate,' next day.

Bassus asked what he was charged with, his name, and profession. Dasius gave his name, profession, and religion. Bassus (who appears to have been a mild kind of man) bade him revere the images of the Emperors, whose salt he ate ($\delta\omega\rho o\upsilon\mu\acute{\epsilon}\nu\omega\nu$ $\acute{\eta}\mu\hat{\iota}\nu$ $\tau\grave{a}$ $\sigma\iota\tau\eta\rho\acute{\epsilon}\sigma\iota a$). Dasius, in a covenanting spirit, replied that he served no earthly monarch. Bassus again invited him to adore the images of the Emperor, 'which

[1] Urbino, 1727, vol. i. p. 198.

homage even barbarous nations pay.' Dasius defied the devil, and anticipated, in his confession, the still unformulated Nicene Creed. Bassus, keeping his temper to a marvel, said that every man must obey constituted authority. Dasius answered, ' Do to me whatever your filthy and impious Emperors command.' Bassus then offered him two hours for reflection, ' that you may consider in yourself *how you may live among us with honour.*' Dasius refused the respite in vulgar and insolent terms. Bassus then ordered him to be decapitated. He had a last chance, being offered incense to burn before the Imperial effigies, but he threw it on the ground, and was done to death.

Not a word about the mock-kingship passed between Dasius and Bassus, who merely asked him to perform the customary sacrifice, that he might 'live honourably in the regiment' (ὅπως δυνηθείης ζῆν μεθ' ἡμῶν ἐν δόξῃ). How could Dasius live on if he was to be sacrificed ' at any rate ' ? Why did not Dasius tell Bassus the supposed facts of the case—that he objected to a month of unhallowed revelry, followed by self-sacrifice to Cronos ? Bassus obviously knew nothing about all that. A soldier only has his orders ; Dasius insulted the religion and the head of the State : he declined to retract, and Bassus had to administer the law. If Dasius did not like the law he need not have enlisted.

The two brief MSS. give us none of this conversation between Bassus and Dasius. That foul-tongued confessor, according to Mr. Frazer, ' refused to play the part of the heathen god and soil his last days by debauchery. The threats and arguments of his commanding officer, Bassus, failed to shake his constancy, and accordingly he was beheaded.' [1] But Bassus, a perfect gentleman, never asked Dasius to soil his last days by debauchery, or to play the part of a heathen god. He merely offered to Dasius the usual test, just as Claverhouse might have offered the Abjuration Oath. The position of Dasius was exactly that of a dragoon of 1684 who 'refused the abjuration.'

In my opinion, Dasius probably was executed for his scruples, insolently expressed, if we believe his biographer ; and, if we do not believe his biographer, the evidence ceases to exist. The biographer, knowing about the usual King of the Saturnalia

[1] *Golden Bough*, iii. 141.

in every Roman household, and wishing to check the survivals of pagan revelry at the new year, declared that the King of the Saturnalia was actually sacrificed to Saturn. But in his own account of the conversations between Dasius and his commanding officer not a word is said about the Saturnalia and the sacrifice of the mock-king. On the other hand, the commanding officer, or military judge, labours to save the life of Dasius, not being aware that it is in any way endangered—except by his recusancy. This hardly appears in Mr. Frazer's brief summary. But a glance at the original ' Acts of St. Dasius ' shows the nature of the evidence.[1]

If any part of it has an official basis, as M. Cumont supposes, that part must be the examination of Dasius by Bassus. Here occurs no hint of sacrificing Dasius as Saturn ; Bassus expects him to throw incense on the flame, and to continue an honourable soldier of the Empire. He knows nothing about sacrificing Dasius. Thus, as historians regard evidence, the statement about the yearly victim of Saturn, a statement made long after the event, and after the establishment of Christianity, is weak indeed. For it has no corroboration in the works of Latin or Greek historians or antiquaries. But anthropology is not history, and Mr. Frazer argues, 'the martyrologist's account of the Saturnalia agrees so closely with the accounts of similar rites elsewhere, which could not possibly have been known to him, that the substantial accuracy of his description may be regarded as established.' [2]

Now we have the Aztec case and the Sacæan case. But the Aztec victim is a captive, not a free soldier, whose life Bassus is most anxious to preserve. The Sacæan victim is not sacrificed, and is a condemned criminal. Now Mr. Frazer has said ' when a nation becomes civilised, if it does not drop human sacrifices altogether, it at least selects as victims only such wretches as would be put to death at any rate.' [3] But a valuable soldier, like Dasius, is not a wretch who would be put to death at any rate. Again, among the numerous cases of periods of licence, like the Sacæa, we know only one instance

---

[1] *Analecta Bollandiana*, xvi. pp. 5–16. The precise position of a ' Legatus ' like Bassus is rather indistinct. If an officer, he need not have asked Dasius what his ' profession ' was.

[2] *G. B.* iii. 142.   [3] *G. B.* iii. 120.

of sacrifice, and that of a criminal, in Ashanti. Our business is to prove that free Roman soldiers voluntarily sacrificed themselves at the Saturnalia. The Aztec sacrifice of a captive, the Persian execution of a criminal, with folklore rites of analogous description, scarcely make the Roman custom probable, while the direct evidence is only that of the martyrologist. His evidence merely asserts, as to the death of Dasius, that he perished for refusing the usual test. Again, as M. Parmentier argues, the sacrifice, if it existed, may have been of Oriental importation. In this condition of the evidence, especially as it allots thirty days to the Saturnalia, an otherwise unheard-of period, suspension of judgment seems prudent.

APPENDIX C

THE RIDE OF THE BEARDLESS ONE

MR. FRAZER's argument about the Ride of the Beardless One, and the possible traces of a similar burlesque performance preluding to or succeeding the Crucifixion, is not easy to follow. Perhaps, in the text, I may have misconceived my author's meaning. We know the ride of the beardless one in Persia through the work of Hyde, published at Oxford in 1700, and again in 1760. I condense Hyde's account as given by Mr. Frazer.[1] The date of the festivity of the beardless one was 'the first day of the first month, which in the most ancient Persian calendar corresponds to March, so that the date of the ceremony agrees with that of the Babylonian New Year Festival of Zakmuk.' In Mr. Frazer's third volume, the Sacæa synchronise with Zakmuk, though in his second volume the Sacæa are of June–July. We shall suppose him, in the present passage, to adhere to the date of March for the Sacæa. The ride of the beardless one, if so, occurs at the Sacæan date. But Hyde found that some Persians regarded the ride of the beardless one as of recent institution; if they were right, it has no traceable connection with the ancient Sacæa. Nor was there any mock-king concerned in the ride of the beardless one ; and there was no probable sacred harlot; still less were

[1] *G. B.* iii. 181, 182.

there two beardless ones, with two sacred harlots, as in Mr. Frazer's theory of the Sacæa. At all events Hyde says no more about the sacred harlots than Dio Chrysostom or any other ancient author records in the case of the Sacæa. Far from being attired as a king, the beardless buffoon was led about naked, on a horse, mule, or ass, fanning himself and complaining of heat, while people soused him in ice, snow, or cold water. Attended by the household of the king or governor, he extorted contributions. The goods seized between dawn and morning prayers fell to the governor or king; what the buffoon took between the first and second prayers he kept; and then he vanished. The populace might beat him later, if they caught him.

Now if this holiday farce existed, at the Sacæa and at Zakmuk, during the time of the exile, the Jews could not borrow the Sacæan custom of hanging a mock-king, for, on Mr. Frazer's theory (if I do not misunderstand it), the ride of the beardless one came in ' after the serious meaning of the custom ' (the hanging of the mock-king) ' had been forgotten.' The ride of the beardless one is ' a degenerate copy of the original '—of the Sacæan whipping, hanging, and scourging a condemned criminal—which had fallen out of use, I presume. Lagarde is not of that opinion : he thinks that the author of the Book of Esther knew and combined the colours of the Persian Magophonia, the Sacæa, and the ride of the beardless. In fact, Dio Chrysostom does not tell us that the Sacæan mock-king rode, whether naked or in splendour, through the city; nor that he made a forced collection, which he was not allowed to live to enjoy. These things may have occurred, but no record proves them. Yet Mr. Frazer has, provisionally, to conjecture that the Sacæan victim had a ride of honour, and made a collection, and that our Lord enjoyed the same privileges. ' The description of His last triumphal ride into Jerusalem reads almost like an echo of that brilliant progress through the streets of Susa which Haman aspired to and Mordecai accomplished.' Our Lord does not appear to have been either naked, like the beardless one, or clad in splendour, like Mordecai, or crowned and robed, or attended by the men-at-arms of Pilate or Herod. He borrowed an ass, with her colt, and the multitude strewed

branches and cried, ' Hosanna to the Son of David.'   He then
' overthrew the tables of the money-changers, and cast out all
them that sold and bought in the Temple: ' a raid,' as Mr.
Frazer says.   But it is not on record that He seized any
property, and His motive has been regarded as an objection to
commercial transactions in a sacred edifice.

It may seem a little arbitrary to connect these acts of
Christ, not with what the Sacæan victim, to our knowledge, ever
did, but with what was done by the beardless buffoon, his
degenerate copy.   We have first to guess that the Sacæan
mock-king acted like him whom we have to guess to be his late
' degenerate copy; ' and then to read into the Gospels an idea
derived from accounts of the ancient or modern buffoon.
Moreover, while Christ represents the mock-king of the Sacæa
in ' the high tragedy of the ancient ceremony '—for *He* is put
to death—his counterpart, Barabbas, has a conjectural ride
which is mere ' farce,' like that of the beardless buffoon.   Now
Mr. Frazer says that, ' after the serious meaning of the
Sacæan custom had been forgotten, and the substitute was
allowed to escape with his life, the high tragedy of the ancient
ceremony would rapidly degenerate into farce.' [1]

The degeneration was rapid indeed : in the twinkling of an
eye.   Christ was *not* allowed to escape with his life: ' the
high tragedy of the ancient ceremony ' existed in his case.   But
instantly ' the high tragedy ' was forgotten ! Barabbas, Christ's
counterpart, in Mr. Frazer's theory, ' may very well . . . have
been going about the streets, rigged out in tawdry splendour,
with a tinsel crown on his head, and a sham sceptre in his
hand, preceded and followed by all the tag-rag and bobtail
of the town, hooting, jeering, and breaking coarse jests at his
expense, while some pretended to salute his mock majesty, and
others belaboured the donkey on which he rode.   It was in
this fashion, probably, that in Persia the beardless and one-
eyed man made his undignified progress through the town, to
the delight of ragamuffins and the terror of shopkeepers whose
goods he confiscated if they did not hasten to lay their peace-
offerings at his feet.' [2]

All this as to Barabbas implies that the ' high tragedy ' of
the Sacæa was already lost in the ' farce ' of the ' degenerate

[1] *G. B.* iii. 183.   [2] *G. B.* iii. 192.

copy,' the ride of the beardless. If so, why did Christ lose
his life? If *He* died solemnly as a recognised god (which Mr.
Frazer seems to me to deny in iii. 120 and asserts in iii. 194–197),
why is his no less sacred counterpart, Barabbas, also and
simultaneously a counterpart of the beardless buffoon?

Either the whole affair was solemn and tragic, the Haman
(Christ) and the Mordecai (Barabbas) being recognised as divine,
or the whole affair was farce, and in neither Christ nor Barabbas
was there any recognised divinity. Mr. Frazer makes the belief
in the divinity of Christ depend on the contemporary recognition of the godhead of the Sacæan victim, whose male issue
was also perhaps recognised as divine.[1] But he also assures
us that the divinity of the Sacæan victim must have been
' forgotten.'[2] In the same way Christ, as victim, was recognised
as divine, and so, necessarily, was his counterpart, Barabbas;
' whether in sober fact, or pious fiction, the Barabbas or Son of
that Divine Father who generously gave his own Son to die for
the world.'[3] Yet this Son of the Divine Father was so remote
from sacred that, just three pages before his Sonhood is
asserted, we have a picture of him riding about on a donkey
among the jeers of the ' tag-rag and bobtail.'[4] It is difficult to
accept both of the theories (not very self-consistent in my
humble opinion), which Mr. Frazer seems able to hold simultaneously or alternately. If Barabbas rode a donkey amid the
jeers of the ragamuffins, then Christ had no triumphal entry
into Jerusalem. He, too, had merely a burlesque ride, if
Barabbas had a burlesque ride, as Mr. Frazer thinks probable.
By the essence of his theory, Christ and Barabbas were counter-
parts, both were divine, or neither was divine, in general
opinion. If Barabbas was a personage in a low farce (as Mr.
Frazer supposes), so was Christ, and no halo of divinity can
accrue from taking part in a burlesque, which cannot also be a
high tragedy, with divine actors. As if difficulties were never
to cease, the beardless buffoon is a degenerate copy of the
Sacæan victim. But while *he* was a proxy for the king, and
also a representative of Humman, or Marduk, or Tammuz, or
Gilgamesh, or Eabani, or a god not yet identified: in his
popular form, as the beardless buffoon, ' his pretence of

[1] *G. B.* iii. 186.　　　　[2] *G. B.* iii. 120.
[3] *G. B.* iii. 195.　　　　[4] *G. B.* iii. 192.

suffering from heat, and his final disappearance, suggest that, if he personified either of the seasons, it was the departing winter rather than the coming summer.'[1]

If so, was the buffoon of the popular ceremony the folklore original of the Sacæan mock-king, or was he a degenerate copy of that versatile victim with a new meaning popularly assigned to him? We are to 'recognise in him the familiar features of the mock or temporary king,'[2] though he has neither crown, sceptre, robes, nor aught to cover his nakedness. If he is not the popular original of the mock-king of the Sacæa, how does he, and how does his magic, put us 'in a position finally to unmask the leading personages in the Book of Esther'?[3] If he is a new popular interpretation of the Sacæan mock-king, a misconstrued survival, he cannot help to explain the Sacæa, or 'Esther,' especially if, as a player in a farce which was a mitigation of the Sacæa, he had not come into existence when 'Esther' was written. But, if the beardless buffoon represents the popular germ of the Sacæan victim, then that victim was originally neither the king's proxy, nor Tammuz, nor Marduk, nor Gilgamesh, nor Eabani, but perhaps 'the departing winter.' He can only serve the theory, in that capacity, if provided with a counterpart to represent the coming summer, while he and his counterpart both have female mates, of whom there is not a ghost of a trace in our authorities, whether in the instance of the Sacæa, the Ride of the Beardless, or the Crucifixion. Nobody says that there were two beardless buffoons, yet there is just as much evidence for them as for the conjectural two sacred characters, with two sacred harlots, at the Sacæa. We must avoid the *multiplicatio entium præter necessitatem.*

---

[1] *G. B.* iii. 184.   [2] *G. B.* iii. 182.   [3] *G. B.* iii. 184.

INDEX

ADONIS. *See* Tammuz
Agathias (Byzantine poet), cited, 130
Ahone (aboriginal N. American god), 20, 39
Alatunjas (Arunta headmen), 101, 259, 260, 265, 267, 269
Alcheringa (mythical heroic age, or period of fabulous ancestors, of the Arunta), 15, 251, 253, 254
Alcheringites (fabulous ancestors), 251, 252
Algonquin deity, 39
Alkna Buma (Arunta clairvoyant), and new-born babies, 262
Amadhlozi (Zulu ancestral spirits), 227, 228
Anahuac : human sacrifices, 193
Anaitis (Persian love goddess), 119, 194
Andamanese : religious beliefs, 231, 232
Andouagni (aboriginal Canadian god), 10 ; no form of prayer addressed to 10, 11, 12, 21, 89
Anthropology, present-day neglect of its study, 7; errors of the 'higher criticism,' 9; gods not addressed in prayer, 10, 11; conflicting evidence of race beliefs, 11 ; coincidence of testimony, 12, 13. *See* under names of tribes and gods
Argyllshire : superstition among women connected with cup-marked rocks, 252, 254
Arician grove of Diana, the, and its ghastly priest, 207 *et seq.*
Arthurian legend : the magical sword, 211
Arunta (tribe of Central Australia), their theory of evolution of our species and the nature of life, 15 ;

scope of their ideas, 16 ; practice of magic, 46, 61, 62, 65 ; magical rites to assist the processes of nature, 82, 83 ; periods of licence, 193, 194, 196, 198 ; totems, 250, 251, 252 ; cited, 67, 68, 101, 259, 263, 264, 265 note, 266, 267
Ashanti : licence at the harvest festival, 188, 189
Asia Minor Greek cities : use of scapegoats in times of calamity, 190
Astarte (Semitic goddess). *See* Ishtar
Atahocan (Huron deity), 42, 89, 238, 296, 297
Athenæus, on the Sacæa, 119, 120, 121 ; cited, 132, 185, 186, 195, 196
Athenian festival of Cronos, 116, 117
Athens : scapegoats killed in times of distress, 190
Atholl, Earl of (pretender to royalty), mock crowning of, 203
Atua (Samoan), tree of protection, 219
Australian blacks : alleged endeavour to delay the course of the sun, 3 ; religious ideas unborrowed, 44 ; attention to the dead, 49 ; Christian Deity identified by them with their own supreme beings, 49 ; religious ideas vary according to fertility of soil, 50 ; invent to please whites, 50, 51 ; emergence of gods from ancestors, 51 ; religious beliefs, 231, 232 ; engraved churinga and rock paintings, 245 *et seq.* ; fire ceremony of, 271. *See* also under tribal names
Aztecs : beliefs, 75 ; human sacrifice at harvest festival, 127 ; 173, 300